Inclusive Practices and Social Justice Leadership for Special Populations in Urban Settings

A Moral Imperative

A volume in
Educational Leadership for Social Justice
Jeffrey S. Brooks, *Series Editor*

Inclusive Practices and Social Justice Leadership for Special Populations in Urban Settings

A Moral Imperative

edited by

M. C. Kate Esposito
California State University Dominguez Hills

Anthony H. Normore
California State University Dominguez Hills

INFORMATION AGE PUBLISHING, INC.
Charlotte, NC • www.infoagepub.com

Library of Congress Cataloging-in-Publication Data

A CIP record for this book is available from the Library of Congress
http://www.loc.gov

ISBN: 978-1-68123-107-5 (Paperback)
        978-1-68123-108-2 (Hardcover)
        978-1-68123-109-9 (ebook)

CONTENTS

SERIES EDITOR'S PREFACE

Jeffrey S. Brooks

I am pleased to serve as series editor for this book series, *Educational Leadership for Social Justice*, with Information Age Publishing. The idea for this series grew out of the work of a committed group of leadership for scholars associated with the American Educational Research Association's (AERA) Leadership for Social Justice Special Interest Group (LSJ SIG). This group existed for many years before being officially affiliated with AERA and has benefited greatly from the ongoing leadership, support, and counsel of Dr. Catherine Marshall (University of North Carolina-Chapel Hill). It is also important to acknowledge the contributions of the LSJ SIG's first Chair, Dr. Ernestine Enomoto (University of Hawaii at Manoa), whose wisdom, stewardship, and guidance helped ease a transition into AERA's more formal organizational structures. This organizational change was at times difficult to reconcile with scholars who largely identified as nontraditional thinkers and who push toward innovation rather than accept the status quo. As the second Chair of the LSJ SIG, I appreciate all of Ernestine's hard work and friendship. Moreover, I also thank Drs. Gaetane Jean-Marie and Whitney Sherman Newcomb, the third and fourth Chairs of the LSJ SIG, for their visionary leadership, steadfast commitment to high standard,s and collaborative scholarship and friendship.

I am particularly indebted to my colleagues on the LSJ SIG's first Publications Committee, which I chaired from 2005 to 2007: Dr. Denise Armstrong, Brock University; Dr. Ira Bogotch, Florida Atlantic University; Dr. Sandra

Inclusive Practices and Social Justice Leadership for Special Populations in Urban Settings, pages vii–ix
Copyright © 2015 by Information Age Publishing
vii

Harris, Lamar University; Dr. Whitney Sherman, Virginia Commonwealth University, and; Dr. George Theoharis, Syracuse University. This committee was a joy to work with, and I am pleased we have found many more ways to collaborate—now as my fellow Series Editors of this book series—as we seek to provide publication opportunities for scholarship in the area of leadership for social justice.

This book, *Inclusive Practices and Social Justice Leadership for Special Populations in Urban Settings: A Moral Imperative*, edited by M. C. Kate Esposito and Anthony H. Normore, is the 16th in the series. The book makes an important contribution by examining complex and varied dynamics related to inclusion and social justice from a variety of perspectives.

Again, welcome to this 15th book in this Information Age Publishing series, *Educational Leadership for Social Justice*. You can learn more about the series at our website, http://www.infoagepub.com/series/Educational-Leadership-for-Social-Justice. I invite you to contribute your own work on equity and influence to the series. We look forward to you joining the conversation.

—**Dr. Jeffrey S. Brooks**
Monash University

OTHER BOOKS IN THE EDUCATIONAL LEADERSHIP FOR SOCIAL JUSTICE BOOK SERIES

Leadership for Social Justice: Promoting Equity and Excellence Through Inquiry and Reflective Practice. (2008). Anthony H. Normore, Editor.

The Emperor Has No Clothes: Teaching About Race and Racism to People Who Don't Want To Know.* (2010). Tema Okun.

Bridge Leadership: Connecting Educational Leadership and Social Justice to Improve Schools. (2010). Autumn K. Cypres & Christa Boske, Editors.

Crises of Identifying: Negotiating and Mediating Race, Gender, and Disability Within Family and Schools. (2012). Dymaneke D. Mitchell.

Defining Social Justice Leadership in a Global Context: The Changing Face of Educational Supervision. (2012). Cynthia Gerstl-Pepin & Judith A. Aiken.

Education-Based Incarceration and Recidivism: The Ultimate Social Justice Crime-Fighting Tool. (2012). Brian D. Fitch & Anthony H. Normore, Editors.

Educational Leadership: Building Bridges Between Ideas, Schools, and Nations. (2012). Christa Boske, Editor.

---

* Winner of the American Educational Studies Association 2011 Critics Choice Award.

Profiles of Care: At the Intersection of Social Justice, Leadership, & the Ethic Of Care. (2012). Jo Bennett.

Educational Leaders Encouraging the Intellectual and Professional Capacity of Others: A Social Justice Agenda. (2012). Elizabeth Murakami-Ramalho & Anita Pankake.

Antiracist School Leadership: Toward Equity in Education for America's Students. (2013). Jeffrey S. Brooks & Noelle Witherspoon Arnold, Editors.

Confronting Racism in Higher Education: Problems and Possibilities for Fighting Ignorance, Bigotry, and Isolation. (2013). Jeffrey S. Brooks & Noelle Witherspoon Arnold, Editors.

Inside Perspective on Education Reform: The Affects and Effects of a "Critical Incident." (2014). Mary Green.

The Place of Disequilibrium in Advocacy Work: Humanitarian Bodies and the Freefall State. (2014). Carol Mullen.

Women Interrupting, Disrupting, and Revolutionizing Educational Policy and Practice. (2014). Whitney N. Sherman & Katherine Mansfield, Editors.

School Leadership in a Diverse Society: Helping Schools to Prepare All Students for Success. (2014). Carlos McCray & Floyd Beachum.

Inclusive Practices for Special Populations in Urban Settings: The Need for Social Justice Leadership. (2015). M. C. Kate Esposito & Anthomny H. Normore, Editors.

Urban Educational Leadership for Social Justice: International Perspectives. (in progress). Jeffrey S. Brooks & Melanie C. Brooks, Editors.

FOREWORD

Peter McLaren
Chapman University

It appears at times that we live inside a revolving world-historical kaleido-scope steadily turned by the Angel of History, forcing us continually to re-focus our imagination as our world converges into yet another entangled pattern of challenges: social, cultural, economic, and spiritual. Yet it is not simply the world that is changing, it is the different ways in which we con-ceive of our positioning in our cosmic voyage through the messy materiality of everyday life. Life does not unfold as some old sheet strewn across a brass bed in the dusky attic of history; our destinies as children, parents, and teachers do not flow unilaterally toward a single vertigo-inducing epiphany, some pyrotechnic explosion of iridescent and refulgent splendor where we lie becalmed, rocking on a silent sea of pure bliss, or where we are held speechless in some wind-washed grove of cedars, in the thrall of an un-bridled, unsullied, and undiluted love of incandescent intensity. Rather, we sling ourselves nervously back and forth across the great Manichean divide of the drab of everyday existence, where, in our elemental contact with the world, our human desires, for better or for worse, tug at us like some glow-in-the-dark hustler in a carnival midway. As critical educators, we take pride in our search for meaning, and our metamorphosis of consciousness has taken us along different paths, to different places, if not in a quest for truth, then at least to purchase a crisper and more perspicuous reality from which to begin a radical reconstruction of society.

Inclusive Practices and Social Justice Leadership for Special Populations in Urban Settings, pages xi–xviii
Copyright © 2015 by Information Age Publishing
xi

But in our protestations against the loss of the fellowship of humanity against whose separation from ourselves we are reacting, we are joined in a common struggle. Those of us who have for some time now rested uneasily with the idea that economic growth and "progress" has brought about a fully formed democracy of inclusion and human and economic rights have revised our view of democracy from a template steeled in the struggle for economic justice and rekindled by new social movements such as Occupy Wall Street, the indigenous struggles of Idle No More, the Zapatistas, the Indignados of Spain, and the Bolivarian revolution brought to the fore by the late Hugo Chavez; we fight now at the headwaters of capitalist production so that the children of the future can be free later on from the overwhelming challenges and obstacles faced by our current generation. By contrast, on the other side of the political aisle, we find those who believe that we live in the best of all possible worlds and who struggle to maintain at all costs the status quo, drawn toward the core notion that we need less regulation of the economy and insisting (often through political sideshows such as Fox News and the Right Wing hate media, especially talk radio) that those "liberals" who seek to change the system are the very ones responsible for most of the problems faced in the United States.

Regardless of what position one takes, few would argue against the idea that today we face an apocalyptic challenge. The challenge is not so much one of the end-of-times drawn forth by the Four Horsemen, harbingers of the last judgment upon humankind, but rather the end of human freedom and creativity brought about by our acquiescence to the social and economic conditions of our own immiseration. We acquiesce to allowing our world to become transformed into a heap of cinders, not because we are willfully ignorant or cowardly quislings with our tails between our legs or because our sapiental compass has been broken but because of our ideological immurement in a thicket of organized stupidity, courtesy of what Althusser (1971) referred to as the ideological state apparatuses. The idea of the ideological state apparatuses is grounded in the contention that ideology represents "the imaginary relationship of individuals to their real conditions of existence" (Althusser, 1971, p. 109) and that ideology has a material existence in that it consists of actions and behaviors governed by their disposition within certain configurations of social forces and institutionalized relations grounded in capitalist relations of exploitation. Individuals, Althusser (1971) contends, are "interpellated," or always already, constituted as subjects ideologically through the process of identity construction by means of various discourses that "speak" to—or "hail"—the subject. In the United States, such discourses are provided by the media, religious organizations, the family, and political affiliations. We affirm ourselves as individual agents through an overarching structure in which we are already positioned as subjects by certain totalizing forces outside of our conscious consideration.

In the United States, individuals generally are hailed as "liberals" or "conservatives" and regard themselves as Democrats or Republicans or Independents, as progressives or conservatives (or a mixture of both), having identified over the years with certain attitudes and ideas inherited from a wide variety of sources, such as family upbringing or exposure to various media propaganda.

In the field of education, we have been struggling under the aegis of the No Child Left Behind generation, and its Race to the Top offspring, whose signatories and proponents remain ensepulcured in abiding and deep-seated assumptions about education and society. In the cognitive framework of many of their supporters, if there is a problem with these policies, these problems are simply anomalies; within their cognitive framework, federal educational policies are generally in the best interests of the country and in no way connected to an institutionally based set of power relationships protecting a dominant racial and class hierarchy where exploitation, racism, and inequality are legitimated and encouraged.

And while such debates intensify throughout the country, capitalism continues to proceed apace, unabated like a wrecking ball, crushing those dependent upon wage labor through the economic and political extraction of surplus labor as surplus value, creating enormous wealth for investors and speculators who not only gleefully disregard their duty to countenance and cure the everyday depredations of capitalist society—hunger, poverty, violence—but who regard the very concept of civic duty to be itself dubious. But the growing ranks of the poor peering from beneath the wreckage, weeping and disconsolate and immobilized inside a putrid silence, steel themselves for yet another day of hardship. Our souls have been deracinated from our ancestral homes and limp toward the future depotentiated, like a torpid carnation in the lapel of a wedding crasher.

We stare at our television and computer screens in the desolate solitude of being "connected" in network society only to witness a staggeringly obscene and dogged defense of the likes of Cliven Bundy and Darren Wilson by the system of White privilege (the largest defender of de facto White privilege being the Republican Party) that distributes its parasitic and racist opinions that exhort us to serve the sentinels of the capitalist class, disguised inside rhetorical bromides, as if they constituted common sense: listen to your elder statesmen and give the actions of our political overseers and officers of the law the benefit of the doubt. Such views, which cocoon an autochthonous mythology of White supremacy and U.S. exceptionalism, have affected the minds of the U.S. public like canisters of sarin gas thrown into a crowd trapped in a windowless room. In a world slouching toward fascism, where so many blithely and smugly follow the arc of White supremacy and aggressively promote the rankest conservatism, racism, sexism, White supremacy, class exploitation, and democracy have become one and the same piece.

The all-important implication of this is that we are facing a choice between socialism or barbarism. As H. G. Wells penned, with such historical prescience, the tragically prophetic words in *The New World Order*, "In the world now all roads lead to socialism or social dissolution" (1940, p. 52). At a time in which morality and politics seemingly cannot go together in what has become, in our own country, a dime-store democracy with quick-drying ideas, a counterfeit public sphere where we gleefully disregard our duty to countenance and cure the everyday depredations of capitalist society—poverty, hunger, racism, violence—education remains in crisis. It can be reconstituted out of the debris left by efforts to privatize, corporatize, and demoralize it only if the social, political, and economic conditions of the larger society significantly change. Whereas advances in critical social theory have helped to provide a language with which to understand our own entrapment within capitalist social relations, its formidable jargon and pronounced tendency to turn off practitioners (transforming it into a selective tradition for mostly academic scholarship), critical pedagogy, with its emphasis on transformative praxis and its roar of dissidence, has helped to take critical theory to the streets, where more tranquil minds fear to tread. Here, critical pedagogy has helped students to navigate and interrogate the unfailingly bewildering rituals of daily survival and the culture industry which capitalism has spawned, empowering them to read the word and the world as agents of their own history. The primary exemplar in this regard is Paulo Freire. However, with each successive iteration of Freire's work, something of the original vibrancy is lost and its theoretical plangency diminished. Nevertheless, Freire's brilliance has exerted an Einsteinian deformation on the practice of pedagogy, bending the light of reason surrounding mainstream conventions by revealing that it is the practices of conventional pedagogy—its banking approach to knowledge production among them—that help to reproduce inequality and injustice in our capitalist society.

My own position, entrusted to Marx but universal in scope, is what I call revolutionary critical pedagogy. The driveshaft of revolutionary pedagogy—transformative praxis—is not the a luminous and imperishable gateway to a restorative oasis floating on the headwaters of creativity, but an agonistic, self-projective pathway to participating in self and social transformation, where the wick and tallow of our teaching is set ablaze in the radiance of our own being and where our students break out of the imprint of their human frailty by naming, challenging, and transcending those forces and relations that both negate and limit our own formation as historical subjects.

Arousing adversarial reactions while at the same time reinforcing the counterintuitive wisdom that being able to feed your family lies on the axis

of the capital/labor relation, that the epicenter of freedom is economic justice, and that class struggle takes priority over identity politics, revolutionary critical pedagogy swims against the liberal undercurrents that would
eventually overpower its more radical tendencies, undercurrents guided by
the staunch intuition that the full wingspan of critical pedagogy should be
occupied with questions of identity politics and cultural struggle and not
with the problems of capitalism and economic injustice.

We, as educators, need to discover sustainable solutions to the deepen-
ing causes of the crisis of global capitalism that is generating protest worldwide, solutions that speak to new strategies and forms of organization. We
will never have equal access to a quality education for all as long as there
exists economic inequality. We don't need increased accountability such as
value-added high-stakes testing and more test data—we need jobs. While it
is true that high child-poverty rates and long-standing economic inequality in the United States are making it impossible for the United States to
compete internationally in PISA rankings, why should we position our educational objectives according to the dictates of the World Bank or the International Monetary Fund? Where poverty rates are below 10%, U.S. students
rank first in the world on PISA in both mathematics and science, and where
poverty rates are between 10% and 24.9 %, U.S. students score 3rd behind
Korea and Finland (Horn & Wilburn, 2013).

John Marsh (2011) notes that the United States does not generate many
more poor people than other countries. European countries achieve lower poverty rates because they provide more social programs aimed at the
poor and unemployed. Without government programs, Sweden would have
26.7% of its population living in poverty, but with their social programs, the
poverty rate is 5.3%. To be sure, education helps some people enter the
labor market and indirectly might create a few more jobs, but what we need
is direct job creation, higher wages, and better redistribution programs.

Marsh (2011) notes that among children whose parents have identical
levels of education, those children who lived in unequal countries performed worse on tests of adult literacy. In general, children of parents with
college degrees perform the same whether they live in Finland, one of the
most equal countries, or the United States, one of the most unequal. But
children in the United States whose parents only attained high school will
perform worse on literacy tests than children in Finland whose parents only
attained high school degrees. This is because economic inequality affects
the quality of family life in areas of health, security, rates of substance abuse,
and in various other dimensions of everyday life.

In 2009, a controversial book, *The Spirit Level*, by epidemiologists Rich-
ard Wilkinson and Kate Pickett, created a toxic stir among U.S. conservatives by arguing that there are "pernicious effects that inequality has on
societies," which the authors meticulously itemized as 11 different health

and social problems that compose the social consequences of income inequality: physical health, mental health, drug abuse, education, imprisonment, obesity, social mobility, trust and community life, violence, teenage pregnancies, and child well-being—outcomes that are far greater in more unequal rich countries.

Tragically, in the United States, education has been made the only available means of addressing injustices that arise from economic disparity, and this to me constitutes one of the worst crimes of capitalism. As a social policy solution to economic exploitation, it is entirely enfeebling. Marsh (2011) makes the case that education should be treated as apolitical—not a market—phenomenon, and I agree. Clearly, we need social programs and noneducational interventions into the market. Some of these could include, for instance, redistributive tax rates, massive public works projects, a living wage law, or a renaissance of labor unions. But it seems clear that more workers with college degrees will not stem the rise of low-wage jobs nor will it reduce inequality. We can't use educational programs per se to reduce inequality, because this just won't work in a capitalist economy. Part of the reason that the United States is one of the most unequal countries in the world is that we have limited economic rights. The ruling elite maintains that our main vehicle for economic success should be connected fundamentally to our right to a decent education. But this is a dishonest ploy, I believe. As Marsh argues, we need more economic rights, and every right we have must have an independent status, such as the right to a useful and remunerative job, the right to adequate food and clothing, the right to a decent education, and so on. In the United States, education is seen as a requirement for all the other rights, and it is assumed that once you are given the right to a good education, all the other rights will take care of themselves. This is a flawed assumption. You can't make these rights dependent upon one another or an outgrowth of one another.

The biggest prohibitive obstacle to organizing the educational left is to develop confidence that an alternative to capitalism can be made viable. Socialism won't succeed unless it can display a socially viable universality, that is, unless it embraces the most developed areas of the world, including, if not especially, in the United States. And that presupposes that we acknowledge the most serious problems affecting contemporary education in the United States. Which is where this compelling book, *Inclusive Practices and Social Justice Leadership for Special Populations in Urban Settings: A Moral Imperative* by M. C. Kate Esposito and Anthony H. Normore, comes into the picture. This is a book that breaks from the compliance of tranquil minds, courageously examining issues that deal with a plethora of challenges to our educational system: mainstream perceptions of immigrants and the effects of education policy on language minority students; the suffocating and restrictive educational environments experienced by deaf and hard-of-hearing (DHH) students due to the oppression and exclusion of deaf people by hearing people, even in "inclusive" schools; experiences of lesbian, gay, bisexual and transgender (LGBT) students who routinely experience bullying in schools in their neighborhood settings and in cyber-space; the struggles of students with autism spectrum disorders, particularly in urban school settings and especially those from low income and under-represented racial minority backgrounds; the current educational experi-ence of disparity and marginalization of "invisible children" within the fos-ter system; the adversity faced by girls in urban settings; the experiences of men and women who have been incarcerated within the nation's prisons; the challenges faced by minority students whose cultures and histories are excluded in school curricula and teaching practices; challenges faced by boys of color in America' urban centers, chemically dependent adolescent Latino offenders, and students with disabilities.

The structural crisis of the capitalist system as a whole only exacerbates the challenges articulated and analyzed so meticulously in Esposito and Normore's important volume by authors uniquely adept and positioned in exposing the exploitative privileges at work in the educational system. Ed-ucation's social and metabolic control over the lives of our youth reflects the policies and practices of the capitalist elite, who target the most vulner-able populations in the poorest countries by means of austerity programs. We need a sustainable ecology of educational practices, that is, epochally sustainable solutions to the crisis of public education today, policies and practices that refuse to squander the lives of our most marginalized com-munities. We cannot let educational leaders and their administrations ac-commodate the objectives of education to the constraining limits of the currently accumulating problems and contradictions of neoliberal capi-talism that are leading to evermore authoritarian forms of "democratic" regulation.

Inclusive Practices and Social Justice Leadership for Special Populations in Ur-ban Settings: A Moral Imperative is a book whose editors evidently are excep-tionally gifted for their success in refusing to let the voices of dissent re-main marginalized in our discussion of education in the 21st century. They have done this by assembling an impressive array of authors who refuse to disregard the context of the external world when planning and plot-ting educational reform. The upshot of their investigations compels us to examine not only how educational policies are produced for the least advantaged in our schools, but how educators and students are themselves produced in the wider institutional, cultural, and economic arrangements of U.S. society. It is a book that will prove invaluable to all who choose to call themselves educators.

REFERENCES

Althusser, L. (1971). Ideology and ideological state apparatuses. In *Lenin and philosophy and other essays* (B. Brewster, Trans., pp. 121–176). New York, NY: Monthly Review Press.

Horn, J., & Wilburn, D. (2013). *The mismeasure of education.* Charlotte, NC: Information Age.

Marsh, J. (2011). *Class dismissed? Why we cannot teach or learn our way out of equality.* New York, NY: Monthly Review Press.

Wells, H. G. (1940). *The new world order.* London, England: Secker & Warburg.

Wilkinson, R., & Pickett, K. (2009). *The spirit level: Why more equal societies almost always do better.* London, UK: Allen Lane.

INTRODUCTION AND OVERALL FRAMEWORK

National figures suggest that millions of students are at risk of dropping out of school. Data further reveals that many of these students are from underserved and underrepresented groups, including students of color, students in foster care, students who are English language learners, students with disabilities and students who are economically poor (Alliance for Excellent Education, 2011). Although progress has been made in advancing equity agendas of access, participation, and academic achievement for individuals with disabilities and/or those from culturally, linguistically diverse, and economically poor backgrounds, significant work remains (Artiles, Bal, & King-Thorius, 2010). This is particularly true in urban schools which overwhelmingly serve students who are economically poor, culturally and linguistically diverse (CLD), and lag significantly behind their peers in academic achievement (Darling-Hammond, 1999). For example, more than ever, schools are enforcing stricter discipline policies (e.g., zero tolerance), which in turn have contributed to the delinquency of minority youth, especially Latino and African American youth, and increased rates of minority incarceration (Bernburg, Gunnar, Krohn, & Rivera, 2006). Minority youth comprise over 60% of children detained by juvenile justice systems across the United States (Hsia, Bridges, & McHale, 2004). These students are more than eight times as likely as their White peers to be housed in juvenile detention facilities (Wordes & Jones, 1998). In all but a few cases, these juveniles passed through traditional educational organizations on their way to incarceration. This path is commonly referred to as the *school to prison*

Inclusive Practices and Social Justice Leadership for Special Populations in Urban Settings, pages xix–xxiv
Copyright © 2015 by Information Age Publishing
xix

pipeline and represents a failure of our educational institutions, and our communities, to serve all students in their care. Truly, a moral and ethical imperative rooted within a social justice framework exists to ameliorate such failures.

The achievement of all urban students must be viewed both as an economic and moral imperative. The majority of the extant educational literature uses the term *Inclusion* to reference the practice of educating students with *identified* disabilities in the general education setting. This concept stems from the Individuals with Disabilities Education Improvement Act (IDEIA) (2004) and its subsequent amendments, which mandate that students with disabilities be educated in the general education setting to the maximum extent possible. The emphasis within the existing special education literature on the legal mandates of IDEIA underscores the fact that individuals with disabilities have faced and continue to face discrimination within schools and society. However, inclusion as we know it today is rooted in a philosophy that emphasizes the uniqueness of all learners, not just students with disabilities. For example, as Fisher and Frey (2001) noted, central to inclusive education is the belief that all students and their families are welcomed and valued members of the classroom, school, and community. An emphasis on high-quality classrooms and schools that are welcoming and affirming to all students, especially those most at risk for failure, is both a moral and ethical obligation for society and school systems alike.

To this end, effective inclusionary practices most certainly benefit all students, including English language learners, those who face gender discrimination, those who are in the foster care system, and those who are gay, lesbian, bisexual, or transgendered (Banks, 2014). The purpose of this edited volume is to examine current realities for special populations in urban schools. The authors in this collection present a broader theoretical inclusive framework rooted in social justice, which, we assert, offers the best practices for a greater number of students who are at risk of minimal academic success. The authors further posit that this broader conceptualization of inclusive schools adds to extant discourses about students with exceptional needs and provides effective strategies school leaders operating from a social justice framework can implement to create more inclusive school environments for all students, especially those in urban centers. It is hoped that lessons learned will improve the preparation and practice of school leaders, thus improving educational outcomes for students from special populations. The book is organized into 11 chapters as follows:

In Chapter 1, "Why Equity Matters in 'Turn White and Speak English' Political Climate: English Language Learners and Educational Trajectories," Irina S. Okhremtchouk explores historical developments and immigration as well as education policies motivating current mainstream perceptions of the nation's immigrants. The readers are invited to examine whether the current landscape of the public education system in the United States fulfills the equity goals of its premise, that is, serving as "the great equalizer" in our society, for the fastest growing segment of student population in the nation's public schools. In order to introduce an authentic voice to the current political and policy landscape, this chapter provides several synopses of interviews with immigrant students sharing their life and schooling experiences through their own words and in their own voices. O'Brien and Brooks present "Deaf Culture and Education: Toward a Culturally Relevant Leadership" in Chapter 2. These authors argue that it is important to understand the experiences of students, particularly Deaf students, not in terms of disability, but through culture. Further, there is little research related to urban minority deaf youth and how Deaf culture and culturally relevant leadership might impact the education of these students.

In Chapter 3, "Creating Inclusive Schools for Gay, Bisexual, Lesbian, Transgender, and Queer/Questioning (GBLTQ) Students: Applying a Social Justice Framework," Thing and Esposito review current research specific to LGBTQ students, examining the best practices educational leaders can implement to improve educational outcomes for LGBTQ students. These authors further provide a theoretical social justice framework school leaders can operate to ensure their setting is truly inclusive. Spence and Peña, in Chapter 4, "Intersections of Autism, Race, and Class: A New Social Justice Agenda for Inclusive Leadership Practices," call attention to the fact that inclusion in general education settings has been a challenge for students with autism spectrum disorders, particularly in urban school settings. They suggest that because families in urban settings tend to lack social and cultural capital to navigate school systems and special education services, they are less likely to advocate for services and interventions for their children with autism. As such, they call school leaders in urban settings to take an active role in supporting the inclusion of students with autism. Recommendations are made for educational leaders to facilitate and lead inclusive educational practices for students with autism spectrum disorders in urban settings. In Chapter 5, "Inclusion Needs of Youth in the Foster Care System Through Strategic Mentoring: A Social Justice Perspective," Susanne M. Foulk examines current educational disparities for youth in the foster system from a social justice lens. In doing so, Foulk highlights the perpetual emotional pain, poverty, and displacement felt by many children and youth within the foster care system. Foulk further highlights the policies, practices, and trends that serve as exclusionary measures, in which the educational needs of children are often left unaddressed as overburdened government systems attempt to respond to basic safety needs. Through mentor engagement, foster youth may more effectively navigate their educational journey, resolve their sense of individual identities as learners, and gain a sense of voice, which assists them in moving beyond their oppression toward successful outcomes and offers hope for their futures.

Dorel and Tejeda, in Chapter 6, "Affect and Resilience in Urban Females: An Emerging Paradigm," explore exclusionary practices of females in urban settings resulting from standards-based reform which seeks to reach students in the cognitive domain. Garfield Dorel and Tejeda examine the role of teachers and administrators in cultivating inclusion through the teaching of resilience. The authors of this chapter posit that females in urban settings experience adversity in everyday life, and it is up to teachers and administrators to harness that adversity into a productive character trait, such as resilience. In Chapter 7, "Educating the Incarcerated Through a Community Jailing Model: A Social Justice Leadership Perspective," Choate and Normore discuss the implications of the fact that 2.2 million inmates in today's jails and prisons will be released. These authors examine models of cultural, restorative, and social justice leadership centered on the idea of "community jailing"—a direct supervision technique allowing for greater and meaningful officer/inmate interaction. Choate and Normore offer suggestions for making positive change, including prison-based/education-based incarceration programs. A new community jailing supervision model is suggested as a social justice response coupled with evidence to corroborate lower incidence of jail violence, a reduction in recidivism, and improved public safety. Berryman, Nevin, SooHoo, and Ford, in Chapter 8, "A Culturally Responsive Framework for Social Justice," assert that today's culturally, ethnically, and linguistically diverse educational system continues to expect all students to be represented within the same curriculum, pedagogy, and testing regimen which has resulted in separate enclaves. Chapter 8 presents an alternative framework the authors termed *culturally responsive inclusion*. Based on key understandings derived from Kaupapa Māori and Freirean philosophies as delineated in *Culturally Responsive Methodologies* (Berryman, SooHoo, & Nevin, 2013), the authors put forth a framework where establishing respectful relationships of interdependence with people is central to both human dignity and praxis. A culturally responsive framework such as this challenges traditional notions of the professional expert working with objectivity; instead, it opens up spaces that call for engagement through the establishment of relational and interdependent discourses.

In Chapter 9, "Our Forgotten Sons: The Underachievement of Boys of Color in America's Urban Centers," Nicole Limperopulos asserts that, 59 years after the *Brown* decision, we stand at a precipice that threatens to undermine the success of our democracy: enduring exclusionary practices that perpetuate the chronic underachievement of boys of color in our nation's urban centers. Limperopulos seeks to catalyze educational leaders to eradicate the exclusionary processes that contribute to the cycle of inferiority and underachievement by adopting best practices that address the discrete needs of this unique population. Calling upon a corpus of literature in urban studies, psychology, adolescent development, and educational leadership, Limperopulos deconstructs the factors that contribute to the underachievement of boys of color, including historic attitudes of racism and classism, the effects of chronic violence exposure, misdiagnosis and disproportionate classification as special education students, and application of harsh discipline policies that lead to increased rates of entry into the criminal justice system. This chapter concludes by imploring educational leaders to implement inclusive practices that eradicate the marginalization of boys of color, thereby enabling them to reach their full academic and personal potential as valued members of the school community. Marietti, Tucker, and Normore, in Chapter 10, "Chemically Dependent Adolescent Latino Offenders: Restorative and Social Justice as Alternatives to Incarceration," demonstrate that Latino youth have disproportionately high contact with the juvenile justice system and that they would benefit from greater access to community-based preventive services and alternatives to detention (Moeller, 2011). Marietti, Tucker, and Normore assert that intervention and treatment options show great promise in reducing a future with the justice system. Chapter 10 further suggests that restorative justice models emphasized by treatment-oriented drug courts and recovery programs promote social justice through reintegration of offenders into the community. The book concludes with Chapter 11, "Implementing a Holistic Approach to Enhance Career Opportunities for Transition Students With Disabilities." Stuntzner and Austin review the critical role of transition in successful employment, career planning, self-determination, and independent living for students with disabilities. Chapter 11 demonstrates that students with disabilities oftentimes fall short and do not succeed following high school. In an effort to change this trend, information pertaining to transition services and ways it can be enhanced are provided. This chapter addresses the necessity of transition services and their relationship to federal legislation, barriers that inhibit students' successful transition to adult life, and the current climate of the public educational system. A framework of recommendations is provided for educators assisting students with disabilities.

—**M. C. Kate Esposito**
Anthony H. Normore

REFERENCES

Alliance for Excellence in Education (2011). *Education and the Economy: boosting the nation's economy by improving high school graduation rates among students of color and native students.* Retrieved on April 7, 2015 from http://all4ed.

org/reports-factsheets/education-and-the-economy-boosting-the-nations-economy-by-improving-high-school-graduation-rates-among-students-of-color-and-native-students/

Artiles, A. J., Bal, A., & King Thorius, K. A. (2010). Back to the future: A critique of Response to Intervention's social justice views. *Theory into Practice, 49,* 250–257.

Banks, J. A. (2014). *An introduction to multicultural education* (5th ed). Upper Saddle River, NJ: Pearson.

Bernburg, J., Gunner, J., Krohn, M. D., & Rivera, C. D. (2006). Official labeling, criminal embeddedness, and subsequent delinquency: A longitudinal test of labeling theory. *Journal of Research in Crime and Delinquency, 43*(1), 67–88.

Berryman, M., SooHoo, S., & Nevin, A. (2013). *Culturally responsive methodologies.* Bingley, UK: Emerald.

Darling-Hammond, L. (1999). Educating teachers for California's future. *Teacher Education Quarterly, 28,* 9–55.

Fisher, D., & Frey, N. (2001). Access to the core curriculum: Critical ingredients for student success. *Remedial and Special Education, 22*(3), 148–157.

Hsia, H. M., Bridges, G. S., & McHale, R. (2004). *Disproportionate minority confinement: 2002 update.* Washington, DC: U.S. Department of Justice, Office of Juvenile Justice and Delinquency Prevention.

Individuals with Disabilities Education Improvement Act of 2004, P. L. 108-446, 20 U.S.C. § 1400 et seq.

Moeller, M. (2011, February). Reauthorizing the Juvenile Justice and Delinquency Prevention Act: The impact on Latino youth. *National Council of La Raza.* Retrieved from http://www.nclr.org/images/uploads/publications/Reauthorizing_the_JJDPA_The_Impact_on_Latino_Youth_1.pdf

Wordes, M., & Jones, S. (1998). Trends in juvenile detention and steps toward reform. *Crime and Delinquency, 44,* 544–560.

CHAPTER 1

WHY EQUITY MATTERS IN "TURN WHITE AND SPEAK ENGLISH" POLITICAL CLIMATE

English Language Learners and Educational Trajectories

Irina S. Okhremtchouk
Arizona State University

ABSTRACT

This chapter explores historical developments and immigration as well as education policies motivating current mainstream perceptions of the nation's immigrants. The readers are invited to examine whether the current landscape of the public education system in the United States fulfills the equity goals of its premise, that is, serving as "the great equalizer" in our society, for the fastest growing segment of student population in the nation's public schools. Furthermore, this chapter examines a stagnation of progress in the upward social mobility of this population, more specifically, in the sector of

Inclusive Practices and Social Justice Leadership for Special Populations in Urban Settings, pages 1–20
Copyright © 2015 by Information Age Publishing
All rights of reproduction in any form reserved.

public education. While discussing policy developments, this chapter high-lights several key facets relating to direct effects on language minority students and the many impacts these policies have on them. And lastly, in order to introduce an authentic voice to the current political and policy landscape, this chapter provides several synopses of interviews with immigrant students sharing their life and schooling experiences through their own words and in their own voices.

INTRODUCTION

You leave and then you come back and they did something amazing and they were doing something together and you miss out on that and you see that they are bonding and the teacher is bonding with them [classmates] and you are missing out on that... I think that's what hurt the most because you want to belong, you don't want to be that Mexican girl... you want to belong, you know?

—Student's reflection on experiences
as an English language learner.

From the very first day English language learners (ELLs) enroll in U.S. schools, they face many disadvantages and inequities, which permeate numerous contexts within the contemporary public education system. Over time, these inequities turn into the status quo, that is, an unavoidable reality for this student population that comes in various forms that often manifest themselves in lack of access to equitable instruction, qualified teachers, appropriate instructional materials, and even meaningful supplemental services intended to better these students' academic trajectories, just to name a few. This is alarming, especially given the fact that more than 10% of students attending the nation's schools are classified ELL (Aud et al., 2013), 25% of all students in the United States identify with Latino/a heritage (Fry & Lopez, 2012), and one in five students in America is a child of immigrants and speaks a language other than English in the home (Capps et al., 2005). And projections show that by 2030, language minority students will compose 40% of student population nationwide (Thomas & Collier, 2002).

In spite of the abovementioned reports and demographic shifts in school composition, ELLs continue to experience high dropout rates, low academic outcomes, and the persisting achievement gap between ELLs and their English-only counterparts has not changed significantly in years (Gándara, Maxwell-Jolly, & Rumberger, 2008). All of these are further coupled with and complicated by other commonly cited practices, stagnating ELLs' academic and social opportunities, such as disproportionate over-representation of ELL students in Special Education programs and under-representation in programs for gifted and talented students (Artiles, Bal & King Thorius, 2010). The urgency to address ELLs' needs is pressing and can no longer be ignored. That being said, however, more often than not, policy attempts to resolve the abovementioned issues have been ineffective, ill-informed, and in some cases even damaging to academic as well as social development of this student population.

To frame this chapter within the social justice framework, throughout this piece I argue (explicitly and implicitly) that it is our collective moral responsibility and, indeed, obligation to ameliorate failures that exist within the U.S. public education system affecting habitually marginalized students, including language minority and ELLs (Banks, 2014). The social justice framework emphasizes the need for professionals who work in educational settings to first embrace, support, and then implement systemic efforts where these professionals play roles of advocates to combat existing social tribulations (Miller & Garran, 2008). That is, educational professionals (i.e., district and school leaders, administrators, and teachers alike) are the ones who are uniquely positioned and have powers to implement change and therefore be an element of that change toward more socially just schools and consequently society at-large.

While reflecting on my own professional trajectory within the U.S. public education system as a teacher, program coordinator, board member, child advocate, and now professor, without a doubt all these roles have had a significant impact on my current work and continue to deepen my understandings of the issues concerning educational equity and social justice. My choice to study the educational experiences of language minority students is in part attributable to my own personal journey as an ELL as well as to further decipher and understand the unique characteristics this rapidly expanding student population brings to the American public education system. Considering my prior and current positionality, this work constitutes an exploration of prominent issues permeating educational contexts as I either personally experienced or witnessed and then later studied. All of which I hope will assist the readers (especially in the education professions) in their examinations of the continued deficit, monolithic perceptions of ELLs, as well as lack of policy response and action to the unconscionable treatment of language minority and ELL students.

In writing this chapter, I first invite the readers to assess the premise of the American public educational system and its goals. Then I present an examination of several key historical developments, recent immigration and education policies motivating mainstream perceptions about the nation's immigrants and thus shaping educational trajectories for this student population, many of whom are in the process of learning the English language. While discussing policy developments, I highlight several key facets relating to the direct and detrimental effects they have on language minority students as manifested within the educational system and society at-large. And lastly, I conclude with snapshots of interviews from my prior work (Okhremtchouk & Carlson, 2013) in this area to illustrate how current educational conditions negatively affect language minority students—and thus shape their life trajectories in "Turn White and Speak English" political climate.

AMERICAN EDUCATION SYSTEM AND ITS GOALS

The constant demographic fluidity in the United States has played a significant role in shaping this nation. Historically, immigrant waves have come and gone as American society continues to grow more diverse. Commonly labeled as a nation of opportunity and the melting pot, the United States perpetuates a notion of the American Dream. This belief, in and of itself, continues to attract people from all walks of life, classes, backgrounds, and heritage to strive for, as perceived, the limitless opportunities this nation has to offer to those who are willing to work hard.

It is through the American public education system that many (including immigrants and citizens) hope to realize the American Dream—the pinnacle of success. Horace Mann, the father of the American public education system, once said, "Education then, beyond all other devices of human origin, is the great equalizer of the conditions of men, the balance-wheel of the social machinery" (cited in Carlton, 1908, p. 50).

Hence, commonly perceived as the great equalizer, the system is looked upon as the remedy for societal inequalities where everyone is treated equally and receives the same opportunities to learn and demonstrate their potential despite one's background or heritage. While this precise notion is cultivated by societal beliefs that public education "goods" are distributed based on equity, it neglects the inequalities perpetuated by the political climate, which inevitably steers the public education system in a desired direction promoted and sustained by the mainstream culture.

Specifically, for language minority, English language learner (ELL) students and their families, this notion is deeply rooted in the perpetuating ideal that the United States is a nation of immigrants, or the "melting pot." To that end, the acquisition and pursuit of the American Dream is the nation's highest commodity sold domestically and worldwide, where one either wants it, is in a constant quest to achieve it, or among the few who have acquired it. In this regard, and for many, the Untied States of America represents economic and social stability, a chance to pursue economic growth and freedom from injustices. These notions are rooted in the belief that the cornerstone of this society is the equality of opportunity, which represents the very foundation of this country—by and for the people where upward social mobility is not only achievable, but is an absolute promise.

That being said, however, there is a significant disconnect between a persistently changing national demographic (a significant part of which has been facilitated by immigration) and the mainstream societal perceptions which have been woven together and catalyzed by the Eurocentric Caucasian male-driven views that perpetuate as well as shape national policies and that of individual states. As a result, a number of misconceptions have surfaced to combat the shifting demographics and changes within society in the United States. Indeed, unlike commonly adopted mainstream perceptions of ELLs as foreigners or foreign-born, remarkably, more than half (57% to be exact) of the adolescent ELLs were born in the United States and more than 75% of elementary-age students are second- or third-generation immigrants (Batalova, Fix, & Murray, 2007).

This ongoing tension between the mainstream Eurocentric hold on power and the nation's immigrants is particularly pronounced in matters of the public sector, where public goods are distributed (e.g., public education system) and evidenced in English-only mandates as well as other anti-immigrant propositions in the contemporary political landscape. Nonetheless, in some sectors of government, policymakers (albeit neglectfully) are attempting to uphold the goals of the American public education system in their efforts to achieve equity and level the playing field for ELLs and other habitually marginalized students. The question remains, however, as to whether these efforts are effective or indeed whether they achieve these goals.

What Is Equity and Why Does the American Education System Advocate for It?

The meaning of equity varies depending on whom one asks. In education, equity has been consistently used to describe fair treatment of all students; specifically, of those students who bring certain academic and other needs into a classroom and who differ from a typical mainstream student or, in other words, their needs are different from that of a typical mainstream student's needs (Artiles et al., 2010; Banks, 2014). A commonly used response to achieving equity in the American K–12 educational system pipeline has been through enactment of policies that would guarantee additional supplemental services and programs to assist students with special needs (e.g., the Individuals with Disabilities Education Improvement Act, 2004). This unequal treatment of unequals or vertical equity approach (Berne & Stiefel, 1999) has been widely utilized by both federal and state governments—one of the oldest and by far largest examples of such are programs sustained by the Elementary and Secondary Education Act (ESEA) of 196,5 subsequently reauthorized and implemented as the No Child Left Behind Act (NCLB, 2001).

These programs, designed to address inequalities in order to achieve equity within the system, come in the form of categorical grants. Categorical programs are restricted funds intended for a specified purpose to address a particular educational need or accomplish a specific educational objective. In the case of ELL students, these funds are designed to promote the academic achievement of this student population and support second language acquisition efforts. In other words, these funds are used to allot resources to address ELL students' needs or provide an incentive for local educational agencies to create, sustain, support, and/or reform an educational program or initiative (Okhremtchouk, 2014). To that end, the overarching aim of categorical funding mechanisms is to ensure access to specified programs, thus maximizing the potential for success of otherwise at-risk students. In doing so, categorical programs are designed to provide supplemental funding to accommodate students' needs without any cost to Local Education Agencies' (LEA) general fund (Okhremtchouk, 2014).

That being said, however, student needs in achieving equity are not always the central focus in formulating categorical programs. As discussed by Thomas Timar (2007), categorical dollars do not consistently follow the needs of students for whom these funds are intended, because the distribution of categorical programs is politicized as a mechanism of competing interests, resulting in targeted programs that favor economically advantaged constituencies instead of populations they were intended to benefit. More specific to ELL students, Okhremtchouk (2011) notes that ELL categorical dollars (both federal and state) are grossly and habitually misused because school district needs (which favor more advantaged students) take precedence over those of students for whom these funds are intended. Moreover, Okhremtchouk notes that these resources are not discussed or allocated for ELL direct services, but rather are used to "keep the system operational" (p. 152). Unsettling is the fact that these supplemental funds were used to supplant—*not supplement*—key educational resources (i.e., textbooks and other obligatory materials to be provided by the district and/or school) as compared to utilizing these categorical dollars on expenditures promoting supplemental academic support programs and direct services for ELLs, as intended by state and federal mandates.

Another dimension—demonstrating the marginalization of students—is the situation of competing interests ascribed to various categorical grants, such as special education, bilingual education, and compensatory education. As indicated by Parrish, Perez, Merickel, and Linquant (2006), competing interests for targeted funds may prevent or stagnate the flexibility required in resource allocation at the local level to more effectively address the complex educational needs of students representing a range of educational needs and characteristics.

Instantiations of social inequities for our most marginalized students are evidenced when at-risk students (e.g., ELLs, those with disabilities or economically poor) are simply used to meet a threshold established by categorical programs and thus generate revenues for their districts. Matsudaira, Hosek and Walsh (2012) found that school sites are disposed to respond to the incentives outlined in the Title I guidelines (NCLB, 2001) to secure a greater amount in federal funds. This tactic manifested in a manipulation of the application sign-up process of those students who were eligible to receive free or reduced lunch in order to meet the threshold required by Title I categorical program (Matsudaira et al., 2012).

Consequently, this pursuit for more equitable education through categorical funding sources proves to be problematic due to the unintended consequences described above and how local entities (school districts and their corresponding schools) respond to the measures designed to equalize the playing field. In short, such tactics at times only increase overrepresentation of minority students in programs tied to categorical funding (e.g., Special Education or Title I) without clear established goals to ameliorate academic achievement among the groups of students for whom these funds are intended.

Another unintended consequence is the labeling of educational needs. While the labeling of educational needs for purposes of identifying the beneficiaries of entitlement-based categorical grants is a standard practice in the field of education, such labeling has the inadvertent consequence of target populations being viewed primarily as deficient in their educational preparation, skills, home cultures, and even potential. Many habitually marginalized students (e.g., ELLs, students with special needs) continue to be disenfranchised by the use of various labels identifying their so-called needs. Such characterizations reflect a pervasive use of cultural-deficit models to identify the educational needs of children and youth in the name of equity.

Yet dollars do not always follow the needs of those for whom these funds are intended and for whom the equity measures are essentially put in place (Okhremtchouk, 2011; Parrish et al., 2006; Timar, 2007). Nevertheless, balancing the concern for avoiding deficit-based labels with accurately identifying educational needs presents a conundrum—categorical programs purported to address the most acute educational gaps in an effort to facilitate comparable benefit (afforded to the mainstream student population) from a common public educational system. In that, even with policy-driven equity measures in place, language minority and ELL students are habitually shortchanged in their acquisition of supplemental resources (Okhremtchouk, 2011; Timar, 2007). The case of which will be further explored in the proceeding sections.

HISTORICAL DEVELOPMENTS: DEMOGRAPHIC SHIFTS
AND RESPONSE TO STUDENT NEEDS

It has been well documented that language minority and ELL students have been and continue to be oppressed as they progress through the American public educational system pipeline. These challenges stretch from basic entitlements, such as availability of needed professional expertise, for example, highly qualified teachers with deep content knowledge needed to address their academic and language needs, adequate instructional materials to facilitate their learning, structural facilities to support and promote their educational engagement (Gándara et al. 2008; Gándara & Merino, 1993; Okhremtchouk & Jimenez, 2013) all the way to political and societal marginalization—manifesting itself in segregation practices (within the public educational system and beyond) (Faltis & Arias, 2012) coupled with lack of access to opportunities that would guarantee upward mobility within the society. Overcoming such oppression is especially challenging for those students and their parents, who are struggling not only in navigating through the educational system, but who are simultaneously learning a new language and educational system itself.

It is a known fact that today our schools are more diverse than ever before, with Latino/as being the fastest growing segment of our nation's population (Camacho Liu, 2011). In fact, the Latino/a population composes the largest segment in both language minority and ELL students (Echevarria, Vogt, & Short, 2014). Border states in particular enroll more Latino/a students in K–12 public schools than any other states.

Using California and Arizona as an example, over half of all students enrolled in K–12 public schools are of Latino/a heritage, the majority of whom being born in the United States (Batalova et al., 2007). That being said, however, although Latino/a students overwhelmingly populate the K–12 public education system in California and Arizona, it is not reflected in postsecondary settings. College enrollments constitute just a fraction of this student population. Roughly 30% of Latino/a-origin students are enrolled in postsecondary schools in California and a mere 15% in Arizona (Trends in Latino College Access and Success, 2011). This disproportionality is not only of national significance but requires a social justice lens to examine its potential impacts on the students and ultimately our nation as a whole. To further examine what could be the reasons for this disfranchisement in the nation's education pipeline, an investigation of what has been the catalyst for shaping educational experiences as well as trajectories for language minority and ELL students is warranted. As such, the following section will address the factors related to the marginalization of language minority students, which perpetuates the new American underclass.

Defining the New American Underclass Through a Decollation of the "Official Language"

Americans have high regard for learning a foreign language or multiple languages when it takes place at an educational institution (i.e., university) or abroad; however, the immigrants' right to pass their language and cultural heritage on to their children is typically met with great hesitation and disapproval (Fishman, 1978). One of the very first examples of this bias was evidenced right around or shortly after World War I, when a number of states passed laws restricting or completely forbidding the support for bilingual and/or foreign language instruction. In fact, by 1923, some 34 states had passed legislation prohibiting public instruction in any language other than English (Toth, 1990). *Meyer v. Nebraska* (1923) is one of the well-known cases involving this issue. The lawsuit challenged restrictions placed on teaching in a foreign language. In the lower courts it was decided that teaching German to children of immigrants was unfavorable to national safety; however, the Supreme Court overturned the decision. The court further established that forbidding foreign language instruction was unconstitutional. Even though the decision in *Meyer v. Nebraska* was powerful and sent a strong message, the ruling itself set a faint precedent for educational rights pertaining to language instruction and language minority students (Wiley, 2007). Essentially, the case was a loss for the immigrants, their children, and language minority rights activists since the case did not justify or rule in support of the right of an individual to use a heritage language (Meyer v. Nebraska, 1923).

Several decades would elapse following *Meyer v. Nebraska* (1923) before Americans started to reexamine foreign language instruction, its value, and its need. It was not until the legendary launch of the Russian spacecraft Sputnik that U.S. policymakers as well as American society would reconsider their views about foreign language, its instruction and value (Lessow-Hurley, 2000). It is important to note, however, that a short-lived tolerance-oriented policy was primarily applied to language minority groups of European origin (Wiley, 2007). As history has shown over and over again, a lack of support for heritage language instruction tends to be racially motivated (Baker & de Kanter, 1983; Crawford, 1989; Portes & Hao, 1998). For example, people of African origin have had a significantly different experience, where restrictive heritage language and literacy policies have been in effect for almost 100 years. Since 1740, slaveholders had perceived literacy (especially literacy in the native/home language among people of African origin) as a threat, resulting in the establishment of compulsory literacy laws, which remained active up until 1846 (Weinberg, 1977).

In the mid-19th century, the notion that all children deserved the right to educational opportunity in publicly supported schools gained favor across the nation (Wiley, 2007). As this movement of access to publicly funded education developed, the right to an equal education was selectively withheld from many children of color, some of whom were also language minorities (Weinberg, 1977). In California, for example, the state's constitution affirmed legal segregation of students who were of Indian, Chinese, Japanese, or Mongolian heritage from the late 19th to mid-20th century (Chin, 1998; Munoz, 2004). It was not until the ruling of *Mendez v. Westminster* in 1946 that the segregation of public schools in California became illegal (Mendez v. Westminster, 1946; Munoz, 2004). While the sate of California became the first state in the nation to officially end segregation in public schools after *Mendez v. Westminster* of 1946, and prior to *Brown v. Board of Education* of 1954, the state had a long history of anti-immigrant provisions, in a more recent example with an English-only twist.

In 1986, Californians, in an overwhelming majority, passed Proposition 63, which declared English as the official language of the state (Dyste, 1989). Dyste (1989), in his review of Proposition 63, asserts, "To many people [Proposition 63] represented a basic social norm of American society—Americans speak English—and in that sense it was very hard to be against it. And for some it was an idea which was already felt to be true" (p. 328). However, Dyste further argues that in fact, this symbol was used deliberately by an organization to promote "U.S. English" and "enact a political agenda to fight the use of languages other than English in the public sector" (p. 329).

Another perfect example of the attempts at language suppression is Arizona's "official language" attempt and later success. Although Arizona's path in declaring English as an official language of the state was not as simple as in California, the same result through a proposition initiative has eventually solidified the fate of the struggle in the "official language" debate. To this end, passed by a narrow 50.5 to 49.5 margin in Arizona in 1988, Proposition 106 declared English as the official language of the state. The Arizona Supreme Court overturned this very proposition citing unconstitutionality 10 years later. In 2005, the second attempt at a similar measure was made and passed the Arizona House as well as Senate, but was later vetoed by then-Governor Napolitano. After polls showed that a majority of Arizonans disagreed with the governor's action, the measure was reintroduced as a ballot initiative in 2006. Now known as Proposition 103, the initiative passed in 2006, declaring English as the official language of the state and significantly reducing government sponsorship as well as funding for bilingual social services and dual-language-printed material for circulation (Proposition 103 – Arizona Law, 2006).

As the above evidence shows, habitually, language minority's rights to speak their heritage language and exercise their heritage along with demands for equal treatment have been constantly questioned and directly tied to one's immigration status. More recently, the matter of one's documented status has permeated the political debate. The terminology alone to describe the immigrant segment of American society has centered on who is considered human as compared to an "alien" and whether that individual is "legal" as compared to an illegal substance. This widely used terminology attached another label to the meaning of what defines a human of certain origin and more importantly, an individual in American society. Sadly but true, these various dehumanizing brands have become synonymous with the Latino/a race, which by default, morphed societal beliefs into new dimensions that, what I argue here, define a new American underclass.

Contemporary Political Climate and the Effects on Language Minority and ELL Students

The negatively charged political climate molded over time by various anti-immigrant propositions and legislation has unquestionably impacted language minority students' educational and life trajectories to a significant degree. Essentially, the expansion of one student population in particular, Latino/a students, has impacted policies in several border states (e.g., California and Arizona) that directly affect educational prospects and ultimately these students' lives. Even though recent political developments are primarily designed to target individuals of Latino/a origin, by default, all immigrant students and children of immigrants are affected by the anti-immigrant sentiment permeating key areas within public societal structures (i.e., education) that these policies target.

Again, to use California and Arizona as examples here, the anti-immigrant propositions and legislation have been facilitated, for the large part, due to xenophobic response to the expansion of the immigrant populations in the last three decades (Crawford, 2008). Although differences in the political affiliations of the voting majority as well as how these two states tackle social issues make them distinctly different—both states have long histories of anti-immigrant sentiment. More notably, matters associated with assimilation, second language acquisition (that of the English language), and one's heritage have played a significant role in impacting educational policies in these two states.

Declaring English as the official language in these two border states was just the first few steps in a series of other English-only, anti-immigrant propositions and legislation. Both states have also passed "English-only School Mandates," also known as "English for Children" initiatives introduced and sponsored by Ron Unz, California businessman, political activist, and unsuccessful candidate for the California governorship in 1994 (Crawford, 2008). Propositions 227 (California) and 203 (Arizona) passed in 1998 and

2000, respectively. Although Proposition 227 did not explicitly forbid bilingual instruction, as special exemptions were made for students to remain in English-immersion or bilingual classes when parents so desire, it placed a number of limitations on bilingual education and instructional strategies for ELLs (Crawford, 2000). Moreover, various teacher disciplinary provisions were implemented under this law, which aim to discipline teachers who refuse to teach solely or predominantly in English (California Secretary of State, 1998). In the case of Arizona's Proposition 203, the choice of bilingual education is a much more complicated feat because of bureaucratic red tape that technically eliminates the option to instruct culturally and linguistically diverse students altogether. Arizona's initiative not only significantly restricts parental rights to choose between bilingual and English-only instruction, but it also restricts the freedom of parental choice (often allotted to parents of mainstream heritage) as it pertains to movement between programs (i.e., school officials may reject waiver transfer requests without explanation or legal consequence) if their student is classified as ELL (Crawford, 2008).

The xenophobic approach did not end with English-only measures. To that end, the English-only initiatives (both in school and beyond) are amongst other more direct and severe anti-immigrant propositions and legislationthat have been enacted in these two states. California's Proposition 187 of 1994, also known as *Save Our State Initiative* (*SOS*), was designed to prohibit access for undocumented citizens to medical care, social services, and public education. As was in the case of California's Proposition 63 (i.e., "U.S. English," declaring English as the official language of the state), an overwhelming majority of California voters supported Proposition 187. However, 3 years later, the federal court found Proposition 187 unconstitutional, stating that this law would inherently perpetuate racial profiling (ACLU, 1999).

Modeled after California's hurtful/racist/discriminatory Proposition 187, Proposition 200 was approved by Arizona voters in 2004. Proposition 200 sought to restrict access to state and local (i.e., city) benefits to undocumented citizens. Although challenged in courts several times over the course of 6 years, the attempts were unsuccessful. By its intent and design, Proposition 200 has paved the road for another, more stringent anti-immigrant legislation.

In 2010, Arizona's governor signed the most draconian nation bill on undocumented immigration into law, Senate Bill 1070. Its aim is to identify, prosecute, and deport undocumented citizens or, as the proposition callously refers to these individuals, "illegal immigrants." Despite the U.S. Supreme Court's ruling in 2012 that immigration and citizenship status are to remain under federal control, the most controversial "show me your papers" clause, was left intact. This section of SB 1070 allows police officers to conduct immigration status checks during lawful stops (e.g., traffic violations), naturally leading to racial profiling of individuals. Fueled by the, at the time, climate and limited opposition, Arizona legislators took an another step through passage of House Bill 2281 (HB 2281, 2010), to not only limit school districts' educational freedoms, but to also substantially limit students' access to culturally relevant literature "deemed" to favor immigrants and their children. The first of its kind in recent history, HB 2281 prohibits public schools (both charter and comprehensive) from offering courses that advocate ethnic solidarity and/or cater to a specific ethnic group, which is coupled with promoting the overthrow of the U.S. government and creating resentment toward a race or class of people (HB 2281, 2010). Section 15-111 of the act justifies this bill, stating, "The legislature finds and declares that public school pupils should be taught to treat and value each other as individuals and not based on ethic background." This very justification serves as an oxymoron based on the simple fact that an individual could never merely divorce one's heritage or one's identity, which often includes linguistic as well as ethnic background. This law placed Arizona public school districts in a bind where they are to choose between the best empirically demonstrated methods and imposed penalties for noncompliance, potentially resulting in up to 10% withholdings of state aid.

Public school districts are not the only public educational entities that have been affected by the political developments driving anti-immigrant mandates. In 2006, Arizona voters approved Proposition 300 (Proposition 300 – Arizona Law, 2006). This law provides that university students who do not have documented immigration status are not eligible for in-state tuition status or financial aid that is funded or subsidized by state dollars. Essentially, the law actively seeks to deny these students an education by restricting access to affordable public college education for those students who are undocumented and further stagnates access to public goods. Moreover, this draconian law requires Arizona institutions of higher learning to report aggregate data on those students who are undocumented, effectively targeting this student population and resulting in avoidance of a public college education altogether by these individuals (even if they can afford to pay out-of-state tuition) due to fear.

Translating Policy Into Practice: ELL Educational Environments

As discussed above, both California and Arizona passed oppressive English-only propositions, which significantly restricts ELLs' experiences in schools and their academic trajectories overall. To further explore and understand how language minority students and, more specifically, ELLs experience educational environments in light of these policies, this subsection of the chapter specifically explores educational conditions as experienced by these subgroups of students.

The proponents of California's Proposition 227 argued that this proposition would not only contribute to better educational programs for ELLs, but also reduce costs associated with funding bilingual coordinators' positions and stipends for bilingual teachers. Consequently, the state government will experience considerable financial relief (California Secretary of State, 1998). However, a study conducted prior to Proposition 227 showed that schools already lacked sufficient resources to execute all their responsibilities (Gándara & Merino, 1993). One of the consequences, as pointed out by Gándara and Merino (1993), was the lack of adequate local resources available to reclassify students from ELLs to fluent proficient. Later reviews of Proposition 227 and its outcomes suggest that the state has largely failed to assess the conditions of education for ELLs by not "adequately mentoring their educational opportunities in terms of access to critical resources such as qualified teachers, appropriate instructional materials, course work, and learning environments" (Gándara & Rumberger, 2008, p. 11). Furthermore in another article, Rumberger and Gándara (2004) argue that the implementation of Proposition 227 was poorly articulated; as a result, the learning conditions for ELLs actually worsened considerably since its implementation.

A 5-year review investigating the effects of Proposition 227 on ELL and the overall educational climate, Parrish et al. (2006) showed that there had been a staggering decline in bilingual services offered to ELLs. For example, bilingual programs across the state of California have declined from 30% to 8% as of 2003. Although, understandably, the decline in bilingual services is expected to be due to legal mandates stemming from passage of prohibitive propositions, this steep decline may also be attributed to confusion about what programs are allowed under Proposition 227. For example, the Proposition 227 provisions do allow for "alternative programs" (i.e., bilingual instruction), however, results suggest that "parents' understanding of their waiver rights and schools' acceptance or rejection of waiver requests are often governed by prior practice and the predisposition of providers toward particular instructional programs" (Parrish et al., 2006, p. viii).

It is important to mention that the option of obtaining bilingual waivers served as a selling point for some language minority and other groups supporting Proposition 227. The waivers were essentially viewed as a viable alternative to the proposed English-only instruction, because parents erroneously believed that they would be the ones to choose appropriate education for their children. That being said, however, other provisions unfavorable to bilingual instruction (embedded in Proposition 227) indicate that the programmatic decision of whether bilingual curriculum is a reasonable program for a given school or district rested with school and district administrators (Cline & Necochea, 2001). Essentially, the waiver issues post–Proposition 227 further chipped away immigrant children' right to an effective education, that is, bilingual education. Bilingual programs continued to decline across the state, from 30% of ELLs receiving bilingual instruction in 1998 to 12% in 2001 and 8% in 2003 (Parrish et al., 2006). The full impact of Proposition 227 on the post–Proposition 227 generation is yet to be seen. However, what is undoubtedly true is that today, California immigrants and children of immigrants have officially lost their once-protected language rights and access to equal education in public schools.

Similar to California, Arizona's draconian educational policies have resulted in an overall decrease of academic outcomes for second language learners. Although both states have, failed their ELL population, Arizona has been in courts for inadequately funding ELL programs and support mechanisms for over 20 years (Flores v. State of Arizona, 1992). Proper identification of ELLs was one of the initial goals of *Flores v. Arizona* in 1992. However, the court's 2006 response to Flores' long-overdue declaratory judgment vis-à-vis HB 2064 made matters for ELLs worse on both programmatic and student identification fronts.

To this end, HB 2064 only guarantees funding for 2 consecutive years. As a result, an HB 2064 taskforce created the Arizona Structured Immersion Program (SEI), which essentially resulted in the segregation of students who are learning the English language for 4 hours of their academic day (Faltis & Arias, 2012). Students enrolled in these programs (4-hour blocks) are taught the English language for only 4 hours during their school day. What is even more alarming is that the students enrolled in these SEI classes are segregated from their English-only peers and not provided instruction in content-specific subject areas and thus have no or very limited exposure to school culture. The restrictive nature of Arizona's 4-hour block English-only instruction is essentially designed to segregate ELL students for, at times, over 85% of their school day. As such, Arizona's SEI environment leads to later student self-segregation practices (where students are more likely to identify with only one group), lack of exposure to core subjects (i.e., math, science, etc.) other than that of English, and naturally lack of academic opportunities later in life (Faltis & Arias, 2012).

LIVING IN "TURN WHITE AND SPEAK ENGLISH" POLITICAL CLIMATE

This chapter would not be complete without snapshots of the stories from real individuals who have gone through the system and experienced first-hand what it is like to live in "Turn White and Speak English" political climate. To give a voice to the realities currently experienced by language minority and ELL students in Arizona, this section depicts several real-life accounts. These snapshots are taken from previous work my colleague and I did on this subject (Okhremtchouk & Carlson, 2013).

To provide a brief context, students' voices depicted in this section are of language minority students who are of Latino/a heritage, were once ELLs, and are now adults pursuing higher education. One of the glaring themes to emerge during the course of these interviews was the extent to which others spurned them due to their background. One interviewee reported that despite a teacher's recommendation, she was prohibited from taking certain courses by her guidance councilor and should instead "take classes that would help you with my English" (Okhremtchouk & Carlson, 2013, p. 3). Essentially, the counselor refused to register her for the course because "I was an ESL student and he [the counselor] felt I was not going to be able to pass an AP exam." Another interviewee described similar experiences in elementary school. When she arrived on her first day of school, she was expecting a translator. Reflecting back on her experiences, she shared that the school was clearly unprepared to educate her. This interviewee did report that after some time, she was taken to the "ESL classroom" and started "reading and watched movies."

In many ways, all interviewees reported that schools repudiated ELL students in many ways, for example, lack of preparation and denying them access to advanced courses. But in addition, the interviewees expressed concerns regarding English-only SEI courses. The interviewees clearly privileged bilingual education.

> My first class was an ESL course with a teacher; he was... it was his first year teaching and yeah, he was very nice. I felt comfortable in that class, but in my math class, the teacher didn't speak Spanish at all and it was horrible. I was... you know... trying to understand what he was saying, but I couldn't.

Later in the interview, this interviewee explained her experiences with SEI.

> Yes, I remember. I was "level one" and then the teacher said, "I will promote you." I went to another SEI class and the teacher would only speak English. And he was not a Hispanic teacher. He knew a little Spanish, but he almost always spoke in English.... I didn't feel like I learned a lot because... SEI class was more about writing and sentences and paragraphs and essays. I felt like I didn't get much help from the teacher. He wanted us to speak in the class, but it was difficult... it was, like, very different from ESL courses. I think he didn't engage us enough.

Another described how she felt when she was pulled out of class to practice English.

> You leave and then you come back and they did something amazing and they were doing something together and you miss out on that and you see that they are bonding and the teacher is bonding with them [classmates] and you are missing out on that... I think that's what hurt the most because you want to belong, you don't want to be that Mexican girl... you want to belong, you know?

The interviewees also made several references to other experiences. The example below is a particular exemplar. It comes from an interviewee who was once undocumented. In this segment, she recalls feeling like a prisoner where she was not able to drive (due to lacking a driver's license) or pursue higher education any further due to restrictive Arizona laws for undocumented citizens.

> My parents decided to move somewhere else [after high school]. Somewhere really far where there's no bus system; you can't even ride your bike from there... and that was during the whole processing with my mom [talks about citizenship paperwork] and I was finishing up community college because you can't go any higher after you get your prerequisites. All you can do is just take fun classes like sociology or psychology.... I was just filling time with other things and I was really not going anywhere. I really felt like a prisoner because I couldn't leave.... my mom was always at work; my step-dad had to work too, so who, who was going to help me out?

In progressing through school, at times in the English-only environment, interviewees reported that speaking Spanish became an act of resistance in an English-only school. An example below illustrates this reality.

> And I remember one day during lunch; we were talking at our table and the assistant principal, she came in and she said, "Oh, this is an English-only school and you shouldn't be speaking Spanish." We didn't even pay attention to her [assistant principal]. We were, like,... after that, when I think about it, even to this day I am, like, there is something wrong in the education system.... like, are we not allowed to be ourselves or express ourselves in the language that we want?

CONCLUSION

This chapter paints a very vivid picture about the abysmal educational conditions that are less than worthy of the American education system, the premise on which the American education system was established (i.e., serving as a great equalizer in our society), and that of the students. In other words, the ways in which the current system operates for language minority and ELL students is appalling. A moral and, more importantly, ethical urgency exists to ameliorate such deplorable conditions and failures (academic and otherwise) for this student population. To that end, educational professionals (i.e., district and school leaders, administrators, and teachers alike) are uniquely positioned to address this urgency and advance social justice goals toward a more equitable educational practice. It is also important not to lose sight of the fact that we, as a nation, are losing generations of talent that language minority and ELL students bring into a classroom, which could potently impact us all in substantive and substantial ways. Put differently, by stagnating the educational process of these individuals, that is, language minority students and ELLs, we are benefiting no one; in fact, we are stagnating our own collective progress by not ensuring equality of opportunity for these students, so they are well positioned to demonstrate many merits they bring to our social structure.

REFERENCES

American Civil Liberties Union [ACLU]. (1999, July 29). *CA's anti-immigrant Proposition 187 is voided, ending state's five-year battle with ACLU, rights groups.* Retrieved from https://www.aclu.org/immigrants-rights/cas-anti-immigrant-proposition-187-voided-ending-states-five-year-battle-aclu-righ

Arizona State House of Representatives. (2010). HB 2281. Retrieved from http://www.azleg.gov/legtext/49leg/2r/bills/hb2281s.pdf

Arizona Secretary of State. (2006). Proposition 103, English as the Official Language. Retrieved from http://www.azsos.gov/election/2006/info/pubpamphlet/english/Prop103.htm

Arizona Secretary of State. (2006). Proposition 300, Public Program Eligibility. Retrieved from http://apps.azsos.gov/election/2006/info/PubPamphlet/Sun_Sounds/english/Prop300.htm

Artiles, A. J., Bal, A., & King Thorius, K. A. (2010). Back to the future: A critique of Response to Intervention's social justice views. *Theory into Practice. 49,* 250–257.

Aud, S., Wilkinson-Flicker, S., Kristapovich, P., Rathbun, A., Wang, X., & Zhang, J. (2013). The condition of education 2013 (NCES 2010-028). *National Center for Education Statistics.* Retrieved from http://nces.ed.gov/pubsearch/pubsinfo.asp?pubid=2013037

Baker, K. A., & de Kanter, A. A. (1983). *Bilingual education: A reappraisal of federal policy.* Lexington, MA: Heath.

Banks, J. A. (2014). *An introduction to multicultural education* (5th ed.). New York, NY: Pearson.

Batalova, J., Fix M., & Murray, J. (2007). *Measures of change: The demography and literacy of adolescent English learners—A report to Carnegie Corporation of New York.* Washington, DC: Migration Policy Institute.

Berne, R., & Stiefel, L. (1999). Concepts of equity: 1970 to present. In H. F. Ladd, R. Chalk, & J. S.

Hansen (Eds.), *Equity and adequacy issues in education finance.* Washington, DC: National Academies Press.

California Secretary of State. (1998). *Proposition 227: English language in public schools: Initiative statute.* Retrieved from http://primary98.sos.ca.gov/Voter-Guide/Propositions/227.htm

Camacho Liu, M. (2011). *Trends in Latino college access and success.* National Conference of State Legislatures (July, 2011). Retrieved from http://www.ncsl.org/documents/educ/trendsinlatinosuccess.pdf

Capps, R., Fix, M., Murray, J., Ost, J., Passel, J. S., & Hernandez, S. (2005). The new demography of America's schools: Immigration and the No Child Left Behind Act. *Urban Institute.* Retrieved from http://www.urban.org/publications/311230.html

Carlton, F. T. (1908). Economic influences upon educational progress in the United States: 1820–1850. *Bulletin of the University of Wisconsin: Economics and Political Science Series, 4*(1), 50.

Chin, G. J. (1998). Segregation's last stronghold: Race discrimination and the constitutional law of immigration. *UCLA Law Review, 46*(1), 1–74.

Cline, Z., & Necochea, J. (2001). Basta ya! Latino parents fighting entrenched racism. *Bilingual Research Journal, 25*(1/2), 89–114.

Crawford, J. (1989). *Bilingual education: History, politics, theory, and practice.* Trenton, NJ: Crane.

Crawford, J. (2008, November). *Frequently asked questions about official English.* Retrieved November 20, 2009, from http://www.elladvocates.org/documents/englishonly/OfficialEnglishFAQ.pdf

Crawford, J. (2000). The Proposition 227 Campaign: A post-mortem. In J. Crawford, *At war with diversity: U.S. language policy in an age of anxiety* (pp. 104–130). Clevedon, England: Multilingual Matters.

Dyste, C. (1989). Proposition 63: The California English Language amendment. *Applied Linguistics, 10*(3), 313–330.

Echevarria, J., Vogt, M. E., & Short, D. J. (2014). *Making content comprehensible for elementary English learners: The SIOP Model* (2nd ed.). Boston, MA: Pearson.

Faltis, C. J., & Arias, M. B. (2012). Research-based reform in Arizona: Whose evidence counts for applying the Castaneda test to structured English immersion models? In M. B. Arias & C. J. Faltis (Eds.), *Implementing educational language policy in Arizona: Legal, historical and current practices in SEI* (pp. 29–38). Tonawanda, NY: Multilingual Matters.

Fishman, J. A. (1978). *Language loyalty in the United States.* New York, NY: Arno.

Flores v. State of Arizona. 42 U.S.C. § 1983 (D. Ariz. 1992).

Fry, R., & Lopez, M. H. (2012, August 20). Hispanic student enrollments reach new highs in 2011. *Pew Research Center.* Retrieved from http://www.pewhispanic.org/2012/08/20/hispanic-student-enrollments-reach-new-highs-in-2011

Gándara, P., Maxwell-Jolly, J., & Rumberger, R. (2008). *Resource needs for English learners: Getting down to policy recommendations.* Santa Barbara: University of California Linguistic Minority Research Institute.

Gándara, P., & Merino, B. (1993). Measuring the outcomes of LEP programs: Test scores, exit rates, and other mythological data. *Educational Evaluation and Policy Analysis, 15*(3), 320–338.

Gándara, P., & Rumberger, R. W. (2008). Defining an adequate education for English learners. *Education Finance and Policy, 3*(1), 130–148.

Lessow-Hurley, J. (2000). *The foundations of dual language instruction* (3rd ed.). Menlo Park, CA: Addison-Wesley/Longman.

Matsudaira, J., Hosek, A., & Walsh, E. (2012). An integrated assessment of the effects of Title I on school behavior, resources, and student achievement. *Economics of Education Review, 31*(3), 1–14.

Mendez v. Westminister School Dist. of Orange County, 64 F. Supp. 544 (D.C.Cal. 1946).

Meyer v. State of Nebraska, 262 U.S. 390 (1923).

Miller, J., & Garran, A. M. (2008). *Racism in the United States: Implications for the helping professions.* Belmont, CA: Thomson Higher Education

Munoz, C. (2004). 50 years after Brown: Latinos paved way for historic school desegregation. *Motion Magazine.* Retrieved from http://www.inmotionmagazine.com/er/cm_brown.html

No Child left Behind (NCLB) Act of 2001. P. L. No. 107-110 § 115, Stat. 1425.

Okhremtchouk, I. S. (2011). *Disjointed continuity: Classification practices for language minority students and implications: A case study.* Davis: University of California.

Okhremtchouk, I. (2014). Categorical grants. In D. Brewer & L. Picus (Eds.), *Encyclopedia of education economics and finance* (pp. 109–115). Thousand Oaks, CA: Sage.

Okhremtchouk, I. S., & Carlson, D. L. (2013). *The affected: Living in "Turn White and speak English" political climate.* San Francisco, CA: American Education Research Association.

Okhremtchouk, I. S., & Jimenez, R. M. (2013). "I Live in a Curled World..." Stories from immigrant students and their teacher. In R. Gabriel & J. Lester (Eds.), *Performances of research: Critical issues in K–12 education.* New York, NY: Peter Lang.

Parrish, T., Perez, M., Merickel, A., & Linquant, R. (2006). Effects of the implementation of Proposition 227 on the education of English learners, K–12: Findings from a five-year evaluation: Final report. *AIR/West Ed.* Retrieved from http://www.wested.org/online_pubs/227Reportb.pdf

Portes, A., & Hao, L. (1998). E pluribus unum: Bilingualism and loss of language in the second generation. *Sociology of Education, 71,* 269–294.

Rumberger, R., & Gándara, P. (2004). Seeking equity in the education of California's english learners. *Teachers College Record, 106,* 2031–2055.

Thomas, W. P., & Collier, V. P. (2002). A national study of school effectiveness for language minority students' long-term academic achievement. *CREDE.* Retrieved from http://crede.berkeley.edu/research/llaa/1.1_final.html

Timar, T. (2007). *Financing K–12 education in California: A system overview.* Stanford, CA: Stanford University Institute for Research on Education Policy and Practice.

Toth, C. R. (1990). *German-English bilingual schools in America: The Cincinnati tradition in historical context.* New York, NY: Lang.

Weinberg, M. (1977). *A chance to learn: A history of race and education in the United States.* Cambridge, UK: Cambridge University Press.

Wiley, T. (2007). Assessing language rights in education: A brief history of the U.S. context. In G. Ofelia & C. Baker (Eds.), *Bilingual education: An introductory reader.* Clevedon, UK: Multilingual Matters.

CHAPTER 2

DEAF CULTURE AND EDUCATION
Toward a Culturally Relevant Leadership

Catherine O'Brien
Gallaudet University

Jeffrey S. Brooks
Monash University

ABSTRACT

Students with disabilities have two primary legal protections in the United States: the right to a free and appropriate public education, and the right of being included "to the maximum extent appropriate" in the general education classroom. Missing from these mandates is a clear definition of all key terms and any guidance on implementation. Importantly, this is also only a legal framework for approaching the education of students with disabilities—it does not address culture, and incorrectly frames them using deficit thinking. In this chapter, we argue that it is important to understand the experiences of students, particularly deaf students, not in terms of disability, but through culture. We explore the intersection of Deaf culture,[1] Deaf education, and also culturally relevant leadership. The last of these recognizes emerging scholar-

Inclusive Practices and Social Justice Leadership for Special Populations in Urban Settings, pages 21–44
Copyright © 2015 by Information Age Publishing
21

ship that acknowledges the importance of leadership in relation to both culture and learning. Further, there is little research related to urban minority deaf youth and how Deaf culture and culturally relevant leadership might impact the education of these students. The remaining part of the chapter describes Deaf culture, culturally relevant leadership, and schooling for deaf students from minority urban populations. The oppression or exclusion encountered by deaf students is the lack of common language that is shared among all parties and the insensitivity of hearing teachers and peers. We hope that this work will both raise awareness of these issues and begin to suggest new ways of conceptualizing leadership in relation to Deaf education.

For at least 50 years, scholars, practitioners and policymakers have all focused on understanding and influencing the unique challenges and opportunities manifest in urban schools (Brooks & Miles, 2008). This focus began in response to educational indicators in such settings that lagged behind nonurban areas (dropout/pushout rates, teacher attrition, attendance, and mobility rates were all higher in urban centers), while performance on standardized assessments were lower (Ravitch, 2010, 2013). Subsequent scholars recognized that these indicators differed sharply along many sociocultural lines (McCray & Beachum, 2014). Many studies suggested that students, teachers, and administrators were treated differently if they were from nondominant racial, ethnic, gender, sexuality, and ability groups and that they received an inferior and often hostile education that did not value or acknowledge difference as a strength, but as a deficit (Bogotch, 2002; Ladson-Billings, 1997). Many studies have explored these and other related issues through various cultural theories, which helped explain both how subcultures worked in and of themselves and how they related to other subcultures and the dominant culture (Brooks & Jean-Marie, 2007; Dimmock & Walker, 2005). At a certain point, scholars began to recognize that educational leaders had the potential to directly and indirectly influence educational cultures by practicing a culturally relevant leadership (Horsford, Grosland, & Gunn, 2011). However, while we acknowledge that the field has come a long way in the past 50 years, there are still significant gaps in our understanding about the experiences of certain cultures and subcultures in schools and how leadership might improve their educational experiences (Brooks, 2012; Ladson-Billings, 1995). This book chapter examines a group whose culture has been marginalized in the educational leadership literature—students who are deaf. Accordingly, the purpose of this chapter is to understand the research on urban deaf students, Deaf culture, and culturally relevant leadership. To date, there is little research related to urban minority deaf youth and how Deaf culture and culturally relevant leadership might impact the education of these students. The remaining part of the chapter describes Deaf culture, culturally relevant leadership, and schooling for deaf students from minority urban populations.

EXPERIENCES OF DEAF STUDENTS IN THE UNITED STATES: SCHOOL AND POLICY

In 2003, Gallaudet Research Institute (2002–2003 data) estimated that of approximately 40,000 deaf and hard-of-hearing (deaf) children and youth (in a survey of U.S. students), only 24.7% (c. 10,800) attended a school for the deaf or a specific center for children who are deaf. Karchmer and Mitchell (2003, p. 23) reported that approximately 72% of K–12 deaf students were enrolled in regular classrooms (31.7%), resource rooms (12.6%), or self-contained classrooms (27.5%). Estimates of the total number of the affected students in the United States have a large variation, from 1 in 1,000 citizens to 4.5 to 11 out of every 1,000 persons (Mitchell, 2005). Often the deaf child is the only such person in these "general education" classrooms. This minority, spread thin among the hearing students, and the fact that many deaf students are not equipped to learn in the mostly oral/aural environment, leads to predictable educational outcomes. Our purpose is to illuminate the unique needs of deaf students and to assess the cultural perspective and opportunities; discovering how leadership, more specifically culturally relevant leadership, can influence their educational outcomes.

Public Law (PL) 94 142 (Individuals with Disabilities Education Act, 1975) was intended to enhance educational opportunities for all students with disabilities. Even with PL 94 142, the education for deaf students has continued to be marginalized with poor outcomes. Blanchfield, Feldman, Dunbar, and Gardner (2001) reported that 18.7% of the U.S. population did not graduate from high school, while 44.4% of the deaf students did not graduate from high school. Completion rates for deaf students vary in postsecondary programs (NLTS2, 2003; Newman et al., 2011).

Deaf students lag significantly behind their hearing peers academically (Moores, 2001; Qi & Mitchell, 2012; Shirmer, 2000). Karchmer and Mitchell (2003, p. 32) reported that the Stanford Achievement scores of deaf students in grades 2 through 9 were consistently lower than the scores of their hearing classmates. According to Qi and Mitchell (2011), academic achievement gaps are noted in reading and mathematics, with reading hovering at the 4th-grade level and mathematics at the at the 6th-grade level for deaf students between the ages of 15 and 18 (high school age). Further, they report that the achievement gap between deaf and hearing student has not improved in the past three decades. Even though these data are dated, neither the United States Department of Education (USDOE) nor the states are required to report or keep a database of disaggregated data on academic yearly progress or standardized test scores of students who are deaf in the public school setting. Currently, there is no database to understand the academic achievement of deaf students, especially deaf urban minority students either nationally or state by state. Given this context, we now consider their collective cultural experiences.

THE CULTURAL LENS: DEAF PEOPLE, CULTURE, AND LANGUAGE

Culture refers to the accumulated values, beliefs, morals, rituals, ceremonies, symbols, art, artifacts, customs, and languages of a group of humans (Harris, 1968; Schein, 2004). One key to identifying a culture is how the members of that culture communicate (Harris, 1968; Manganaro, 2002; Schein, 2004; Spring, 2000). Some scholars argue that language (both verbal and nonverbal) serves to bind members together and helps young or new members learn about culture (Carmel & Monaghan, 1991; Harris, 1968; Spring, 2000, 2008). Language is usually learned both explicitly and implicitly, and is a common way that extant members of the culture transmit values, beliefs, expectations, and such to new members (Hall, 1973; Rutherford, 1988).

Several researchers have drawn parallels between Deaf culture and indigenous cultures, especially in the way they have been treated by the members of dominant cultures (Batterbury, Ladd, & Gulliver, 2007). Batterbury et al., (2007) find parallels between the life experiences and patterns of oppression of "Sign Language Peoples" (SLPs) and First Nations (Canadian indigenous) peoples. They challenged the belief that SLPs should be categorized as fitting the disability model and suggested that the disability label denies the uniqueness of sign language and/or allows colonial-type oppression. These authors contend that the SLPs should be considered indigenous groups, qualifying for rights of protection of culture, education, and language that are offered to other indigenous groups such as First Nations.

The history of the treatment of deaf individuals and communities includes attempts by paternalistic "colonizers" to eradicate their languages and cultures. In the last 300 years, SLPs have commonly been described in demeaning terms such as primitive, dumb, mute, feebleminded, retarded, subhuman, paranoid, and suspicious (Batterbury et al., 2007; Lane, 1999). An unintended consequence of establishing deaf schools, which have been in existence since the 1750s, is that they became important sites for development of distinctive language and culture. Hearing society responded by instituting the "oral method," in which signed language was banned in favor of training deaf children to lip-read and speak so that they could be "restored to society." The 1880 International Congress on Education of the Deaf passed a resolution that sign language was to be forbidden (Lane, 1999). Deaf teachers and sign language usage were phased out in many schools and were replaced with hearing teachers and speech therapy. A decline in academic performance and emotional results ensued and continued for almost a century. Serious linguistic study of American Sign Language (ASL) did not begin until the 1960s, and sign language slowly began to return to schools in the 1970s; a "Deaf resurgence" began after the 1980s (Batterbury et al., 2007).

The sign language resurgence was tempered by three waves of oralism that challenged deaf education. The first wave was mainstreaming, which has been provided for deaf children in public schools since the 1970s; it effectively isolated deaf children by separating them from their deaf peers and their language. Mainstreaming is not "inclusive," as its proponents claim. The other two "neocolonialist" waves of oralism are technological attempts to eradicate deafness: cochlear implant technology and gene therapy (Lane, 1999).

The United Nations Declaration on the Rights of Indigenous Peoples, adopted on September 13, 2007, included specific rights to be accorded to indigenous peoples. Batterbury et al., (2007) identified at least six articles that would help SLPs resist destruction of their languages and culture, and encourage them in developing appropriate education for their children. Each article describes rights that should be afforded to indigenous individuals or peoples (and SLPs):

- Article #7: The rights to life, physical and mental integrity
- Article #8: The right not to be subjected to forced assimilation or destruction of their culture
- Article #13: The right to revitalize, use, develop and transmit to future generations their histories, languages, oral traditions, philosophies, writing systems and literatures
- Article #14: The right to establish and control their educational systems and institutions providing education in their own languages, in a manner appropriate to their cultural methods of teaching and learning
- Article #15: The right to the dignity and diversity of their cultures, traditions, histories and aspirations, which shall be appropriately reflected in education and public information
- Article #31: The right to maintain, control, protect and develop their cultural heritage, traditional knowledge and traditional cultural expressions (United Nations, 2007, pp. 7–12).

Audism and the Deaf Perspective

The term "audism," based on the Latin term "*audire*" meaning "to hear," was first used by an American Deaf educator Tom Humphries in 1975

(Bauman, 2004, 2008; Lane, 1999). It is formally defined as an act of discrimination on the basis of "one's ability to hear" or "to behave in the manner of one who hears" (Bauman, 2008, p. 240).

Humphries described audism as follows:

[Audism] appears in the form of people who continually judge deaf people's intelligence and success on the basis of their ability in the language of the hearing culture. It appears when the assumption is made that the deaf person's happiness depends on acquiring fluency in the language of the hearing culture. It appears when deaf people actively participate in the oppression of other deaf people by demanding of them the same set of standards, behavior, and values that they demand of hearing people. (p. 240)

Harlan Lane (1999) used the term "audism" to describe the hearing society's paternalistic and condescending treatment of deaf people and further described it as

dealing with deaf, dealing with them by making statements about them, authorizing views of them, describing them, teaching about them, governing where they go to school, and in some cases where they live; in short audism is the hearing way of dominating, restructuring, and exercising authority over the Deaf community. (p. 43)

In a brief discussion of the origins of audism, Bauman (2004) notes that one source is the linking of spoken language to what it means to be human. Human beings are perceived as "speaking animals." If one cannot speak, then he or she is less than a human being. This perception serves as a powerful legitimatizing force for institutions such as education and medicine to attempt to make deaf individuals more "normal," that is, "fully speaking" human beings. The dynamics of audism are often compared to colonialism. The parallels include attempts to eradicate indigenous languages, educational values, and history, and replace them with those of the dominant culture.

Deaf Culture

Deaf culture is a group of linguistic minorities in which people express themselves using a visual language. The largest, most sophisticated and publically visible Deaf culture in the world is based on ASL and has developed in the United States (Christiansen & Barnartt, 1995; Lane, Hoffmeister, & Bahan, 1996; Moore & Levitan, 2005). Common language as well as shared norms, meanings, values, beliefs, rituals, and ceremonies that are exclusive to the Deaf community hold members together (Hall, 1973). Importantly, deaf people are not loosely organized on the basis of a similar sensory loss but are organized around a visual orientation.

While ASL is clearly a central facet of Deaf culture, the question of whether proficiency in ASL is a requirement for membership in Deaf culture is debatable. There are now members who claim to be culturally Deaf but do not sign fluently. They claim the Deaf cultural status because of their similar experiences of oppression and their positive attitude toward being Deaf. One particular member has been identified as being in "a culture made up of immense and intense imagination, illustrating Deaf identity in the making" (Bruggemann, 2004). Some members consider those who wear hearing aids as "not Deaf enough" and thus marginalize them (Edwards, 2010). Deaf people value and are proud of themselves as Deaf individuals, their language, and cultural heritage. They wish to preserve their history, language, norms, values, and beliefs as integral parts of their cultural and personal identities (Baynton, Gannon, & Bergey, 2007; Lane, 1999; Lane et al., 1996).

Cultural Identity

Deaf culture is "a social, communal, and creative force of, by, and for Deaf people based on ASL. Deaf culture encompasses communication, social protocol, art, entertainment, recreation (e.g., sports, travel, and Deaf clubs), and worship" (Moore & Levitan, 2005, p. 325). Deaf culture is also an attitude, one that demonstrates a "can do" approach to life (Christensen & Barnhartt, 1995). It is important to note that Deaf culture and Deaf identity are positive terms, whereas terms like hearing-impaired do not connote any particular pride or sense of community (Leigh, 2009; Moore & Levitan, 2005).

Deaf culture also represents a sense of cultural belonging. ASL is a complete language, fully accessible and naturally used by many Deaf people. It brings about cultural awareness, unity, communication, and pride. What Deaf culture represents is the opposite of the outsider view of deafness—a condition of hearing impairment or hearing disability, which implies that something is broken and must be fixed. Deafness as a pathology entails investigating and measuring the quality of hearing that an individual possesses and giving the person a label (mild, moderate, severe, or profound hearing loss) to describe the ability to auditorially hear and understand the spoken word. Historically, the dominant hearing culture has relegated people who are deaf or hard of hearing to social categories such as handicapped, disabled, or outsider (Moore & Levitan, 2005; Munoz-Baell & Ruiz, 1999).

Not all culturally Deaf people are completely deaf. Just as there are variations of skin color among African Americans, there are variations in hearing status among culturally Deaf people. Some culturally Deaf people are born into the culture, as in the case of Deaf children born to Deaf parents.

These children learn their parents' language and other traditions of Deaf people from their families and their Deaf communities. Unfortunately, cultural learning as described is relatively rare. Nearly 90% of deaf children are born to hearing families (Ladd, 2003; Lane et al., 1996; Moore & Levitan, 2005). They learn sign language and Deaf culture outside the family, typically at residential schools or from members of the Deaf community.

Cultural Definers: Characteristics

Deaf culture manifests itself in terms of language, behaviors, norms, and rituals. Deaf culture also consists of the system of beliefs held by the people, their principles of life, and their moral values. Some basic characteristics of Deaf culture are discussed below.

Language

The American Deaf cultural world values ASL as its one and only language; it is an integral part of the identity of Deaf people (Lane et al., 1996; Moore & Levitan, 2005; Munoz-Baell & Ruiz, 1999). Padden and Humphries (1988) noted that language is the primary identifier of a culture. ASL is a true language that possesses its own syntax, phonology, notation, morphology, classifiers, and semiology (Humphries & Padden, 1988; Moore & Levitan, 2005; Stokoe, 2005). Because the use of sign language is a natural and effective way of communicating, Deaf people do not see themselves as disabled but as culturally different from the mainstream. Consequently, culturally Deaf people tend to emphasize their linguistic and cultural heritage and eschew the "disability" label. The view that culturally Deaf people have of themselves distinguishes them from adults who lose their hearing later in life and feel the loss of hearing more acutely.

Although culturally Deaf people use sign language, not all signers are deaf (Lane, 1999; Moore & Levitan, 2005); many hearing signers grow up in or interact with culturally Deaf communities (Groce, 1985; Lane et al., 1996; Moore & Levitan, 2005). Hearing children of Deaf parents learn spoken English from relatives, friends, and other English-speaking contacts in their neighborhood. They grow up bilingual in ASL and English, and move between the two cultures.

Values and Beliefs in Deaf Culture

Shared values, defined and nurtured by the culture, cause members of a culture to be deeply committed to what is important to them (Deal & Peterson, 1999). Members of the Deaf cultural community value their history, their hands and eyes, and Deaf children, whether they are children with Deaf parents or hearing parents (Cohen, 1995; Ladd, 2009; Lane et al.,

1996; Moore & Levitan, 2005; Wrigley, 1996). The Deaf cultural community cherishes its history and development (Lane, 1999). Many state schools for the Deaf have museums in which they display the rich history of development of the Deaf community (Reed, 2000). People who are Deaf value their hands and eyes (Lane, 1999), since they are essential for communication. ASL not only requires the use of the hands but also the use of body movements and facial expressions; it can only be understood by seeing all three movements together. The Deaf community values Deaf children (Baynton et al., 2007; Lane, 1999). When a Deaf couple learns that their baby is Deaf, the parents are joyful and excited. The child will grow up in a family where ASL is taught and learned, and the opportunity is treasured because many of these parents did not have that advantage when they were children.

Norms and Behaviors

Members of the Deaf community transmit the norms for socially acceptable practices. Facial expressions and body language are critical for conveying essential meaning and ensuring quality communicative exchange (Lane et al., 1996). Eye contact is essential when communicating with Deaf people. It is acceptable for Deaf people to maintain eye contact while they're signing to each other, because the eyes communicate feeling and provide feedback, often indicating whether the addressee is following the conversation. Good eye contact and the maintenance of personal space are important to make signing efficient and comfortable. While eye contact is critical for conversation, head nods and specific gestures of understanding, agreement, or disagreement are also necessary (Lane et al., 1996). Often, before a Deaf person leaves a room where there are with other Deaf people, he or she will notify friends of where he or she is going. If he or she is simply going to another location in the building, it is proper to notify his/her friends before moving out of sight. On the other hand, gaining the attention of another requires specific body language and movement. Attention-getting behaviors include waving hands with arms extended and standing in the person's field of vision, flipping of the lights, stomping feet, and tapping one on the shoulder.

Rituals are formal or informal actions performed mainly for their symbolic value. Residential schools are the points of contact for Deaf culture and help to nurture and maintain rituals and ceremonies (Padden & Humphries, 1988, 2005). Residential students are immersed in the genre of deafness and exchange stories and folklore of the residential school and Deaf culture (Ladd, 2009; Lane et al., 1996; Lane, Hoffmeister, & Bahan, 2002; Moore & Levitan, 2005; Reed, 2000). Students at these schools have developed literary associations and small theater groups that create traditions of sign poetry and storytelling (Baynton et al., 2007; Ladd, 2009; Lane et al., 1996, 2002; Moore & Levitan, 2005; Reed, 2000). The National Theatre of the Deaf (which tours throughout the United States and the world) and the Deaf West Theatre, which is based in Los Angeles, California, are outgrowths of activities begun in schools for the deaf (Baynton et al., 2007).

Most graduates from residential schools develop strong bonds with their alma mater and attend many ceremonies at the schools, such as homecoming, athletic games, and graduation. Many alumni also attend activities and support the schools in many ways, bringing Deaf culture community influence to the schools (Lane, et al., 1996, 2002; Moore & Levitan, 2005; Reed, 2000). It is important then to connect these cultural dynamics to the work of educational leaders.

TOWARD A CULTURALLY RELEVANT LEADERSHIP

As American schools become more and more diverse, it is imperative that teachers and other school leaders become culturally proficient. Lindsey, Robins, and Terrell (2009) begin their book, *Cultural Proficiency*, with an overview of changes in views about diversity over the last six or seven decades. American culture has moved from segregation to multiculturalism to diversity and cultural proficiency. Culture is inclusive and broadly includes all shared human characteristics (age, gender, language, abilities, sexual orientation, race, ethnicity, etc.). Recognizing the importance of these differences and working toward ways to enrich understanding within the school are two of the first steps to helping young people become more aware of the diverse global community in which they live.

Lindsey et al. (2009) provided a list of culturally proficient behaviors toward which teachers and other leaders should strive. These qualities are important in the classroom or any other setting where members of the school community interact. The characteristic behaviors are (a) assessing one's own culture and that of the students, (b) valuing the diversity observed, (c) managing the differences, (d) adapting to the diversity by continuously learning about the different cultures, and (e) working to influence the culture of the entire school toward cultural proficiency. These characteristics of strong collaborative culture ought to also identify goals for culturally proficient leaders: enhancement of mutual trust, possessing empathy, giving access to support and assistance, being willing to take risks, and sharing proactive knowledge.

Brooks and Normore (2010) describe culturally relevant leadership as a part of the preparation for educational leaders of the 21st century. They identify and describe nine "literacies that must be developed" (p. 53) in the education of leaders so that they are aware of and use glocal literacy in "their pedagogy and practice" (p. 52). These literacies "are (a) political literacy, (b) economic literacy, (c) cultural literacy, (d) moral literacy, (e) pedagogical literacy, (f) information literacy, (g) organizational literacy, (h) spiritual and religious literacy, and (i) temporal literacy" (pp. 53–54). These "glocally" educated leaders must understand that people in the 21st century live in multiple cultures, nestled one within another and interacting simultaneously in numerous ways. They must practice the kind of culturally relevant pedagogy (CRP) advocated by Ladson-Billings (1994, 1995) and others.

Leadership is a phenomenon and an organizational quality (Ogawa & Bossert, 1995; Pounder, Ogawa, & Adams, 1995). Leadership studies offer many definitions or characterizations of leaders. An effective leader utilizes a "toolbox" of leadership skills adaptable to different situations. Though different from management theory, most leadership theories share the notion that leaders must have followers or they are not leaders, and the leaders influence the behavior of their followers. Within leadership, there are four types of leadership categories (Boje, 2003).

The first of the four groups are the trait or universal principal theories. Qualitative differences, either innate or exogenous, fit the leader for his/her role and define the individual as a leader. Some of the differences may be character qualities such as drive to succeed or honesty, while others may be behavioral qualities such as organizing efficiently or acting assertively (or passively) (Boje, 2003).

The second category includes contingency theories or situational theories. These claim that the situation will determine the leader (and his/her style). No leadership style will work in all situations; rather, success depends on a number of contingent variables. Most students of leadership refer to influence of the situation today but do not see these ideas containing explanatory power (Boje, 2003).

The third category of leadership theories is the behavioral or process models. Most of these theories have some form of sharing among leaders. Leaders may be appointed or be informal leaders. One might lump transactional, participative, distributed, and collaborative leadership models under this category (Boje, 2003). However, we also see that Burns (1978) and others contend that transactional leadership and transformational leadership are two ends of a spectrum of behaviors that any leader may express, and we may identify these as a fourth category.

The fourth category of leadership theories includes transactional, transformational leadership, heroic and "charismatic" leadership theories. This grouping implies that change results from the work of the leaders. Some proponents of each theory characterize representatives of their favorite theory with desirable traits (Boje, 2003).

Importantly, while these somewhat traditional ways of thinking about leadership provide a foundation for thinking about practice, writ large, scholars have begun to introduce models of leadership that put cultural relevance at the center of practice. For example, Horsford et al., (2011) suggest a framework of culturally capable leadership that highlights the interconnected nature of professional duty, personal journey, pedagogical approach, and the political context (see Figure 2.1).

It is significant that the authors include cultural proficiency, equity, engagement, and excellence as part of their model. This represents a culture-centered approach to leadership that is a much-needed shift in a field long characterized by theories that ignored such constructs (Brooks & Miles, 2008, 2010). Given these advances, we turn now to what is known about Deaf leadership.

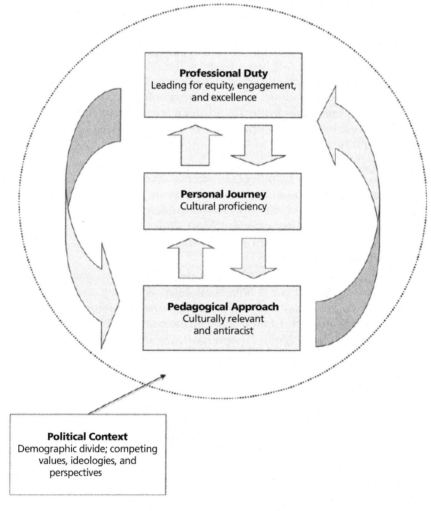

Figure 2.1   Framework for culturally capable leadership.

DEAF LEADERSHIP

In a residential school for the Deaf, the practice of school leadership will be influenced by leadership practices within Deaf culture. Deaf leadership, sometimes denied by the hearing community, has emerged in many places, along with organizations that further enable the Deaf to control their own destinies and to lobby for equal rights. Lane et al. (1996) studied leadership and how it emerges in the Deaf community and found that two very small groups within the community play a large role in leading. The leaders are those who were born Deaf to Deaf parents and those who lost their hearing after acquiring English or another audile language. Leaders who were born to Deaf parents are the most knowledgeable about the history of Deaf culture and ASL. Often these leaders are called "grassroots" leaders, and many have attended residential schools for the deaf (Lane et al., 1996, p. 172). The residential school is said to be the initial location for emerging grassroots leaders (Lane et al., 1996).

The second group, those who lost their hearing after acquiring a verbal language such as English, are leaders who are able to interact with the hearing and Deaf communities. Lane et al. (1996) call these leaders "inter-cultural leaders" (p. 172), noting that they essentially have "a foot in both worlds." Many intercultural leaders possess excellent skills in reading and writing and many are able to speak and communicate in both English and ASL.

Deaf community leaders realize that they must struggle for power and change if they wish to advance in areas where hearing people have previously oppressed them (Lane, 1999; Wrigley, 1996). Lane et al. (1996) state, "Considering all the powerful forces that bind Deaf people together in the Deaf-World, from language, schools and sports, to organizations, arts and oppression, it is no surprise that well-acculturated Deaf men and women find great strength in their Deaf identity" (p. 173). An example of Deaf leadership having an impact on education, including selection of a Deaf president of a prominent university, was the "Deaf President Now" campaign at Gallaudet University in Washington, DC.

Deaf President Now

In 1988, for the first time in the history of the United States and the world, members of the Deaf community and the students at Gallaudet University protested the denial of their rights to be equal citizens under the Title VII of the 1964 Civil Rights Act (Christiansen & Barnartt, 1995). Four Deaf student leaders, Tim Rarus, Jerry Covell, Bridgetta Bourne, and Greg Hlibok, from Gallaudet University in Washington, DC, organized and led the "Deaf President Now" protest. They were revolting against the board of trustees' presidential hiring practices (Baynton et al., 2007; Christiansen & Barnartt, 1995). The students at Gallaudet University asserted their right to seek the hiring of a Deaf president to govern and educate their own. The Deaf President Now movement began when the Board of Trustees at Gallaudet University refused to consider the hiring of a president of the university who was Deaf (Baynton et al., 2007; Christiansen & Barnartt, 1995; Cohen, 1995; Ladd, 2009; Lane, 1999; Lane et al., 1996, 2002; Moore & Levitan, 2005; Padden, 2003; Schein, 1989). The final six applicants included three hearing candidates and three Deaf candidates. The vote was 10 to 4 to hire a hearing woman over the three candidates who were Deaf. When explaining why a Deaf person was not chosen to be Gallaudet University's next president, chairman of the Board of Trustees, Jane Spilman, stated that "Deaf people are not able to function in a hearing world," thus signifying her belief that the Deaf community is not able to govern its own higher education institution (Christiansen & Barnartt, 1995, p. 55).

Gallaudet University students protested by shutting down the campus, barricading the entrance gate, and Deaf community leaders gave numerous speeches. Finally, a protest march to the capitol building was planned and executed. The students of Gallaudet University presented four demands to the school's administrators: the selection of a Deaf president, the resignation of Jane Spilman, a 51% majority on the Board of Trustees to be Deaf, and no reprisals (Christiansen & Barnartt, 1995). In the end, all of these demands were met. For the first time in the history of the most prestigious university in the world for the Deaf, Gallaudet University was governed by one of its own (Christiansen & Barnartt, 1995). I. King Jordan became the first Deaf president of Gallaudet University in 1988 (Christiansen & Barnartt, 1995).

Prior to the highly publicized Deaf President Now campaign, there were few Deaf researchers and little sensitivity to the idea of Deaf culture. Since the Deaf President Now protest, the Deaf have formed a number of new organizations and programs (e.g., Deaf Studies Programs in colleges and universities) that have purposes related to building relationships among the Deaf and obtaining treatment consistent with their abilities and sense of value. This includes an interest in the culture and leadership of schools for the Deaf.

Deaf Organizations

The Deaf cultural community has many organizations that are part of the shared historical development of what Deaf culture is today. These organizations provide structure and assist the Deaf community in becoming stronger educationally, politically, and culturally. The most prominent organization in the United States, and perhaps the oldest, is the National Association of the Deaf (NAD). NAD was founded in 1880 in Cincinnati, Ohio (Lane et al., 1996; Padden & Humphries, 1988, 2005); it is currently headquartered in Silver Spring, Maryland. The NAD is a nonprofit organization for Deaf people and run by Deaf people to advocate for Deaf rights

(Ladd, 2009; Moore & Levitan, 2005; Padden & Humphries, 1988, 2005). The NAD is credited for advocating and legally insuring quality in interpretation; qualified interpreters are trained and certified through programs such as the Registry of Interpreters for the Deaf (RID) (Lane et al., 1996; Moore & Levitan, 2005).

Another organization of the Deaf is the World Federation of the Deaf (WFD). The NAD in the United States is a member of the WFD, which has over 120 national associations of Deaf people as members (Lane et al., 1996). WFD grew out of the International Congress of the Deaf, and its purpose is to ensure the preservation of Deaf language and Deaf culture (Lane et al., 1996). The WFD is a policymaking body with a general assembly including two members from every national association of the Deaf. The WFD General Assembly meets every 4 years to elect members to the board and to adopt policies (Lane et al., 1996).

Deaf athletes around the world are also organized. Athletic organizations are much like the NAD and are represented both nationally and internationally. The U.S. athletic organization is called the American Athletic Association of the Deaf (AAAD). Athletic organizations are nurtured in the residential schools for the Deaf; they are a source of Deaf pride and shared experiences, and acclimate Deaf students to Deaf Culture (Lane et al., 1996). There are local, regional, state, national, and international athletic associations of the Deaf. It is important to mention that many Deaf teams compete with hearing teams. They challenge the hearing societal view of Deaf people as isolated or limited in their abilities (Lane et al., 1996). The athletic teams play nationally and internationally, and the AAAD sponsors world games for the Deaf (Lane et al., 1996). World games for the Deaf, called Deaflympics, are held every 4 years in cities around the world and are sanctioned by the IOC. They are scheduled so that they do not coincide with the International Olympics or the Special Olympics. Part of the motivation for the separate scheduling was to allow the participants to have time for fellowship and sharing in addition to the competitions. The next Deaflympics summer games will be held in Vancouver, Canada, in 2015.

The NAD, WFD, and AAAD are the largest organizations of the Deaf, but smaller organizations of the Deaf exist, including church organizations, social organizations, political organizations, organizations for the arts including performing arts such as theater (National Theatre of the Deaf), storytelling performance, mime, and literature. These organizations encourage cultural awareness, pride, and belonging within the Deaf community. Deaf organizations assist in defining and identifying the Deaf cultural community (Baynton et al., 2007; Christiansen & Barnartt, 1995; Cohen, 1995; Ladd, 2009; Lane, 1999; Lane et al., 1996, 2002; Moore & Levitan, 2005; Padden, 2003; Schein, 1989). These organizations have had an influence over schools and the education for the Deaf.

MINORITY DEAF STUDENTS

Teaching and learning are powerful social foundations for all children. Students who are deaf have the same needs as their hearing peers in that they need opportunities to learn, use, and engage in language every day (Ramsey, 1997). Communication that occurs in inclusive educational environments between students who are deaf and their teachers and peers must include a common understanding of needs and language that is shared among all parties (Marschark, Lang, & Albertini, 2002; Ramsey, 1997). Ramsey (1997) said,

> The generally low school achievement of deaf children may have many sources, but from my observation, it is often imposed upon normally intelligent deaf children by well-meaning educators who place them in settings where they cannot interact meaningfully with others and thus cannot learn and develop. (pp. 3–4)

As with language learning in any humans, the language development of students who are deaf or hard of hearing is a cognitive and expressive process that needs to be supported in a social context that assists children with the knowledge of their culture's language forms and uses (Ramsey, 1997; Stinson & Antia, 1999).

In one study, Ramsey (1997) stated that placement of deaf minority students in public schools was likely due to their ethnic backgrounds. Holt (1995) had also noticed that only 30% of ethnic minority students who were deaf compared to 58% of White students who were deaf were placed in mainstream classrooms for more than 6 hours per week. In another study, Cerney (2007) interviewed teachers and discussed the achievement of deaf students from minority backgrounds in urban schools. One teacher interviewed by Cerney reported about the difficulty of deaf students in poor socioeconomic situations. This teacher explained that none of the deaf students could afford hearing aids; however, the school has an FM system in the school that is used to communicate with the students. There was no mention of what occurs with students who do not have residual hearing and are unable to use hearing aids or an FM system. These factors reduce the opportunity for academic success. A teacher in Cerney's study expressed the concern that her peers believed that they decrease their curricular expectations. In addition, this teacher observed that there was a general lack of discipline in many of these classrooms. None of the studies we have cited mention school leadership or the role of leadership in the education of deaf students. The terms "culturally relevant knowledge," "cultural proficiency," "leadership," and the role that school leaders play in these schools are missing in these studies. However, more concerning is that current studies clearly indicate that leadership is the second most critical factor in student success next to teaching (Darling-Hammond, LaPointe, Meyerson, Orr, & Cohen, 2007).

Cultural proficiency is the ability to demonstrate one's personal norms and behaviors in a way that is inclusive of the cultures of others and of the school organization. Cultural proficiency recognizes differences and embraces them—it is a way of being. In a school, cultural proficiency allows individuals and organizational members to interact effectively with people who differ from them. They are able to practice cultural norms and embrace the values of others in order to understand the importance of their actions (Lindsey et al., 2009). Common barriers for the teacher desiring cultural proficiency and diversity in the classroom are the feeling that there must be "power over" the students and the feeling that the students need to adapt or change (Lindsey et al., 2009). This is possibly because of the ways that educators are prepared and then socialized into the profession (Britzman, 1986).

In a study of a mainstreamed/inclusion school setting, it was reported that the principal relied heavily on the classroom teacher of the deaf students and the resource teachers' knowledge of deafness and the deaf students before making any decisions (Slobodzian & Lugg, 2006). Though he was lacking knowledge of Deaf culture and the deaf students, he did consult with someone who had some knowledge. However, the same principal placed the deaf students in the same category as with special education students with cognitive disabilities and failed to recognize Deaf culture and the language of Deaf people. For example, his before-school norms required the special education student to be segregated to enter the school's front entrance while the rest of the student population socialized and played together before school and entered the school from the rear of the building. The school building separated these students and prevented them from socializing or engaging with each other before school. The principal failed to ensure that all staff could communicate with the deaf students in spite of the teachers' objections.

In a study of a school for the deaf, O'Brien (2011) also found a lack of understanding of cultural proficiency by administration. Culturally relevant knowledge and leadership and leadership in understanding the minority population enrolled in the school were lacking. One Deaf staff member explained,

> I believe that there are gaps in understanding Deaf culture. I think when you have a hearing teacher teaching a Deaf student they don't fully understand their perspective or their culture and that is a tough place to be in. They don't understand what it is like to be in their shoes, so to speak. A good example would be, suppose you have a white teacher with a black student, there can be conflict, just because they are of different ethnicity. They don't necessarily understand each other one hundred percent. There is a barrier to their com-

munication and that is sort of my way of thinking. I believe that Deaf teachers need to be in a Deaf school because they understand what it is like to walk in their shoes. It [having Deaf teachers] reduces the amount of frustration; there is that rapport.

This staff member is speaking of cultural proficiency; this means not just having the knowledge of Deaf culture and other cultures of the students but also being able to practice and demonstrate the cultural norms.

Ignoring the cultural background of students rather than identifying it, learning about diversity, celebrating, and nurturing the differences can cause misunderstandings. In one particular school for the deaf (O'Brien, 2011), there was a lack of understanding of urban deaf students and their backgrounds. For example, one administrator explained that cultural differences have implications in schooling and described,

> We do occasionally have a child that leaves because he can't live in the dorm. He misses his family so much and needs to be home and taken care of by mom... Most of the time when that happens we find it to be the Hispanic families because of their strong cultural views of family.

While other teachers and staff have cited a lack of parental involvement and communication with the student(s) in O'Brien 2011, an administrator explained, "It doesn't matter when a kid comes in, if they are black or white, or where they come from, a rural or urban area or some surrounding areas. Each individual comes from their own culture, their own family background." Another administrator explained,

> All those dynamics are brought here to school and they affect the staff and students. Their economic situation or life style doesn't matter, and how they were raised doesn't matter either. You see all different kinds of backgrounds; there are many variations, more variations than in public schools.

Yet there was no mention of celebrations of diversity of the students, the organization of events such as Black history, or how the economic situations are addressed. While ignoring the racial differences among students can have negative consequences, the school can also be positive in some ways.

In an observation in a school for the deaf, O'Brien (2011) noted that all of the students—Black, White, Asian, Hispanic; it did not matter what race—were all sitting together in groups of their own choosing. They were all conversing in ASL, teasing, joking, and chatting with one another. When asked about this observation, a staff member who was African American explained that race does not matter to these students. The students intermingle and enjoy the friendships and even the dating experience. Further,

There is no segregation, you've got black and white kids sleeping in the same room, same dorm. There is no segregation. You need to find the commonality. You can see that in how kids choose their partners. For dating partners, it is less of a factor to date someone of another race... I think the parents still focus on separation. Those kids sometimes have to be secret about who they are dating because their parents may not want them to date someone of another race... When that happens, I see kids ignore their parents, and date outside their race in secret.

Investigator: Everyone seems to get along very well in that respect.

Staff: We don't see the racial tensions here that you see in the "hearing world." Yes, there are some issues in both the hearing and Deaf worlds. It's important to remember that the issues out there do affect the school but maybe not in the same way or to the same magnitude... Most students that are black come from the cities.

Deafness places students in a small minority. That minority is at a disadvantage in the classroom that is not aware of Deaf culture and pedagogy. Students of cultural minority backgrounds who are deaf are an even smaller minority. Issues of communication (facility of administrators and faculty in ASL), differential treatment by race, and discipline issues (in urban schools) all have roles in reducing the quality of the educational experience of deaf students (especially in the urban schools). Our contention is that culturally proficient leadership could help to ease some of the problems. Interestingly, race was not perceived as a barrier among students of a school for the deaf. This could be both positive and problematic for minority deaf students. Learning and valuing a common language was apparently the primary factor breaking down interracial and socioeconomic barriers.

FINAL THOUGHTS

Prior to O'Brien's 2011 dissertation study, there were no systematic studies of leadership practices at schools for the deaf. Leadership theory, particularly theories of collaborative and culturally relevant/proficient leadership, is an appropriate yet limited way to study these schools. However, the unique contribution of this chapter is the lens—Deaf culture—which leads to a different perspective when understanding culturally relevant leadership and cultural proficiency as they relate to the deaf student population. The evidence for the existence of Deaf culture includes its language, its values, and its organizations. Those who have been studying Deaf culture indicate that the culture is transmitted in residential schools for the deaf. However, with more than 75% of deaf students attending public, mainstreamed, inclusionary schools, more studies are needed to understand the development of culturally proficient leadership and schooling for the vast majority of deaf students in the United States. Such new studies would provide greater insight for understanding the role of deaf students within the school and how Deaf culture influences student academic achievement, school leadership, and school culture. Finally, Deaf culture as a lens gives greater insight into the school setting and how we ought to rethink the education of deaf children is the mainstream setting, especially those in diverse and impoverished areas.

The laws that have produced inclusive programs for deaf students often do not provide the most conducive cultural environments for learning or for educational access to occur. Current applications of the laws have not stimulated conversations on race, class, disability, culture, and spiritually culturally relevant pedagogical knowledge or practice. Yet it is our hope that with focused study and with new theoretical perspectives that help us make sense of Deaf culture in education, leaders will have a better perspective on what it means to support and guide students and educators in both public and private school settings.

NOTE

1. In this chapter, the word "deaf" is used in either lowercase or uppercase depending on the meaning related to each. The capital "D" is used to signify culture. Elsewhere, when culture is not signified, the lowercase "d" is used (Padden & Humphries, 2005).

REFERENCES

Batterbury, S. C. E., Ladd, P., & Gulliver, M. (2007). Sign language peoples as indigenous minorities: Implications for research and policy. *Environment and Planning, A 39,*2899–2915. doi:10.1068/a388

Bauman, H. L. (2004). Audism: Exploring the metaphysics of oppression. *Journal of Deaf Studies and Deaf Education, 9*(2), 239–246.

Bauman, H. L. (Ed.). (2008). *Open your eyes: Deaf studies talking.* Minneapolis: University of Minnesota Press.

Baynton, D., Gannon, J., & Bergey, J. (2007). *Through deaf eyes.* Washington, DC: Gallaudet University Press.

Blanchfield, B. B., Feldman, J. J., Dunbar, J. L., & Gardner, E. N. (2001). The severely to profoundly hearing-impaired population in the United States: Prevalence estimates and demographics. *Journal Academy of Audiology, 12,* 183–189.

Bogotch, I. E. (2002). Leadership for socially just schooling: More substance and less style in high-risk, low-trust times. *Journal of School Leadership, 12,* 198–222.

Boje, D. (2003, August 16). Theatrics of leadership: Leaders as storytellers and thespians. Retrieved May 2, 2014, from http://business.nmsu.edu/~dboje/teaching/338/theatrics_of_leadership_links.htm

Britzman, D. (1986). Cultural myths in the making of a teacher: Biography and social structure in teacher education. *Harvard Educational Review, 56*, 442–472.

Brooks, J. S. (2012). *Black school, White school: Racism and educational (mis) leadership.* New York, NY: Teachers College Press.

Brooks, J. S., & Jean-Marie, G. (2007). Black leadership, White leadership: Race and race relations in an urban high school. *Journal of Educational Administration, 45*(6), 756–768.

Brooks, J. S., & Miles, M. T. (2008). From scientific management to social justice…and back again? Pedagogical shifts in educational leadership. In A. H. Normore (Ed.), *Leadership for social justice: Promoting equity and excellence through inquiry and reflective practice* (pp. 99–114). Charlotte, NC: Information Age.

Brooks, J. S., & Miles, M. T. (2010). The social and cultural dynamics of school leadership: Classic concepts and cutting-edge possibilities. In S. D. Horsford (Ed.), *New perspectives in educational leadership: Exploring social, political, and community contexts and meaning* (pp. 7–28). New York, NY: Lang.

Brooks, J. S., & Normore, A. (2010, January). Educational leadership and globalization: Literacy for a global perspective. *Educational Policy, 24*(1), 52–82. Retrieved from http://epx.sagepub.com/cgi/content/abstract/24/1/52 doi:10.1177/0895904809354070

Brueggmann, B. (2004). *In literacy and deaf people.* Washington, DC: Gallaudet University Press.

Burns, J. (1979). *Leadership.* New York, NY: Harper and Row.

Carmel, S., & Monaghan, L. (1991). Studying Deaf culture: An introduction to ethnographic work in Deaf communities. *Sign Language Studies, 73*, 411–420.

Cerney, J. (2007). *Deaf education in America: Voices of children from inclusion settings.* Washington, DC: Gallaudet University Press.

Christiansen, J., & Barnartt, S. (1995). *Deaf president now: The 1988 revolution at Gallaudet University.* Washington, DC: Gallaudet University Press.

Cohen, L. H. (1995). *Train go sorry: Inside a deaf world.* New York, NY: Vintage Books.

Darling-Hammond, L., LaPointe, M., Meyerson, D., Orr, M. T., & Cohen, C. (2007). *Preparing leaders for a changing world.* Palo Alto, CA: Stanford University, Stanford Educational Leadership Institute.

Deal, T., & Peterson, K. (1999). *Shaping school culture: The heart of leadership.* San Francisco, CA: Jossey-Bass.

Dimmock, C., & Walker, A. (2005). *Educational leadership: Culture and diversity.* Thousand Oaks, CA: Sage.

Edwards, R. A. R. (2010). Hearing aids are not deaf: A historical perspective on technology in the deaf world. In L. Davis (Ed.), *The disability studies reader* (3rd ed., pp. 402–416). New York, NY: Routledge.

Gallaudet Research Institute. (2003, December). *2002–2003 regional and national summary.* Retrieved from http://research.gallaudet.edu/Demographics/2003_National_Summary.pdf

Groce, N. (1985). *Everyone here spoke sign language.* Cambridge, MA: Harvard University Press.

Hall, E. T. (1973). *The silent language.* New York, NY: Doubleday.

Harris, M. (1968). *The rise of anthropological theory.* Boston, MA: Crowell.

Holt, J. A. (1995). Efficiency of screening procedures for assigning levels of the Stanford Achievement Test (8th ed.) to students who are deaf or hard of hearing. *American Annals of the Deaf, 140*(1), 23–27.

Horsford, S. D., Grosland, T. J. & Gunn, K. M. (2011). Pedagogy of the personal and professional: Considering culturally relevant and antiracist pedagogy as a framework for culturally capable leadership. *Journal of School Leadership, 21*(5), 582–604.

Karchmer, M. A., & Mitchell, R. E. (2003). Demographic and achievement characteristics of deaf and hard of hearing students. In M. Marschark & P. E. Spencer (Eds.), *Oxford handbook of deaf studies, language, and education* (pp. 21–37). New York, NY: Oxford University Press.

Ladd, P. (2003). *Understanding Deaf culture: In search of deafhood.* Clevedon, UK: Cromwell.

Ladd, P. (2009). *Understanding Deaf culture: In search of deafhood.* Tonawanda, NY: Multilingual Matters.

Ladson-Billings, G. (1994). *The dreamkeepers.* San Francisco, CA, Jossey-Bass.

Ladson-Billings, G. (1995). Toward a theory of culturally relevant pedagogy. *American Educational Research Journal, 32*(3), 465–491.

Ladson-Billings, G. (1997). I know why this doesn't feel empowering: A critical race analysis of critical pedagogy. In P. Freire, J. W. Fraser, D. Macedo, T. McKinnon, & W. T. Stokes (Eds.), *Mentoring the mentor: A critical dialogue with Paulo Freire* (pp. 127–141). New York, NY: Lang.

Lane, H. (1999). *The mask of benevolence.* New York, NY: Knopf. (Original work published 1992)

Lane, H., Hoffmeister, R., & Bahan, B. (1996). *A journey into the Deaf-world.* San Diego, CA: DawnSignPress.

Lane, H., Hoffmeister, R., & Bahan, B. (2002). Educational placement and the deaf child. In M. A. Byrnes (Ed.), *Taking sides: Clashing views of controversy in special education* (pp. 220–228). Boston, MA: McGraw-Hill.

Leigh, I. W. (2009). *A lens on deaf identities.* New York, NY: Oxford University Press.

Lindsey, R. B., Robins, K. N., & Terrell, R. D. (2009). *Cultural proficiency: A manual for school leaders* (3rd ed.). Thousand Oaks, CA: Corwin.

Manganaro, M. (2002). *Cultures, 1922: The emergence of a concept.* Princeton, NJ: Princeton University Press.

Marschark, M., Lang, H., & Albertini, J., (2002). *Educating deaf students.* United Kingdom: Oxford University Press.

McCray, C., & Beachum, F. (2014). *School leadership in a diverse society: Helping schools to prepare all students for success.* Charlotte, NC: Information Age.

Mitchell, R. (2005, February). A brief summary of estimates for the size of the Deaf population in the USA based on available federal data and published research. *Gallaudet University.* Retrieved from http://research.gallaudet.edu/Demographics/deaf-US.php

Moore, M., & Levitan, L. (2005). *For hearing people only.* Rochester, NY: Deaf Life.

Moores, D. F. (2001). *Educating the deaf: Psychology, principles, and practices* (5th ed.). Boston, MA: Houghton Mifflin.

Munoz-Baell, I., & Ruiz, M. (2000). Empowering the deaf: Let the deaf be deaf. *Journal of Epidemiology & Community Health, 54*(1), 40–44. Retrieved from http://www.ncbi.nlm.nih.gov/pmc/articles/PMC1731537/

National Longitudinal Transition Study 2 (NLTS2). (2003). *Data tables.* Retrieved from http://www.nlts2.org/data_tables/index.html

Newman, L., Wagner, M., Knokey, A.-M., Marder, C., Nagle, K., Shaver, D., & Schwarting, M. (2011). *The post-high school outcomes of young adults with disabilities up to 8 years after high school. A report from the national longitudinal transition study-2 (NLTS2)* [NCSER 2011-3005] (NCSER 2011-3005). Menlo Park, CA: SRI International.

O'Brien, C. (2011). The influence of Deaf culture on school culture and leadership. A case study of a school for the deaf (Doctoral dissertation, University of Missouri, Columbia). Available from ProQuest Dissertations and Theses database.

Ogawa, R., & Bossert, S. (1995). Leadership as an organizational quality. *Education Administration Quarterly, 31*(2), 224–243.

Padden, C. (2003). The expansion of sign language education. In J. Bourne & E. Reid (Eds.), *World yearbook of education, 2003* (pp. 49–60). London, UK: Kogan-Page.

Padden, C., & Humphries, T. (1988). *Deaf in America: Voices from a culture.* Cambridge, MA: Harvard Education Press.

Padden, C., & Humphries, T. (2005). *Inside Deaf culture.* Cambridge, MA: First Harvard University Press.

Pounder, D., Ogawa, R. T., & Adams, E. (1995). Leadership as an organization-wide phenomena: Its impact on school performance. *Administration Quarterly, 35*(4), 564–588.

Qi', S., & Mitchell, R. (2012). Large-scale academic testing of deaf and hard-of-hearing students: Past, present and future. *Journal of Deaf Studies and Deaf Education, 17*(1), 1–18. doi: 10.1093/deafed/enr028.

Ramsey, C. (1997). *Deaf children in public schools.* Washington, DC: Gallaudet University Press.

Ravitch, D. (2010). *The death and life of the great American school system: How testing and choice are undermining education.* New York, NY: Basic.

Ravitch, D. (2013). *Reign of error: The hoax of the privatization movement and the danger to America's public schools.* New York, NY: Knopf.

Reed, R. (2000). *Historic MSD: The story of the Missouri school for the deaf.* Fulton, MO: Ovid Bell.

Rutherford, S. (1988). The culture of American Deaf people. *Sign Language Studies, 59,* 129–147.

Schein, E. (2004). *Organizational culture and leadership* (3rd ed.). San Francisco, CA: Jossey-Bass.

Schein, J. (1989). *At home among strangers.* Washington, DC: Gallaudet University Press.

Schirmer, B. R. (2000). *Language and literacy development in children who are deaf* (2nd ed.). Boston, MA: Allyn and Bacon.

Slobodzian, J. T., & Lugg, C. (2006) "He's a nice man, but it doesn't help": Principal leadership, school culture, and the status of deaf children. *Journal of School Leadership, 16*(3), 292–318.

Spring, J. (2000). *The universal right to education: Justification, definition, and guidelines.* Mahwah, NJ: Erlbaum.

Spring, J. (2008). *The American school: From the Puritans to No Child Left Behind* (7th ed.). New York, NY: McGraw-Hill.

Stinson, M., & Antia, S. (1999). Considerations in educating deaf and hard-of-hearing students in inclusive settings. *Journal of Deaf Studies and Deaf Education, 4*(3),163–174. doi:10.1093/deafed/4.3.163

Stokoe, W. (2005). Sign language structure: An outline of the visual communication systems of the American Deaf. *Journal of Deaf Studies and Deaf Education, 10,* 3–37. (Original work published 1960)

United Nations (UN). (2007). *United Nations Declaration on the Rights of Indigenous Peoples.* General Assembly resolution 61/295. Retrieved from http://www.un.org/esa/socdev/unpfii/en/drip.html

Wrigley, O. (1996). *The politics of deafness.* Washington, DC: Gallaudet University Press.

CHAPTER 3

CREATING INCLUSIVE SCHOOLS FOR GAY, BISEXUAL, LESBIAN, TRANSGENDER, AND QUEER/QUESTIONING (GBLTQ) STUDENTS

Applying a Social Justice Framework

James Thing
University of Arizona

M. C. Kate Esposito
California State University Dominguez Hills

ABSTRACT

Research consistently demonstrates that lesbian, gay, bisexual, transgender, and queer (LGBTQ) youth are consistently marginalized in schools, in neighborhoods, homes, and in cyberspace. Among the deleterious outcomes experienced by gay youth are bullying, psychological distress (e.g., anxiety, depression, low self-esteem, suicidal ideation), health problems (e.g., substance

Inclusive Practices and Social Justice Leadership for Special Populations in Urban Settings, pages 45–61

abuse, sexual risk-taking behavior), lowered academic performance (e.g., absenteeism, low academic achievement), and social isolation. This chapter proposes a social justice framework of inclusion that informs the development and implementation of antibullying and antidiscrimination practices and policies in the classroom and at our schools more generally. The authors review the current research specific to academic and social realities for LGBTQ students in secondary school settings, discuss how the application of a social justice framework will help ensure that schools do not perpetuate the marginalization of sexual minority youth (SMY), and discuss specific strategies educators at all levels, including colleges and universities, can implement to provide inclusive, safe schools for all students. This research adds to the extant literature by examining strategies for creating inclusive schools for all of our students, especially those who have been historically, systematically, and structurally excluded.

Educators most frequently use the term "inclusion" to refer to a philosophical instantiation of teaching students with disabilities in the same classroom setting and curriculum as their peers who do not have disabilities (Hallahan, Kauffman, & Pullen, 2015). Although the term stems from a specific educational context—that of the education of students with disabilities—it is not outside the larger geopolitical context in which schools operate. For example, Udvari-Solvner (1997) noted that inclusion necessitates a critique of contemporary school cultures that results in the realization of more just, humane, and democratic communities. As part of a larger social justice–based effort aimed at alleviating inequalities within the educational system, and to make the system more responsive to all students, lesbian, gay, bisexual, transgender, and queer/questioning (LGBTQ) activists and allies have for the past three decades advocated for the inclusion of LGBTQ students (e.g., Uribe, 1994). In short, inclusive school environments bring inequities in treatment and opportunity to the forefront so that differences are valued and respected (Udvari-Solvner, 1997). From this perspective, inclusion is concerned with *all* students—especially those who are marginalized (Artiles, Kozleski, Dorn, & Christensen, 2006)—and is situated in a social justice framework (Artiles, Bal, & King Thorius, 2010) that can be applied to any marginalized population within educational settings. For the purpose of this chapter, these authors define social justice within the context of the educational system as a "critique of educational systems in terms of access, power, and privilege based on race, culture, gender, sexual orientation, language, background, ability and/or socioeconomic position" (Brown, 2004, pp. 79–80).

INCLUSION AS A CALL TO INTERROGATE EXISTING EDUCATIONAL REALITIES

One of the most marginalized populations within society and the educational system are students who are lesbian, gay, bisexual, transgendered, or queer/questioning (LGBTQ). Researchers consistently conclude that sexual minority youth (SMY)—those who do not identify as heterosexual—are at increased risk for peer rejection, limited school support, and verbal and physical attacks within school settings (Kosciw, Greytak, Bartkiewicz, Boesen, & Palmer, 2012). Academically, LGBTQ youth are at higher risk for underachievement, absenteeism, diminished educational aspirations, and leaving high school early (Satcher & Schumacker, 2009). It is clear that interrogating the school system with an "inclusionary lens" steeped within a social justice framework is necessary if SMY are to be truly "included" in the educational system and thus have the opportunity to reach their full potential.

As such, this chapter will review the current research specific to academic and social realities for LGBTQ students in secondary academic settings, discuss how the application of a social justice framework will help ensure that schools do not perpetuate the marginalization of SMY, and discuss specific strategies educators can implement to provide inclusive, safe schools for all students. Furthermore, this chapter will add to the extant literature examining strategies for providing inclusive schools to all of our students, especially those who have been historically, systematically, and structurally excluded. Given the paucity of literature specific to the application of a social justice framework to meet the needs of SMY (Hernandez & Fraynd, 2014), this chapter further seeks to provide a framework from which to operate when seeking to mitigate the harsh realities LGBTQ students—youth and young adults—experience in school settings.

Schools as Danger Zones

Secondary schools (middle and high schools) are very often unwelcoming environments for LGBTQ youth (Bidell, 2011; Kosciw et al., 2012; Mahdi, Jevertson, Schrader, Nelson, & Ramos, 2014). Schools have been characterized as "hostile environments for a distressing number of LGBTQ students, the overwhelming majority of whom hear homophobic remarks and experience harassment or assault...because of their sexual orientation or gender expression" (Kosciw et al., 2012, p. 5). For example, recent data from the 2011 GLSEN national school climate survey (Kosciw et al., 2012) indicated that 81% of LGBTQ secondary students experienced verbal harassment (e.g., being called names or being threatened), and 38.3% SYM reported physical harassment (e.g., being shoved) in the previous academic year. Verbal and physical bullying of LGBTQ students can cause emotional, psychological, and educational difficulties for victims, bystanders, and the perpetrator (Bidell, 2011). Alarmingly, 18.3% of LGBTQ youth surveyed reported physical assault (e.g., kicked, harmed with a weapon) because of their perceived or actual sexuality. Likewise, students with nonconforming gender expression—those who do meet societal norms for their gender (Roberts, Rosario, Slopen, Calzo, & Austin, 2013)—reported similarly high rates of physical abuse at the hands of their schoolmates. Finally, 63.5 % LGBTQ youth respondents reported that they felt unsafe at school, which led to 31.8 % of these SYM students to skip a day or more of school (Kosciw et al., 2012).

Unfortunately, bullying and harassment do not stop when students leave the school facilities. More than half of students surveyed reported being the victim of electronic harassment or cyberbullying outside of the school setting (Kosciw et al., 2012). Cyberbullying is a significant concern, because, as D'Auria (2014) notes, one act of cyberbullying can quickly escalate when it is sent to thousands of bystanders in cyberspace who join in or forward the harmful information. Because the wounding information is available 24 hours a day, seven days a week "the victim is unable to escape the abuse at home or at school" (p. 19). This sometimes constant harassment as well as the general vulnerability of LGBTQ students in cyberspace can be very detrimental to the health and well-being of SMY (CDC, 2013).

Findings from the Gay, Lesbian and Straight Education Network (GLSEN) national school climate survey are consistently replicated in the extant literature. For example, the CDC (2013) has emphasized that SYM youth are more vulnerable to threats or injuries by a weapon at school than are their heterosexual peers. Furthermore the research has identified many detrimental academic and psychological problems and risk behaviors (e.g., substance abuse) associated with a hostile school climate (D'Auria, 2014; Kosciw et al., 2012; Roberts et al., 2013). The following section will discuss the outcomes in the abovementioned three areas.

Academic Outcomes

The academic outcomes of LGBTQ youth—especially those who are from multicultural, multilinguistic, and economically poor backgrounds—are often vulnerable because considerable cognitive, emotional, and physical resources are spent avoiding victimization within school settings, thus limiting the amount of resources that can be spent on academics and school involvement. Due in large part to being bullied, many LGBTQ students are less attached to schools, as evidenced by several indices, resulting lower academic achievement (i.e., lower grades), truancy, and skipping certain classes (Hillard, Love, Franks, Laris, & Coyle, 2014; Kosciw et al., 2012). Clearly, bullying and harassment put LGBTQ at an academic disadvantage, as their number of hours and sense of safety in school is diminished, which ultimately compromises SMY's opportunities to thrive in school.

Psychological Well-Being and Stress

Research has consistently shown that the psychological well-being of LGBTQ youth can be strained due to social stigma associated with sexuality and gender (CDC, 2013). Social stigma permeates the educational experiences, neighborhood environments, and often familial systems of LGBTQ youth, often leaving them with few sources of social support. As a result, studies consistently show that LGBTQ youth are at greater risk for self-harm, suicidal ideation, depression, and other mental health concerns such as PTSD (see Dragowski, Halkitis, Grossman, & D'Augelli, 2011; Haas et al., 2011) and have higher rates of substance abuse and sexual risk behavior, which often go hand-in-hand (Kecojevic, et al., 2012; Marshal et al., 2008).

As discussed above, LGBTQ youth are victimized in schools by their peers at alarmingly high rates (Kosciw et al., 2012; Toomey, Ryan, Diaz, & Russell, 2011). Further, research shows that families are often unwelcoming to their LGBTQ children and siblings (Švab & Kuhar, 2014). School and family are two vitally critical sources of social support for all youth. Given that many LGBTQ youth are victimized at school and online, and are unable to find the support available to heterosexual youth from their families, their self-esteem and well-being are significantly strained (e.g., Švab & Kuhar, 2014). It is clear that interventions and programs need to be implemented to ensure that schools are safe and provide inclusive environments where SMY can thrive—which should be a birth right.

THE ROLE OF SCHOOL PERSONNEL

Teachers on the Frontlines

The literature concerning school climate suggests that school personnel have a profound effect on the educational climate of a given school. This is especially true with regard to fostering classrooms and schools which accept individual differences among K–12 students and their families. Some 12% of secondary students identify as lesbian, gay, bisexual, transgender, or queer/questioning (Russell, 2006), which, given a typical class size of 30, students, suggests that teachers will have on average three LGBTQ students per class. Sadly, many school personnel have perpetuated and in some cases encouraged unsafe school climates (Kosciw et al., 2012; Milburn & Palladino, 2012). For example, startlingly, more than half of the students' surveyed in the 2011 National School Climate reported hearing homophobic remarks from school faculty and staff (Kosciw et al., 2012). Additionally, students in Hillard and associates' (2014) study reported that teachers took limited actions to educate those students who engaged in harassment. Thus, it is not surprising that most students surveyed in Hillard and associates' study (2014) believed that reporting incidents of victimization would result at best in only minimal intervention by administration (Dykes, 2010; Hillard et al., 2014; Kosciw et al., 2012).

SooHoo (2004) asserts that students glean different lessons from their teachers' (in)actions such that students come to view bullying as acceptable and learn that staying silent in an oppressive situation is appropriate behavior. Teachers' participation in bullying by ignoring it creates hostile environments where all students are adversely affected. Bullies learn that bullying is acceptable. Students learn that bystanderism, the "response of people who observe something that demands intervention on their part, but they choose not to get involved" (SooHoo 2004, p. 200), is acceptable. Finally, targets of bullying suffer the consequences of homophobic bullying that could, if teachers were to work toward creating truly inclusive environments, be avoided or at least diminished. The linchpin role teachers play in reducing bullying (Kosciw et al., 2012) or in perpetuating homophobia (Kosciw et al., 2012; Milburn & Palladino, 2012) for students from marginalized groups—those from sexual minorities and students with disabilities—warrants investigation into the factors that prevent teachers and administrators from intervening (Larrabee & Morehead, 2010).

Teachers may not intentionally perpetuate homophobia in the classroom, however homophobia and heterosexism pervade many classrooms. For example, preservice and in-service teachers report limited knowledge about the academic, psychological, or health risks associated with sexual minority students. Milburn and Palladino (2012) report that teachers (preservice and in-service) "failed to recognize bullying as an antecedent for emotional distress and potential health risk behaviors" (p. 97). Larrabee and Morehead (2010) further note that teachers express concern about the appropriateness of LG-BTQ issues within the K–12 curriculum. This is troubling because educators' ignorance often results in a "hands-off" approach in confronting issues affecting SMY (Dykes, 2010; Hillard et al., 2014). This hands-off approach may be due to teachers' fear, intimidation, or limited interaction with individuals who are LGBTQ (Larrabee & Morehead, 2010). Studies assessing teacher attitudes indicate that teachers generally have moderate (as opposed to positive or negative) attitudes toward lesbian and gay individuals (Wyatt, Oswalt, White, & Peterson, 2008). These researchers further indicate that teachers held more negative attitudes toward gay males than lesbian females. It is clear that much work remains if teachers are to be prepared to work with and improve the educational setting for SMY (Dykes, 2010; Larrabee & Morehead, 2010; Milburn & Palladino, 2012).

Although teacher education programs address diversity with regard to class, gender, race, and ethnicity, attention to sexuality and gender[1] expression are considerably absent (Banks, 2014; Dykes, 2010; Larrabee & Morehead, 2010). Athanases and Larrabee (2003) identified several factors impeding the attention given to sexual minority youth within teacher preparation programs; among them are the newness of articulated guidelines to address marginalized youth, limited scope of multicultural agendas which do not adequately address heterosexism, and a limited theoretical base for effectively preparing teachers to advocate for sexual minority youth. Other researchers assert that addressing issues of sexuality within the framework of multicultural classes runs the risk of being additive in nature (Banks, 2014). Additional concerns emerge when including information on SMY is at the discretion of the instructors who may choose to "ignore" this important topic (Wyatt et al., 2008).

Given that queer youth are among the most underserved student populations within our educational system (Kosciw et al., 2012), an ethical imperative and legal precedents exist which necessitates that teacher preparation programs devote the adequate resources and time needed to effectively prepare teachers to not only practice inclusivity but to become advocates for the needs of all marginalized students—including SMY (Bishop & Casida, 2011).

School Health Professionals

School health professionals—social workers, school counselors, school nurses, and other school faculty associated with the healthcare industry—play a central role in providing safe and inclusive educational environments for SMY (Bidell, 2011; Mahdi et al., 2014; Murphy, 2012). School health professionals can educate teachers, staff, administrators, and students about LGBTQ issues and school policy and practices, as well as individual teacher and staff practices that impact the school climate for LGBTQ youth (and ultimately all youth). Further, school health professionals should advocate for equality for all students, including LGBTQ students. Unfortunately, recent research suggests that school health professionals do not feel adequately prepared to address the behavioral health concerns or harassment of LGBTQ students (Bidell, 2011; Mahdi et al., 2014). For example, as Mahdi et al. (2014) found, school counselors and health workers had limited experience discussing at-risk behaviors with LGBTQ students. Further, the majority of respondents in Mahdi's study reported limited or no experience in intervening to address harassment based on actual or perceived sexual identity. It is clear that because of their training, school psychologists and counselors are uniquely positioned to address issues confronting SMY within school settings (Bidell, 2011). As asserted by Griffin and Steen (2011),

> If our educational system intends to fulfill its commitment to serving all students, especially those on the fringes of society, and intends to live up to its promise of providing vital avenues of access and opportunity, school counselors, in conjunction with other important school stakeholders must use their unique educational backgrounds and strategic positioning within schools to make meaningful change in their schools. (p. 75)

School Administrators—School Leaders

As school leaders, principals have tremendous influence on the climate of teaching and learning in their schools (Lynch, 2012). Although the existing literature examining school settings for LGBTQ youth has consistently demonstrated that schools are fraught with bullying, school leaders underestimate the pervasive nature of the problem (Hernandez & Fraynd, 2014; Kosciw et al., 2012). In a national study GLSEN and Harris Interactive (2008) found that the overwhelming majority of principals reported having heard students make sexist or homophobic remarks. Discerning is the fact that most secondary school principals report that male students who do not fit the "typically masculine" image as well as LGBTQ students would feel unsafe at their school (GLSEN & Harris Interactive, 2008).

Central to the role of an effective administrator is the ability to understand school faculty and related personnel's professional development needs. Although research findings consistently demonstrate professional development specific to creating safer environments for LGBTQ youth is critical to the creation of a safe environment, few principles report providing this type of training (GLSEN & Harris Interactive, 2008; Kosciw et al., 2012; Slesaransky-Poe, 2013). For example, although 60% of school principals reported providing professional development for their staff who addressed bullying or harassment, only 5% of those surveyed reported their professional development specifically addressed LGBTQ issues (GLSEN & Harrison Interactive, 2008).

Lynch's (2012) review of the changing responsibilities of school leaders highlights the important roles school leaders play in implementing policies to ensure legal mandates stemming from the state and federal level are met (e.g., No Child Left Behind Act [2001] and IDEIA [2004]). Although principals have a legal obligation to implement antibullying policies, many policies do not specifically address sexual orientation or gender identity (GLSEN & Harris Interactive, 2008; Kosciw et al., 2012) According to Hernandez and Fraynd (2014), "unlike other antidiscrimination measures where school leaders are hyper-vigilant, LGBTQ policies have yet to be implemented" (p. 117). If schools are to meet legal mandates of NCLB and IDEIA, which call for increased student learning outcomes for all students, including those who are LGBTQ, school leaders will need to develop and implement policies specific to this population (GLSEN & Harris Interactive; Kosciw et al., 2012; Pazey & Cole, 2012; Slesaransky-Poe, 2013). From a social justice equity perspective, policies should be implemented not to meet legal mandates but out of an ethical and moral concern for all students. When this is not the case, school districts and school leaders must be held responsible by the court system for their failure to protect SMY students from harassment (Bishop & Casida, 2011). It should be noted that many states have passed legislation specific to LGBTQ youth, which will be addressed in more depth below

THE INTERSECTIONS OF ETHICAL BEHAVIOR, INCLUSION, AND SOCIAL JUSTICE

Federal law (NCLB, 2001, Safe Schools Provisions) entitles all students to a free, safe, and effective education. If the school system is to fulfill its promise to provide an education to all students, we must create an educational environment that is inclusive to all, including those who have disabilities and those who are LGBTQ, or LGBTQ students with a disability. As evidenced in the extant literature, students with disabilities and students who are gay have been systematically marginalized and excluded (as opposed to included) from an education that meets their unique needs. These current authors profess that inclusion can only occur when the educational program is equitable, that is, tailored to meets a student's specific needs. As asserted by Artiles (2005, as cited in Artiles et al., 2010), an equity-difference socially just approach strives to deliver justice by providing all learners with the same treatment (e.g., a high-quality standards-based education) while recognizing individual differences (e.g., specific learning disabilities) and tailoring education to meet one's need. Further assertion is made that "this approach is ultimately consistent with the justice discourse advanced in the disability social movement" (Artilles et al., 2010, p. 252). In situating LGBTQ students in this social justice narrative, these authors advocate an equity-difference approach, which provides all students with a safe environment and acknowledges the fact that they are part of a marginalized sexual minority group which necessitates that supports are provided to ensure schools are welcoming. Further, we agree with Liassidou's (2013) concern that confronting specific issues in isolation from others (e.g., separately focusing on sexuality or race/ethnicity or class, etc.) is a "futile endeavor" that cannot lead to sustainable systematic change for marginalized groups because such efforts are too narrowly focused. However, we assert that this application of the social justice framework to the improvement of educational realities for LGBTQ youth not only acknowledges that change is possible, but provides a vision for how such change can be accomplished and ultimately how inclusive environments can be constructed. As such, the subsequent sections will address strategies that when implemented will interrogate existing school structures, thus creating inclusive environments.

Support of and Implementation of GSAs

It has been well documented that SMY are frequently physically and verbally victimized at school (Kosciw et al., 2012; Murphy, 2012; Slesaransky-Poe, 2013). Research findings (for complete review, see Toomey et al., 2011) have also consistently demonstrated that one of the most successful strategies—currently available for implementation—to help ensure a safe school climate is the creation of Gay-Straight Alliance clubs (GSAs). GSAs are secondary school student-led groups, held at individuals' school sites, which support and advocate for students who are gay, lesbian, bisexual, transgendered, questioning their sexuality, and/or who have gay family members or are allies (GLSEN, 2007). GSA clubs are open to all students regardless of sexual identity and are intended to improve the school climate for all students through education, support groups, and advocacy (GLSEN, 2007). These clubs seek to (a) provide a supportive and safe space in schools for LGBTQ students, allies, and students who have family members who are gay; (b) educate students about their rights; (c) educate faculty and staff; and (d) foster advocacy and activism (GLSEN 2007; Poteat, Sinclair, DiGiovanni, Koenig, & Russell, 2012). For example, because they are student led (GLSEN, 2007), GSA members can provide support to their peers who may be experiencing difficulties, such as bullying or familial rejection (Poteat et al., 2012). Additionally, they may provide settings for youth to engage in social activities (Poteat et al., 2012) or in advocacy initiatives designed to mitigate inequities at the school or community level (GLSEN, 2007).

The first GSA was formed in 1988 by a straight student who sought to reduce bullying and harassment of LGBTQ students (GLSEN, 2007). Although many schools have attempted to prevent the formation of such groups, they are protected by the Equal Educational Access Act of 1984 (Lambda Legal, 2013). As Murphy (2012) notes, the attempts to stifle or prevent GSA groups from forming is indicative the importance of such organizations. Today GLSEN estimates there are more than 4,000 GSAs across all 50 states and Puerto Rico, Guam, and Washington, DC (GLSEN, 2007) in both middle and secondary settings.

Positive outcomes of GSAs include institutional- and individual-level changes that can become protective factors for LGBTQ youth. Overall, schools with GSAs report a reduction of harassment based upon actual or perceived (homo)sexuality and/or gender expression, as well as a school-wide reduction of homophobic remarks. For individuals, whether LGBTQ or an ally, participation in GSAs potentially precipitates an increased sense of safety, belonging and connectedness, and feelings that the school is less sexually prejudiced, as well as the development of leadership skills, improved grades, and better interpersonal relationships (GLSEN, 2007; Murphy, 2012; Toomy et al., 2011). Support for LGBTQ youth and/or having a GSA in the school is endorsed by several leading professional associations including the American Academy of Pediatrics, the American Association of School Administrators, the American Counseling Association, the American Federation of Teachers, the American School Counselor Association, the National Association of School Nurses, and several other national organizations (Murphy, 2012).

Credentialing Programs Have Obligation to Address LGBTQ Issues

The literature examining the preparation of school personnel demonstrates that teachers (e.g., Larrabee & Morehead, 2010; Wyatt et al., 2008), school health professionals (e.g., Mahdi et al., 2014) and administrators (e.g., Hernandez & Fraynd, 2014) are unprepared to address the unique needs of SMY within the school system. If P–12 schools are to become more inclusive, personnel preparation programs (e.g., policymakers, state and federal legislators, school leadership programs, teacher credentialing programs) must provide a robust curriculum specific to the unique needs of LGBTQ students so that upon graduation, future teachers, health personnel, and administrators are well prepared to meet the needs of LGBTQ students. As Averett and Hedge (2012) so aptly conclude "in an inherently heterosexist society such as the US... programs of higher education have a responsibility to educate and prepare their students for nondiscriminatory practice within schools" (p. 547).

The extant literature addressing the preparation of school personnel suggests that one approach to ensuring school personnel are well prepared to actively engage in the work needed to ensure inclusive schools is the application of a social justice framework to existing credentialing programs. For example, as Pazey and Cole (2012) note, "Central to the standards within educational administration is the concept of social justice, which is advanced in the language of inclusion" (p. 253). The infusion of social justice is also evident in school counseling credential programs (Griffin & Steen, 2011) and integral to the preparation of special education teachers because they are trained advocate for students with disabilities (Dykes, 2010). We agree with Bidell (2011), who asserted that counselors who operate from a social justice framework are uniquely prepared to serve as GSA leaders and hope that all school personnel would be prepared to serve not only as GSA leaders, but as advocates for all students, especially those who are marginalized within the current educational system.

The literature has established a clear need for school personnel to be better prepared to meet the needs of SMY. This is particularly true with the development and implementation and institutionalization of inclusive curriculum. For example, as Burdge, Snapp, Laub, Russell, and Moody (2013) note, only recently have states begun to adopt curriculum that is specific to LGBTQ issues. Larrabee and Morehead (2010) suggest credential candidates be provided with many opportunities to discuss and understand inclusive curriculum if they are going to internalize the skills needed to effectively implement inclusive curriculum. These authors agree and suggest that faculty—across all credentialing programs—will need additional training. If issues pertaining to SMY are to be brought to the forefront of credentialing programs, educators must first acknowledge that the need for such an agenda exists. Secondly, future leaders must reflect upon their existing knowledge base with regard to the unique needs specific to GLBTQ in schools and seek to increase such knowledge.

Schoolwide Training Specific to LGBTQ Issues

In order to provide a safe, supportive, and inclusive environment for sexual minority youth, all of the school faculty, staff, administration, and support teams (e.g., school nurses, counselors, and community liaisons) must receive training at the local school or district level. As Slesaransky-Poe (2013) aptly notes, the training must be "inclusive and comprehensive sex, gender and sexuality education (p. 41)" for all adults who work in the school. This training is particularly vital for school personnel who have not received training in their certification programs. Further, schools leaders must actively work to ensure such training is implemented on an ongoing basis (Mahdi et al., 2014).

Development and Implementation of Antidiscrimination Policies

In order to create and ensure an inclusive environment exists for all students, district leaders must implement strong policies specific to the protection of SMY (Bishop & Casida, 2011). As indicated by Kosciw et al.'s (2012) national report on school climate, many schools do not have bullying policies which explicitly address LGBTQ students. Although research suggests a greater number of schools and districts have moved to implementing policies specifically addressing LGBTQ students than in years past (Hillard et al., 2014), many schools have not implemented these vital policies (Kosciw et al., 2012). Research findings further suggest that such policies must be "comprehensive and enumerate the categories of gender identity and expression, sexual orientation and family composition" (Slesaransky-Poe, 2013, p. 43). Once developed and implemented, students and adults must be provided with a comprehensive overview of district and school policies and the protocols thus better ensuring antidiscriminatory policies are adhered to (Flemming, 2012). Schools seeking to implement training that is targeted to the needs of the school should assess school personnel and students annually (Hillard et al., 2014) with respect to their knowledge and abilities to create safe and inclusive environments.

Implementation of Inclusive Curriculum

School climate research suggests that the implementation of inclusive curriculum promotes greater feelings of student safety, health, and well-being

(Burdge et al., 2013; Kosciw et al., 2012). Findings further suggest that SMY absenteeism is reduced and academic achievement is increased (Burdge, Sinclair, Laub, & Russell, 2012). Drawing on research findings associated with inclusive curriculum and in efforts to interrogate the harsh realities of schools for LGBTQ youth, the Fair, Accurate, Inclusive, and Respectful Education Act of 2011 (FAIR Act, 2011) was signed into law. This Act requires California's P–12 schools to include age-appropriate, factual information about social movements, current events, and the history of people with disabilities, and LGBTQ individuals in school curriculum. The implementation of the FAIR Act further seeks to ensure that contributions of both men and women, people of color, diverse ethnic communities, and other historically underrepresented groups are represented in the textbooks and curriculum for P–12 students. The Act further prohibits instruction or school-sponsored activities that promote a discriminatory bias based on race or ethnicity, gender, religion, disability, nationality, and sexual orientation, or other characteristics (Penan, 2013). As Burdge, Snapp, Laub, Russell, and Moody (2013) note, a broad approach to the implementation of an LGBTQ inclusive curriculum "likely has the greatest impact on school climate" (p. 5). As such, we encourage school leaders and policymakers across the nation to pass legislation similar to California and to actively seek to implement an inclusive curriculum.

CONCLUSIONS

Schools are in many ways unwelcoming environments for LGBTQ youth. Structurally, LGBTQ youth are excluded with respect to representation in curriculum, unprepared teachers, administrators, and other personnel, and overall heterosexist school climates. Interpersonally, LGBTQ youth often experience verbal and physical harassment from bullies. Structural and interpersonal marginalization manifest simultaneously when school personnel do not intervene to stop bullying of LGBTQ students. The discrimination and marginalization SMY face in school settings can be a barrier to full participation in school activities and success in middle and high schools.

Situating this chapter in a social just framework provides the impetus for change based on ethical and moral obligations that are outside the mandates of the legal system. Research findings from disabilities research, social and behavioral health research, and educational research has provided tangible solutions that when implemented, have the power to dramatically improve the lives of not only LGBTQ youth, but all youth from marginalized backgrounds. It is up to educators themselves and the educational system more broadly to put social justice into practice by fully integrating solutions already available, such as forming and supporting Gay-Straight Alliance clubs on campus, addressing LGBTQ issues in credentialing programs, providing schoolwide training specific to LGBTQ issues, developing and implementing antidiscrimination policies and protocols on how to handle LGBTQ discrimination on campus, and developing inclusive curriculum. These tools can be implemented by policymakers, principals, teachers, and school personnel who should, in the spirit of a social justice of inclusion, seek out new solutions that fit the specific needs of their district, school, and classroom.

Legal protections do exist to protect SYM youth; however, alone, legal mandates are insufficient to bring about the depth of change needed to create environments that foster inclusivity. In addition to legal protections, school personnel are integral to the creation of a truly inclusive school climate since they are on the front lines with students daily. School personnel interact with students throughout the day and are thus in the unique position to model a social justice approach to inclusion. Further, school personnel observing students interacting can intervene when homophobic remarks are made, even if the remarks are not aimed at an LGBTQ student. Finally, school personnel can develop, implement, and support several structural mechanisms (e.g., trainings, inclusive curriculum) designed to educate school personnel and students about the importance of creating inclusive and welcoming environments for all students.

NOTE

1. These authors recognize that these aspects of identity are not mutually exclusive, but rather are intersecting (e.g., Black lesbian).

ACKNOWLEDGMENT

This research has been supported by the Frances McClelland Institute at the University of Arizona and an NIH T32 CA 9492-28 Training Grant

REFERENCES

Artiles, A. J., Bal, A., & King Thorius, K. A. (2010). Back to the future: A critique of response to intervention's social justice views. *Theory Into Practice, 49*, 250–257.

Artiles, A. J., Kozleski, E. B., Dorn, S., & Christenson, C. (2006). Learning in inclusive education research: Re-mediating theory and methods with a transformative agenda. *Review of Research in Education, 30*, 65–108.

Averett, P. E., & Hegde, A. (2012). School social work and early childhood student's attitudes toward gay and lesbian families. *Teaching in Higher Education, 17*(5), 537–549.

Athanases, S. Z., & Larrabee, T. G. (2003). Toward a consistent stance in teaching for equity: Learning to advocate for lesbian- and gay-identified youth. *Teaching and Teacher Education, 19*(2), 237–261.

Banks, J. A. (2014). An introduction to multicultural education (5th ed.). Upper Saddle River, NJ: Pearson.

Bidell, M. P. (2011). School counselors and social justice advocacy for lesbian, gay, bisexual, transgender, and, questioning students. *Journal of School Counseling, 9*(10), 1–22.

Bishop, H. N., & Casida, H. (2011). Preventing bullying and harassment of sexual minority students in schools. *The Clearing House, 84,* 131–138.

Brown, K. M. (2004). Leadership for social justice and equity: Weaving a transformative framework and pedagogy. *Educational Administration Quarterly, 40,* 77–108.

Burdge, H., Sinclair, K., Laub, C., & Russell, S. T. (2012). Research Brief No. 14: Lessons that matter: LGBTQ inclusivity and school safety. *Gay-Straight Alliance Network and California Safe Schools Coalition.* Retrieved September 29, 2014, from https://www.gsanetwork.org/files/aboutus/PSH%20Report%206_2012.pdf

Burdge, H., Snapp, S., Laub, C., Russell, S. T., & Moody, R. (2013). Implementing lessons that matter: The impact of LGBTQ-inclusive curriculum on student safety, well-being, and achievement. *Gay-Straight Alliance Network/Frances McClelland Institute.* Retrieved September 29, 2014, from http://www.gsanetwork.org/files/aboutus/ImplementingLessons_fullreport.pdf

Centers for Disease Control and Prevention (CDC). (2013). *2012 Division of Adolescent and School Health: Success stories.* Retrieved May 30, 2014, from http://www.cdc.gov/healthyyouth/stories/pdf/ss_booklet_0713.pdf

D'Auria, J. P. (2014). Cyberbullying resources for youth and their families. *Journal of Pediatric Healthcare, 28*(2), 19–22.

Dragowski, E. A., Halkitis, P. N., Grossman, A. H., & D'Augelli, A. R. (2011). Sexual orientation victimization and posttraumatic stress symptoms among lesbian, gay, and bisexual youth. *Journal of Gay and Lesbian Social Services, 23*(2), 226–249.

Dykes, F. (2010). Transcending rainbow flags and pride parades: Preparing special education preservice educators to work with gay and lesbian youth. *SRATE Journal, 19*(2), 36–43.

Fair, Accurate, Inclusive, and Respectful (FAIR) Education Act SB 48. (2011) Retrieved September 29, 2014, from http://www.eqca.org/atf/cf/%7B34f258b3-8482-4943-91cb-08c4b0246a88%7D/FAIR%20education%20fact%20sheet%20final.pdf

Flemming, J. (2012, March/April). Bullying and bias: Making schools safe for gay students. *Leadership,* 12–14.

GLSEN. (2007). Research Brief: Gay-straight alliances: Creating safer schools for LGBT students and their allies. *Gay, Lesbian and Straight Education Network.* Retrieved September 16, 2014, from http://glsen.org/sites/default/files/Gay-Straight%20Alliances.pdf

GLSEN & Harris Interactive. (2008). The principal's perspective: School safety, bullying and harassment: A survey of public school principals. New York, NY: GLSEN.

Griffin, D., & Steen, S. (2011). A social justice approach to school counseling. *Journal for Social Action in Counseling and Psychology, 3*(1), 74–85.

Haas, A. P., Eliason, M., Mays, V. M., Mathy, R. M. Cochran, S. D., D'Augelli, A. R.,...Clayton, P. J. (2011). Suicide and suicide risk in lesbian, gay, bisexual and transgender populations: Review and recommendations. *Journal of Homosexuality, 58*(1), 10–51.

Hallahan, D. P., Kauffman, J. M., & Pullen, P. C. (2015). *Exceptional learners: An introduction to special education* (13th ed.). Upper Saddle River, NJ: Pearson.

Hernadez, F., & Fraynd, D. J. (2014). Leadership's role in inclusive lgbtq-supportive schools. *Theory into Practice, 53*, 115–122.

Hillard, P. L., Love, L., Franks, H. M., Laris, B. A., & Coyle, K. (2014). "They were only joking": Efforts to decrease LGBTQ bullying and harassment in Seattle public schools. *Journal of School Health, 84*(1), 1–9.

Individuals with Disabilities Education Improvement Act (IDEIA) of 2004, P. L.108-446, 20 U.S.C. § 1400 et seq.

Kecojevic, A., Wong, C. F. Schrager, S. M., Silva, K. Bloom, J. J., Iverson, E., & Lankenau, S. E. (2012). Initiation into prescription drug misuse: Differences between lesbian, gay, bisexual, and transgender (LGBT) and heterosexual high-risk young adults in Los Angeles and New York. *Addictive Behaviors, 37*, 1289–1293.

Kosciw, J. G., Greytak, E. A., Bartkiewicz, M. J., Boesen, M. J., & Palmer, N. A. (2012). *The 2011 National School Climate Survey: The experiences of lesbian, gay, bisexual and transgender youth in our nation's schools.* New York, NY: GLSEN.

Lambda Legal. (2013). *Know your rights: Your legal right to form a GSA.* Retrieved September 15, 2014, from http://www.lambdalegal.org/know-your-rights/lgbtq-teens-young-adults/your-legal-right-to-form-a-gsa

Larrabee, T. G., & Morehead, P. (2010). Broadening views of social justice and teacher leadership: Addressing LGB issues in teacher education. *Issues in Teacher Education, 19*(2), 37–52.

Liasidou, A. (2013). Intersectional understandings of disability and implications for a social justice reform agenda in education policy and practice. *Disability & Society, 28*(3), 299–312.

Lynch, J. M. (2012). Responsibilities of today's principal: Implications for principal preparation programs and principal certification policies. *Council on Rural Special Education, 31*(2), 40–47.

Mahdi, I., Jevertson, J., Schrader, R., Nelson, A., & Ramos, M. M. (2014). Survey of New Mexico school health professionals regarding preparedness to support sexual minority students. *Journal of School Health, 84*(1), 18–24

Marshall, M. P., Friedman, M. S., Stall, R., King, K. M., Miles, J., & Gold, M. A. (2008). Sexual orientation and adolescent substance use: A meta-analysis and methodological review. *Addiction, 103*(4), 546–556.

Milburn, W., & Palladino, J. (2012). Preservice teachers' knowledge, skills, and dispositions of LGBTQ bullying intervention. *The American Association of Behavioral and Social Sciences Journal, 16*, 86–100.

Murphy, H. E. (2012). Improving the lives of students, gay and straight alike: Gay-straight alliances and the role of school psychologists. *Psychology in the Schools, 49*(9), 883–891.

No Child Left Behind (NCLB) Act of 2001. P. L. No. 107-110 § 115, Stat. 1425.

Pazey, B. L., & Cole, H. A. (2012). The role of special education training in the development of socially just leaders: Building an equity consciousness in educational leadership programs. *Educational Administration Quarterly, 49*(2), 243–271.

Penan, H. (2013, June 3). FAIR Education Act. *The Notice.* Retrieved September 29, 2014, from http://thenoticeca.com/2013/06/03/fair-education-act/

Poteat, V. P., Sinclair, K. O., DiGiovanni, C. D., Keonig, B. W., & Russell, S. T. (2012). Gay-straight alliances are associated with student health: A multischool comparison of LGBTQ and heterosexual youth. *Journal of Research on Adolescence, 23*(2), 319–330.

Roberts, A. L., Rosario, M., Slopen, N., Calzo, J. P., & Austin, S. B. (2013). Childhood gender nonconformity, bullying victimization, and depressive symptoms across adolescence and early adulthood: An 11-year longitudinal study. *Journal of the American Academy of Child and Adolescent Psychiatry, 52*(2), 143–152.

Russell, S. T. (2006). Substance use and abuse and mental health among sexual-minoirty youths: Evidence from Add Health. In A. M. Omoto & H. S. Kurtzman (Eds.), *Sexual orientation and mental health: Examining idendity and development in lesbian, gay, and bisexual people* (pp. 13–35). Washington, DC: APA.

Satcher, J., & Schumacker, R. (2009). Predictors of modern homonegativity among professional counselors. *Journal of LGBT Issues in Counseling, 3*(1), 21–36.

Slesaransky-Poe, G. (2013). Adults set the tone for welcoming all students. *Kappan, 94*(5), 40–44.

SooHoo, S. (2004). We change the world by doing nothing. *Teacher Education Quarterly, 31*(1), 199–211.

Švab, A., & Kuhar, R. (2014). The transparent and family closets: Gay men and lesbians and their families of origin. *Journal of GLBT Family Studies, 10*(1/2), 15–35.

Toomey, R. B., Ryan, C., Diaz, R. M., & Russell, S. T. (2011). High school gay-straight alliances (GSAs) and young adult well-being: An examination of GSA presence, participation and perceived effectiveness. *Applied Developmental Science, 15*(4), 175–185.

Udvari-Solner, A. (1997). Inclusive education. In C. A. Grant & G. Ladson-Billings (Eds.), *Dictionary of multicultural education* (pp. 141–144). Phoenix, AZ: Oryxg.

Uribe, V. (1994). Project 10: A school-based outreach to gay and lesbian youth. *High School Journal, 77*, 108–112.

Wyatt, T. J., Oswalt, S. B., White, C., & Peterson, F. L. (2008, Spring). Are tomorrow's teachers ready to deal with diverse students?: Teacher candidates' attitudes toward gay men and lesbians. *Teacher Education Quarterly*, 171–185.

CHAPTER 4

INTERSECTIONS OF AUTISM, RACE, AND CLASS

A Social Justice Agenda for Inclusive Leadership Practices

Melissa Spence
Los Angeles Unified School District

Edlyn Vallejo Peña
California Lutheran University

ABSTRACT

Despite becoming a federal mandate, inclusion in general education has been a challenge for students with autism spectrum disorders, particularly in urban school settings. The needs of students in urban settings are complicated by issues of low income, language minority, and underrepresented racial minority status. School leaders in urban settings are called upon to take an active role in supporting the inclusion of students with autism. Utilizing a social justice framework, this chapter will explore how administrators and teacher leaders can promote inclusion as an ethical practice in urban settings. Recommendations are made for educational leaders to facilitate and lead in-

Inclusive Practices and Social Justice Leadership for Special Populations in Urban Settings, pages 63–81

clusive educational practices for students with autism spectrum disorders in urban settings.

The successful inclusion of children with disabilities and special needs in our school system relies on the belief that all children have equal access to a quality education. Inclusive education isn't a program, a place or a classroom. It is a way of understanding and living in the real world. Because, in fact, this is a world that has people of all different sizes, shapes, colors and abilities.

—Nicole Eredics (2012, para. 2)

Schools in the United States are experiencing dramatic increases in enrollment of students with autism spectrum disorders (ASD). The impetus behind the compelling and urgent need to support students with ASD stems from the surprising exponential growth in school children diagnosed with the disorder. As of 2014, the Centers for Disease Control (CDC) reported that 1 in 68 children in the United States are diagnosed with ASD, a 30% increase from the previous two years. Further, the CDC (2013) found that 1 in 50 school-aged children (ages 6–17 years) are identified with ASD, equivalent to nearly 2% of the school-aged population. This trend indicates that school leaders will require a greater understanding of students with ASD, and most teachers can expect to teach students identified with autism, if they have not done so already. Despite becoming a federal mandate (Almazan, 2009; IDEIA, 2004; NCLB, 2001), including students with ASD in general-education settings has created real and perceived challenges for school leaders, particularly in urban environments. Students in urban settings are more likely to come from low income and underrepresented racial minority families who tend to lack the social and cultural capital to navigate school systems and special education services (Oesterreich & Knight, 2008). The result is inequitable educational opportunities and outcomes for families from historically marginalized backgrounds. As such, school leaders in urban settings are called upon to take an active role by assisting parents to navigate the system and supporting the inclusion of students with autism in the general-education classroom. Utilizing a social justice framework, this chapter will explore how school leaders can promote inclusion as an ethical practice in urban settings. Recommendations are made for educational leaders to facilitate and lead inclusive educational practices for students with autism spectrum disorders in urban settings.

Understanding Autism and Inclusion

Autism is a developmental disorder in which individuals experience communicative, behavioral, and social challenges (CDC, 2013). As a spectrum disorder, individuals express the characteristics of ASD differently and to varying degrees of severity, making no two individuals with ASD identical. ASD is five times more likely in boys than girls, although it is unknown why such gender disparity occurs (CDC, 2013). Early symptoms typically manifest by 24 months and can include delayed speech, avoidance of eye contact, becoming upset by minor changes (environmental and/or routine), not responding to one's name, perseverative interests, and hypo- or hyperactivity to sensory input (CDC, 2013). These behaviors can lead to difficulties in navigating social and educational environments.

Historically, students with ASD have been relegated to special education programs. More recently however, students with ASD are accessing inclusive learning environments, and yet minimal discussion and significant confusion persists throughout the professional community as to what inclusion looks like and how to best implement the practice (Anastasiou & Kauffman, 2011; Renzaglia, Karvonen, Drasgow, & Stoxen, 2003; Williams, Johnson, & Sukhodolsky, 2005). Administrators, teachers, and parents typically utilize three terms interchangeably to describe inclusionary practices: *mainstreaming, integration,* and *inclusion.* Yet the literature contains discrete definitions for each term, indicating that the interchangeable utilization of terms is inappropriate (Renzaglia et al., 2003).

Mainstreaming indicates a separate educational placement. The student is enrolled in a special education classroom for core academic instruction and mainstreamed into the general-education setting for activities deemed appropriate and accessible (Renzaglia et al., 2003). Integration and inclusion both imply the full-time placement of a special education student into a general-education classroom, but they differ in an ideological framework. *Integration* refers to physical proximity, which does not always engender ideological, inclusive thinking. Inclusion reaches beyond integration as it embodies the belief that everyone belongs and can learn from each other (Renzaglia et al.,). *Inclusion* is the embracing of a progressive educational culture, a culture valuing diversity in learning styles, behavior, and social aptitude. This means that educating students with disabilities is not relegated to special education teachers alone but rather becomes the shared responsibility of all teachers and staff. True inclusion is the ultimate ambition "that crosses all environments and social settings where people with disabilities learn, work, live, and play" (Renzaglia et al., 2003, p. 140). Regardless of ideological differences, legal and political documents commonly use the term *inclusion* when referring to *integration* (Barton, Reichow, Wolery, & Chen, 2011; IDEIA, 2004; von der Embse, Brown, & Fortain, 2011). For the purposes of this chapter, the term *inclusion* will be utilized to indicate the full-time placement of a student with special needs into a general-education environment that embodies the belief that the student belongs and is a fully participating member of the classroom

Significant Legislation

Two key pieces of legislation spurred the practice of inclusionary practices: NCLB (2001) and IDEIA (2004). NCLB requires administrators and teachers to increase academic achievement for students in subgroups, such as students with disabilities (NCLB, 2001). Integration is thus viewed as a vehicle to increase academic achievement by exposing students with ASD to rigorous curricular content to a greater extent than possible in a special education classroom (Barton et al., 2011; van der Embse et al., 2011). IDEIA (2004) mandates the inclusion of students with disabilities as much as possible within a least restrictive environment (LRE) (Barton et al., 2011; IDEIA, 2004; von der Embse et al., 2011). Although IDEIA (2004) did not create the idea of LRE, the legislation shifted the focus from a nebulous best practice toward a mandate wherein school districts and teachers are now held directly accountable for the academic achievement of all students (Barton et al., 2011; von der Embse et al., 2011). Both NCLB (2001) and IDEIA (2004) changed instructional delivery for students with ASD, where included placements are becoming the expected norm (Barton et al., 2011; Renzaglia et al., 2003; van der Embse et al., 2011).

Despite becoming a norm, misconceptions prevail regarding the outcomes of inclusion. Positive outcomes for students with disabilities who are educated in inclusive general-education settings are numerous. For instance, students experience higher levels of achievement in math and reading when they learn in a general-education curriculum (Cole, Waldron, & Majd, 2004; Cosier, Causton-Theoharis, & Theoharis, 2013). Students with intellectual disabilities, which may include students with autism, make more progress in literacy skills when fully included in general education compared to their peers in special-education settings (Dessemontet, Bless, & Morin, 2012). Such outcomes lead to higher graduation rates and more capable and contributing citizens in our communities. When students are included, the message is that they belong and can thrive among and alongside typical peers, who also benefit from inclusive experiences themselves. Inclusion is therefore an important aim for educational leaders.

Challenges to Inclusion in Urban Settings

Several major issues pose added complexities to successful inclusion of students with autism in urban school settings. First, low-income, language minority, and ethnic minority children—who make up a significant portion of students in urban schools—tend to enter school systems having received fewer early intervention services and quality preschool compared to their peers (Iland, Weiner, & Murawski, 2012; Tek & Landa, 2012). Symptoms of autism in ethnic minority and language minority children are more likely to go undetected by families during critical years of early development and thus result in later diagnoses (Tek & Landa, 2012). Late detection of symptoms and diagnoses results in a ripple effect of delayed intervention. Exacerbating this problem are publicly funded developmental services that are disproportionately distributed across families from different racial and socioeconomic groups. The *Los Angeles Times* revealed the disparities in a featured article about the stratification of services in California: "For autistic children 3 to 6—a critical period for treating the disorder—the state Department of Developmental Services last year spent an average of $11,723 per child on whites, compared with $11,063 on Asians, $7,634 on Latinos and $6,593 on blacks" (Zarembo, 2011, para. 9).

To complicate matters, disparities in school services exist in large urban districts like the Los Angeles Unified School District (LAUSD), the second-largest school district in the United States. Again, public spending on school services varies across socioeconomic status and race.

> Data from [Los Angeles] public schools, though limited, shows that whites are more likely to receive basic services such as occupational therapy to help with coordination and motor skills. The divide is even starker when it comes to the most coveted service—a behavioral aide from a private company to accompany a child throughout each school day, at a cost that often reaches $60,000 a year. In the state's largest school district, Los Angeles Unified, white elementary school students on the city's affluent Westside have such aides at more than 10 times the rate of Latinos on the Eastside. (Zarembo, 2011, paras. 10–12)

Other studies have reported the gross overrepresentation of traditionally marginalized groups of students in segregated special education classes, creating exacerbated conditions of systemic segregation for students of color (Losen & Orfield, 2002). The act of placing students in special education is complicated by issues of race, gender, native language, and socioeconomic status. Boys, especially boys of color, are more likely to be placed in special education compared to girls (Johnson & Shelton, 2014). Public LAUSD data on ASD students enrolled in the 2013–2014 academic school year show that Latinos and English language learners with ASD spend a significantly greater amount of time in segregated special education classes compared to White and native English learners. Further, students with ASD who attend schools in the southern and eastern regions of LAUSD, areas in which more low-income families reside, spend significantly more time in special education classes compared to students in the western and northern regions of LAUSD. The literature suggests that low-income and underrepresented ethnic minority (URM) students with disabilities "often receive inadequate services, low-quality curriculum and instruction and unnecessary isolation from their nondisabled peers" (Lawrence-Brown & Sapon-Shevin, 2013, p. 74). Families from educated and upper income backgrounds tend to have the capital—human, social, and cultural capital—to advocate for better and more intensive services. These conditions stifle the educational and occupational opportunities of children with autism and other disabilities from already marginalized backgrounds, perpetuating a cycle of unequal opportunities.

Important factors in the equation of successful inclusion are school culture and educators' beliefs about inclusion. Research suggests that teachers' attitudes toward students with disabilities and their inclusion in general-education settings dramatically influence the effectiveness of their instruction (Cassady, 2011). Teachers may feel unequipped to teach and respond to learning and behavioral challenges and that attention to these matters can detract from the learning of students without disabilities in the classroom. Contrary to these misperceptions, research has refuted the idea that academic performance suffers for students without disabilities who are educated in classrooms in which students with disabilities are included (Ruijs, Van der Veen, & Peetsma, 2010; Sermier Dessemontet & Bless, 2013). Still, without leadership and administrative support to include children with disabilities, "tension, stress, and strain [can arise] for both teachers and students alike in inclusive settings" (Ross-Hill, 2009, p. 189). Administrative support for inclusion directly impacts general educators' behaviors and teaching methods. That is, proper support from administrators has the potential to increase teacher collaboration with special educators and overall acceptance of inclusion (Ross-Hill, 2009).

The good news is that following the tenets of NCLB (2001) and IDEIA (2004), many large school districts are pushing for more inclusion of their special-education students (Castellanos, 2013; Jones, 2013; Phillips, 2013). This shift is creating dramatic cultural changes to large institutions. Beginning at the start of the 2013–2014 academic school year, the Los Angeles Unified School District began a multistep plan to close its special-education centers, integrating these students into traditional campuses (Castellanos, 2013; Jones, 2013). Of the 82,765 special-education students enrolled in LAUSD, only 2,190 (or 2.6%) will remain at special-education centers (Castellanos, 2013). Similarly, the Stockton Unified School District (SUSD) is working toward what Assistant Superintendent Tom Anderson refers to as a "massive culture shift" (Phillips, 2013, para. 2). SUSD is in the process of developing learning centers throughout their K–8 campuses. All students, including students with disabilities, will begin their school day in a general-education classroom, leaving only to attend the learning centers as needed (Phillips, 2013). While far from full inclusion, it is a step "back to the idea that every kid belongs to every teacher and every kid starts as a general-education kid" (Phillips, 2013, para. 3). Some 10% of SUSD's student population have an eligibility of ASD, and ultimately the district's plan aims to increase teacher expectations of students, boost the social opportunities provided to students with special needs, and foster compassion amongst general-education students (Phillips, 2013).

Including the Student Perspective

It is important to acknowledge that while inclusion literature focuses on effective leadership, teacher practices, and instructional strategies, much of this knowledge comes from the perspective of school leaders and teachers. What is missing is a student perspective. What do students with ASD perceive to be important factors to an inclusive education? This is particularly important for students in urban schools with large populations of traditionally marginalized groups. These students and families "ought to be included in decision-making regarding these practices..., [giving] voice to the perspectives of those defined as outsiders in the process of problem-setting and solving" (McKinney & Lowenhaupt, 2013, p. 322).

In a rare study that documented the perceptions of students with autism about schooling, Saggers, Hwang, and Mercer (2011) interviewed nine high school students with ASD to determine which school factors had positive and negative effects on their educational experience. The researcher found six influential factors: teacher characteristics, curriculum-related issues, support mechanisms, friendships, environmental considerations, and teasing/bullying. Students reported that instruction was beneficial when teachers had a firm understanding of ASD and students' needs, thereby creating a structured learning environment and knew how to make learning fun. Students indicated a need for teachers to consider environmental considerations, as noise levels, light sensitivity, and crowding could be problematic. A heavy academic workload was deemed too overwhelming and stressful, as were assignments involving handwriting (in the presence of fine motor difficulties). Students communicated a need for support outside of the classroom (social skills, academic, behavioral) but expressed a desire for this support to be subtle and did not want much attention called upon themselves. These findings further support the need for school leaders and teachers to not only have a solid foundation and training regarding the characteristics of ASD and best instructional practices but also in how to best implement such knowledge and practice to best benefit students with ASD within inclusive settings.

Toward a Social Justice Framework for Inclusion

The operating paradigms and frameworks about students with autism and other disabilities shape educational leaders' approaches and practices.

Society is slowly progressing from viewing students with ASD from a medical to a social constructionist model (Anastasiou & Kauffman, 2011; Renzaglia et al., 2003; Silverman, 2007). A medical perspective frames students with ASD as having abnormalities and deficits needing correction. Segregated special education classrooms became bastions of "curing" these deficits, resulting in labeling, isolation, and stigmatization (Anastasiou & Kauffman, 2011). The social constructionist model emerged as a direct reaction against the medical model and its ableist assumptions (Anastasiou & Kauffman, 2011; Reid & Knight, 2003; Renzaglia et al., 2003). Social constructionism views the behavioral, social, and academic challenges inherent with students with ASD as social constructions (Anastasiou & Kauffman, 2011). The idea is that society constructs social and physical barriers for people with disabilities "that result in pathologizing, infantilism, exclusion, and poverty" (Reid & Knight, 2003 p. 18). For example, hand flapping does not cause injury to an individual's self or others, yet the behavior is considered problematic or socially unacceptable because society has labeled the behavior as such. In contrast, through a social constructionist lens, students with ASD are no longer viewed as needing to be cured. Instead, the focus shifts from interventions on the individual to society and systems, while still providing opportunities for individual empowerment and the development of self-efficacy skills to become productive members of society (Renzaglia et al., 2003).

The overarching goals of a social constructionism framework are to challenge widespread belief systems related to ableism and to realize the democratic ideals of social justice. In this socially just framework, all children are deserving of quality and equal educational opportunities. Toward this end, successful inclusion goes beyond the simple placement of students within a general-education classroom with the proper supports. School leaders must be at the forefront to carry out this movement in school settings. McKinney and Lowenhaupt (2013) assert that "School leaders play a key role in promoting a vision, structure, and the culture to support the pursuit of social justice" (p. 311). A social justice framework must therefore extend beyond instructional strategies to truly examine how inclusive cultures are built within school systems.

Though socially just leaders have a unified "mission to motivate change to improve the educational experiences of and outcomes for all students, particularly those who have traditionally been marginalized in schools" (McKinney & Lowenhaupt, 2013, p. 309), the shifts in educational culture have left schools without a strong understanding of how to implement true inclusive practices. Without a set of guiding principles or framework to realize a socially just culture, school leaders have little in the way of a roadmap to guide their leadership practices. The absence of a roadmap is compounded by the fact that literature on socially just leadership has been extraordinarily silent about disability and inclusion issues (McKinney

& Lowenhaupt, 2013). Moreover, there is no roadmap or set of directions for general-education teachers, resulting in disparate inclusive practices throughout classrooms. This is evidenced by the varying vernacular used to describe inclusion (e.g., mainstreaming, integration, inclusion). Instead, school leaders, staff, and teachers are largely left to their own devices to decipher not only the intricacies of ASD, but also what inclusion entails and how to best enact the practice (Anastasiou & Kauffman, 2011; Renzaglia et al., 2003; Williams et al., 2005).

Very few frameworks exist in the literature that center on inclusion or make mention of students with disabilities. Winzer and Mazurek (2012) present one of the few models aimed at aiding schools in analyzing and enacting inclusive schooling practices. Their model includes five major components that bring together the complexities to be considered in examining and realizing inclusive schooling. While the model aims to examine inclusion from a macro or national and international perspective, its application is useful at the school level, particularly in urban schools. The central component that undergirds inclusive schooling in Winzer and Mazurek's model is social justice.

> The overarching aim is to produce a conceptual shift in the way in which individuals with disabilities are perceived in terms of their place in society and how educational rights are provided. Once it is agreed that diverse groups have a natural rightful place in society, then it follows that schools should mirror that broader commitment. (p. 16)

Without this philosophical ideal in place, school leaders will struggle to achieve real inclusion.

The four themes that surround social justice in the model are dimensions of time, cultural parameters, school transformation, and policy and outcomes. Drawing from these themes, school leaders should first consider and document the school's history of inclusive policies and practices, the resiliency of these practices, and the age and evolution of the reform. Considering these dimensions of time requires that school leaders consider contexts—national, state, and local policies that impact practices of inclusion over time. School leaders might ask, what can be learned from the implementation of inclusion practices and reforms in our school's history? Second, school leaders must understand and consider cultural parameters. In what ways do the local history, culture, identity, religion, and ideologies about equality shape the perceptions of families and school personnel? From this perspective, school leaders look beyond technical policies to acknowledge cultural expectations of what it means to have a disability and what it means to be inclusive. Winzer and Mazurek (2012) reiterate that "it is the manner by which societies construct and respond to disabilities, gender, race, and cultural differences that determine how inclusive that society can be" (p. 18). Third, the school transformation theme requires school leaders to reconceptualize school systems and organizational structures that contribute to long-standing inequities. This theme challenges school leaders to abandon segregated schools and classes of students with disabilities. General educators will need the support to create fundamental changes in teaching and learning processes. Fourth, school leaders are asked to examine school policies and the outcomes of those policies. Policies include multiple strands: leadership, teacher recruitment, teacher training and professional development, early identification and early intervention, teacher working conditions, evaluation of implemented programs, among others. Examining their outcomes is just as important. Winzer and Mazurek emphasize that "outcomes rest on the proposition that ultimately educational inclusion means making a difference in the opportunities and lives of all students, particularly those traditionally marginalized, segregated, or excluded" (p. 20).

The inclusion model by Winzer and Mazurek (2012) suggests that change is complex, takes time, and involves interwoven processes. This inclusive agenda is supported by research and has the potential to guide school leaders toward a more inclusive vision and school culture.

Educational Leadership as a Catalyst for Change

Visionary leadership is a crucial element for changing school culture to one that fosters inclusion (Crosland & Dunlap, 2012; Lynch & Irvine, 2009; Waldron & McLeskey, 2010). In other words, strong leaders play a critical role in the cultivation of inclusive culture at schools sites, guiding teachers, increasing receptivity, and articulating a clear vision for integrative practices (Crosland & Dunlap, 2012; Kasa-Hendrickson & Kluth, 2005; Saggers et al., 2011; Schein, 2004). School site administrators consequently become important players in the development and maintenance of an inclusive school culture (Crosland & Dunlap; 2012; Waldron & McLeskey, 2010). School administrators employ several mechanisms to move schools toward not only procedural changes but changes in consciousness, perception, and understanding of students with ASD. These mechanisms include setting explicit goals, guiding collaborative decision making, developing a climate of trust, supporting staff both within and out of the classroom, and ensuring programs and supports are appropriately executed (Waldron & McLeskey, 2010). Most importantly, the leaders must be explicit in stating his or her own values and assumptions when establishing the emerging culture (Saggers et al., 2011; Schein, 2004). Such transparency builds the assumption that an oft-ignored group on campus will begin receiving rapt attention in terms of academic instruction and achievement. School leaders are thus sending a clear, unequivocal message regarding their expectations of an inclusive culture, quality programs, and effective instruction.

Waldron and McLeskey (2010) advocate for the use of Comprehensive School Reform (CSR) as one vehicle for leaders to utilize in building transparency. CSR requires school leaders to engage the entire school community in the inclusive discussion, examining critical questions such as what does inclusion look like within our school and what is expected of school staff in order to create and maintain inclusive classrooms? Under the principles of CSR, school administrators are building inclusive cultures within their schools by simultaneously empowering and promoting ownership of inclusive practices among teachers, staff, and parents.

Kasa-Hendrickson and Kluth (2005) examined the importance of leadership in the development of inclusive culture. The researchers examined one inclusive school site and the mechanisms employed by its leaders to engender inclusive practices and empowerment amongst staff. This particular school had engaged inclusive practices since the 1970s, long before the legal tenets of IDEIA (2004) and NCLB (2001) dominating today's educational landscape. The school served a rather severe ASD population; however, these students experienced inclusion, and successfully so, since preschool. The teachers strongly believed in, and adhered to, the ideology of inclusion: its social import, improved academic outcomes, and the idea that all students are competent learners (Kasa-Hendrickson & Kluth, 2005). Inclusive practices were enhanced by the structure of both the school and classrooms (addressed sensory needs, predictable daily routines, and visual supports); however, these researchers concluded that it was the actions of the administration that truly set the stage for inclusive practices. Leaders at the school promoted a culture where classroom environments and curriculum were accessible to all students, nondisabled peers were taught to understand ASD and related behaviors, and the acceptance of all students and their needs was automatic and never questioned. In short, school leaders successfully reconstructed the school's perception of normalcy and routine in order to foster the belief that disability is part of society's natural diversity.

Presidio Middle School in San Francisco and Charlotte Valley Central School in New York are two more examples of effective school leadership promoting inclusion (Koplen, 2014; NPR, 2014). Administrators at both sites have diligently worked to change the school's culture of inclusion. Within Presidio Middle School, the students with mild to moderate disabilities receive academic instruction while seated amongst their nondisabled peers. Teachers accommodate course material, and students work together so the students with disabilities receive assistance from their peers. The students with more profound disabilities are routinely mainstreamed for gym, art, and other electives (NPR, 2014).

Charlotte Valley Central School provides more structured supports. The school formed an inclusion staff, created a sensory room, and provides iPads for students to participate in and respond to their classroom environment (Koplen, 2014). However, the administrative leadership at Presidio Middle School has encountered pushback from teachers. These teachers are apprehensive about instructional integrity. In particular, the teachers have expressed concern rooted in the misperception that the level of academic instruction may be compromised in order to accommodate students with disabilities, and that the benefit to both general- and special-education students will therefore become nullified (NPR, 2014). These reactions demonstrate that despite strong leadership and research demonstrating the gains for all students (e.g., Cole et al., 2004; Ruijs et al., 2010; Sermier Dessemontet et al., 2013), general-education teachers may not feel prepared to tackle inclusion within their classrooms (Cassady, 2011). Further, such reactions pinpoint the need to promote inclusion as more than an academic endeavor, but one of cultural change and societal import. Teachers must therefore not only have the appropriate knowledge and skills but also subscribe to an epistemological perspective that promotes inclusive practice.

Developing Teachers as Leaders: Teacher Preparation Programs

Despite increasing and intensifying teacher training, preparing teachers to provide the best inclusive environment for their students with ASD remains a challenge (Anastasiou & Kauffman, 2011; Beecher & Darragh, 2011; Silverman, 2007; Whalon & Hart, 2010). Inclusion has transformed the necessary skills of general-education teachers as each student presents unique learning, behavioral, and social challenges (Barton et al., 2011; Beecher & Darragh, 2011; Silverman, 2007). The current education environment expects teachers to possess an understanding of ASD while simultaneously creating and maintaining structured learning environments excelling in explicit instruction (Barton et al., 2011). Yet many teachers believe they do not possess the knowledge and skills to sufficiently support students with ASD (Beecher & Darragh, 2011; Cassady, 2011; Leach & Duffy, 2009).

Teachers must have the appropriate skillset to successfully implement their knowledge and instruct students with ASD (Leach & Duffy, 2009). Inclusive environments will achieve success if teachers are supplied with pertinent and sufficient knowledge regarding the growing population of students with ASD (Guldberg, 2010). Preparation programs should place increased emphasis on supplying teachers with an understanding of the various challenges presented by students with ASD and best instructional practices. Providing future teachers with a strong ASD background better prepares them to provide quality, direct instruction in terms of academics, social skills, and behavior. Further, a holistic understanding of ASD allows for the creation of a supportive classroom environment in terms of adjusting to individual students' sensory needs, collaborating with appropriate service providers, and following and adapting to each student's developmental progression, as not all students with ASD follow identical developmental pathways (Guldberg, 2010).

This literature surrounding inclusive best practices for students with ASD (Guldberg, 2010; Leach & Duffy, 2009) places a large emphasis on disability-specific interventions while providing little information for building epistemological perspectives. Yet, when examining the inclusion of students with ASD from a social justice framework, it is not enough to explore instructional practices such as prompting hierarchies, visual schedules, behavior plans, and such (Barton et al., 2011; Kasa-Hendrickson & Kluth, 2005). These supports should be utilized within all classrooms regardless of the presence of students with ASD, as they benefit from multiple learning needs and provide universal access to the academic environment. Such a myopic examination of instructional practices deviates from a social justice perspective. More work is needed in examining and building social justice into both leadership practice and teacher preparation programs.

Recommendations

Major obstacles hinder the development and realization of a sustainable culture of inclusion in schools. Educational leadership and administrator preparation programs must be more purposeful about including content and learning outcomes related to inclusion. Pazey and Cole (2012) note that content about students with disabilities and special education law "has been a long neglected area within university-based administrator preparation programs and has been strangely absent in conversations relevant to the creation of administrator preparation programs that embrace a social justice model of leadership" (p. 243). The absence of special education topics in administrator preparation program curricula can lead future administrators to mistakenly assume that special education and students with disabilities do not fall within their professional purview. The reality is that educational leaders have an ethical and legal responsibility to educate students with disabilities, especially in light of the assertion that special education is a highly litigated educational law issue (Pazey & Cole, 2012). Administrators must contend with the complicated task of navigating the legal landscape, responding to the needs of all learners, and holding students accountable within an environment of competing resources.

In addition to rethinking educational leadership and administrator preparation programs, opportunities for self-reflection are necessary for school leaders to become effective change agents. Segall and Campbell (2012) found administrators with more experience with students with ASD also displayed greater positive attitudes toward students with disabilities as well as greater awareness and use of effective strategies. However, the majority of administrators do not have the type of experience with students with ASD that warrant increases in positive attitudes and strategy awareness and implementation (Segall & Campbell, 2012); therefore, self-reflection is necessary to bridge the gap between experience and implementation. Webster-Smith (2011) proposes a pyramid of self-reflection for leaders. The process of self-reflection includes examination of the heart, thoughts, emotions, attitudes, words, actions, habits, and character. Put simply, the pyramid guides leaders in examining their own perceptions, preconceived notions, and expectations of students with disabilities. Regularly employing self-reflection allows leaders to dissolve internal conflicts created by biased thought processes while maintaining focus on inclusion.

Leading schools in urban settings adds another layer of complexity to being a socially just leader. Urban school leaders—wherein a large number of English language learners, ethnic minorities, and low income students enroll—require increased sensitivity to the cultural needs of families of students with autism. An essential part of social justice leadership is informing and empowering families to advocate for appropriate resources and supports (Pazey & Cole, 2012). Developing community leadership and building partnerships with urban families strengthens the relationship between schools and families. Further, this effort aims to give voice to traditionally marginalized groups of students and families who have historically been voiceless.

Further, school-based professional development is key to cultivating an inclusive culture. An effective school leader must empower staff, developing their ownership of the inclusive process. An important step in the empowerment process is providing quality, relevant professional development (Waldron & McLeskey, 2010). The ways in which professional development has commonly been presented, however, will not be effective in developing inclusive environments. Traditionally, professional development is presented in a linear, rigid fashion, to large groups of people within a limited time frame, with little to no follow-through to ensure the provided information, strategies, knowledge, and such are implemented with fidelity within classrooms (Waldron & McLeskey, 2010). Professional development must engage staff, shifting teacher roles from passive listeners to active participants. It is essential that content is focused, addresses ASD knowledge and instructional practices, developed collaboratively with teachers, and includes follow-up and coaching within classrooms (Brock, Huber, Carter, Juarez, & Warren, 2014; Waldron & McLeskey, 2010). Most importantly, professional development must have the support of all staff to ensure each of these factors are recognized and adhered to; for "when these activities are deeply situated within collaborative school cultures, they are much more effective in changing teacher practices" (Waldron & McLeskey, 2010, p. 63).

Moreover, teacher credential programs must up the ante on developing inclusive teacher leaders. Teacher preparation programs are given the dauntless task of preparing teachers to work within a diverse and challenging environment. For teachers to become effective inclusion leaders, they must enter the profession with the necessary skillset to successfully instruct students with ASD (Barton et al., 2011). Whalon and Hart (2010) state that programs "must ensure that future and practicing...teachers (a) are aware of how the characteristics of children with ASD impact learning and instruction and (b) implement the most up-to-date, evidence-based practices" (p. 254). More in-depth, specific preservice training is mandated, especially in the areas of learning styles, rigidity, behaviors, and social impairments (Beecher & Darragh, 2011; Whalon & Hart, 2010). For example, general education classrooms tend to heavily use oral discourse; therefore, teachers should be prepared to deliver instruction using additional modes of instruction (i.e., visuals, models) and not overly rely on oral presentation (Whalon & Hart, 2010). Teachers should be well prepared before they are hired by a school district so that the district does not carry the full burden of providing comprehensive professional development for effective instruction strategies to support students with ASD.

While arming prospective teachers with knowledge and best instructional practices is necessary, it is far from the only responsibility falling on the shoulders of teacher preparation programs. Preservice teachers must also believe in and adhere to the ideology behind inclusion. No amount of instructional skillsets or knowledge will push teachers to become inclusive leaders; yet the adoption of a social justice epistemology will ensure a step in the right direction. Further, epistemological beliefs are more likely to be shaped by the inclusion policies and attitudes of a school and once engaged, it becomes difficult to change teacher attitudes and beliefs (Jordan, Schwartz, & McGhie-Richmond, 2009). These findings necessitate the need for teacher preparation programs to incorporate social justice in practice. It should not be assumed that all entering candidates have the same thoughts and beliefs toward inclusion. Programs should assess teacher candidates with respect to their epistemological beliefs at the beginning (Silverman, 2007).

Moving the Inclusion Agenda Forward

Cultivating the capacities of educational leaders to become active agents in the inclusion agenda is a tall order. To be sure, adopting the preceding suggestions to improve administrative and teacher preparation programs and professional development opportunities sounds deceptively simple. It is a much more difficult task to restructure one's epistemology and to go against the exclusionary norm exemplified in society. However, these steps must be in place to change the inclusive culture within our educational systems. Addressing the disparities in our school systems can happen with the provision of richer experiences (both knowledge and practical) of administrators in educating students with ASD, ongoing opportunities for self-reflection, and continuing professional development that is relevant to a school site's needs. This is especially critical in urban schools, where the intersections of autism, race, and class both complicate and enrich the path toward inclusion. In these settings, school leaders have the incredible responsibility to transform school communities into ones where all children have access to quality educational opportunities and spaces in which they belong and thrive. This is, after all, the ultimate aim of the inclusive educational leader who is grounded in an ethic of social justice.

REFERENCES

Almazan, S. (2009). Inclusive education and implications for policy: The state of the art and the promise. *TASH Congressional Briefing on Inclusive Education,* 1–30.

Anastasiou, D., & Kauffman, J. M. (2011). A social constructionist approach to disability: Implications for special education. *Exceptional Children, 77*(3), 367–384.

Barton, E. E., Reichow, B., Wolery, M., & Chen, C.-I. (2011). We can all participate! Adapting circle time for children with autism. *Young Children, 14*(2), 2–21.

Beecher, C. C., & Darragh, J. J. (2011). Using literature that portrays individuals with autism with pre-service teachers. *The Clearing House, 84,* 21–25.

Brock, M. E., Huber, H. B., Carter, E. W., Juarez, A. P., & Warren, Z. E. (2014). State-wide assessment of professional development needs related to educating students with autism spectrum disorder. *Focus on Autism and Other Developmental Disabilities, 29*(2), 67–79.

Cassady, J. M. (2011). Teacher's attitudes toward the inclusion of students with autism and emotional behavioral disorder. *Electronic Journal for Inclusive Education, 2*(7), 1–23.

Castellanos, D. (2013, June 23). Changes in special ed draw outrage. *Los Angeles Times,* p. A25.

Centers for Disease Control and Prevention (CDC). (2013). Changes in parent-reported autism spectrum disorder in school-aged U.S. children: 2007 to 2011–2012. *National Health Statistics Report, 65,* 1–11.

Cole, C. M., Waldron, N., & Majd, M. (2004). Academic progress of students across inclusive and traditional settings. *Journal Information, 42*(2), 136–144.

Cosier, M., Causton-Theoharis, J., & Theoharis, G. (2013). Does access matter? Time in general education and achievement for students with disabilities. *Remedial and Special Education, 34*(6), 323–332.

Crosland, K., & Dunlap, G. (2012). Effective strategies for the inclusion of children with autism in general education classrooms. *Behavior Modification, 36*(3), 251–269.

Dessemontet, R. S., Bless, G., & Morin, D. (2012). Effects of inclusion on the academic achievement and adaptive behaviour of children with intellectual disabilities. *Journal of Intellectual Disability Research, 56*(6), 579–587.

Eredics, N. (2012, July 15). Why would we want inclusive education? [Blog post]. *ollibean.* Retrieved from http://ollibean.com/2012/07/15/why-would-we-want-inclusive-education-2/

Guldberg, K. (2010). Educating children on the autism spectrum: Preconditions for inclusion and notions of 'best autism practice' in the early years. *British Journal of Special Education, 37*(4), 168–174.

Iland, E. D., Weiner, I., & Murawski, W. W. (2012). Obstacles faced by Latina mothers of children with autism. *Californian Journal of Health Promotion, 10*, 25–36.

Individuals with Disabilities Education Improvement Act (IDEIA), 20 U.S.C. § 1400 *et seq.* (2004).

Johnson, B., & Shelton, J. (2014, May). *My brother's keeper task force report to the president.* Retrieved from http://www.whitehouse.gov/sites/default/files/docs/053014_mbk_report.pdf

Jones, B. (2013, June 14). More special-ed kids head to traditional schools. *San Jose Mercury News.* Retrieved from http://www.mercurynews.com/news/ci_23464708/more-special-ed-kids-head-traditional-schools

Jordan, A., Schwartz, E., & McGhie-Richmond, D. (2009). Preparing teachers for inclusive classrooms. *Teaching and Teacher Education, 25*, 535–542.

Kasa-Hendrickson, C., & Kluth, P. (2005). "We have to start with inclusion and work it out as we go": Purposeful inclusion for non-verbal students with autism. *International Journal of Whole Schooling, 2*(1), 2–14.

Koplen, C. B. (2014, April 12). School opens doors on autism program. *The Daily Star.* Retrieved from http://www.thedailystar.com/localnews/x1445042605/School-opens-doors-on-autism-program

Lawrence-Brown, D., & Sapon-Shevin, M. (2013). *Condition critical: Key principles for equitable and inclusive education.* New York, NY: Teachers College Press.

Leach, D., & Duffy, M. L. (2009). Supporting students with autism spectrum disorders in inclusive settings. *Intervention in School and Clinic, 45*(1), 31–37.

Losen, D. J., & Orfield, G. (2002). Introduction. In D. J. Losen & G. Orfield (Eds.), *Racial inequity in special education* (pp. xv–xxxvii). Cambridge, MA: Harvard Education Press.

Lynch, S. L., & Irvine, A. N. (2009). Inclusive education and best practice for children with autism spectrum disorder: An integrated approach. *International Journal of Inclusive Education, 13*(8), 845–859.

McKinney, S., & Lowenhaupt, R. (2013). New directions for socially just educational leadership: Lessons from disability studies. In L. Tillman & J. Scheurich (Eds.), *Handbook of research on educational leadership for diversity and equity.* Washington DC: American Educational Research Association.

National Public Radio (NPR) (Producer). (2014, April 27). *Learning with disabilities: One effort to shake up the classroom* [Audio podcast]. Retrieved from http://www.npr.org/2014/04/27/307467382/learning-with-disabilities-one-effort-to-shake-up-the-classroom

No Child Left Behind (NCLB) Act, 20 U.S.C. 70 § 6301 *et seq.* (2001).

Oesterreich, H. A., & Knight, M. G. (2008). Facilitating transitions to college for students with disabilities from culturally and linguistically diverse backgrounds. *Intervention in School and Clinic, 43*(5), 300–304.

Pazey, B. L., & Cole, H. A. (2012). The role of special education training in the development of socially just leaders: Building an equity consciousness in educational leadership programs. *Educational Administration Quarterly, 49*(2), 243–271.

Phillips, R. (2013, July 8). SUSD plans major shift. *Recordnet.com.* Retrieved from http://www.recordnet.com/apps/pbcs.dll/article?AID=/20130708/A_NEWS/307080315/-1/A_NEWS04

Renzaglia, A., Karvonen, M., Drasgow, E., & Stoxen, C. C. (2003). Promoting a lifetime of inclusion. *Focus on Autism and Other Developmental Disabilities, 18*(3), 140–149.

Ross-Hill, R. (2009). Teacher attitudes towards inclusion practices and special needs students. *Journal of Research in Special Educational Needs, 9*(3), 188–198.

Ruijs, N. M., Van der Veen, I., & Peetsma, T. T. (2010). Inclusive education and students without special educational needs. *Educational Research, 52*(4), 351–390.

Saggers, B., Hwang, Y.-S., & Mercer, K. L. (2011). Your voice counts: Listening to the voice of high school students with autism spectrum disorders. *Australasian Journal of Special Education, 35*(2), 173–190.

Schein, E. H. (2004). *Organizational culture and leadership* (3rd ed.). San Francisco, CA: Wiley.

Segall, M., & Campbell, J. M. (2012). Factors relating to education professionals' classroom practices for the inclusion of students with autism spectrum disorders. *Research in Autism Spectrum Disorders, 6*(3), 1156–1167.

Sermier Dessemontet, R., & Bless, G. (2013). The impact of including children with intellectual disability in general education classrooms on the academic achievement of their low-, average-, and high-achieving peers. *Journal of Intellectual and Developmental Disability, 38*(1), 23–30.

Silverman, J. C. (2007). Epistemological beliefs and attitudes toward inclusion in pre-service teachers. *Teacher Education and Special Education: The Journal of the Teacher Education Division of the Council for Exceptional Children, 30*(1), 42–51.

Tek, S., & Landa. R. J. (2012). Differences in autism symptoms between minority and non-minority toddlers. *Journal of Autism and Developmental Disorders, 42*(9), 1967–1973.

von der Embse, N., Brown, A., & Fortain, J. (2011). Facilitating inclusion by reducing problem behaviors for students with autism spectrum disorders. *Intervention in School and Clinic, 47*(1), 22–30.

Waldron, N. L., & McLeskey, J. (2010). Establishing a collaborative school culture through comprehensive school reform. *Journal of Educational and Psychological Consultation, 20,* 58–74.

Webster-Smith, A. (2011). Scaling the pyramid of self reflection: A model and an assignment for the preparation of inclusive leaders. *The International Journal of Educational Leadership Preparation, 6*(1), 1–14.

Whalon, K. J., & Hart, J. E. (2010). Children with autism spectrum disorder and literacy instruction: An exploratory study of elementary inclusive settings. *Remedial and Special Education, 32*(3), 243–255.

Williams, S. K., Johnson, C., & Sukhodolsky, D. G. (2005). The role of the school psychologist in the inclusive education of school-age children with autism spectrum disorders. *Journal of School Psychology, 43,* 117–136.

Winzer, M., & Mazurek, K. (2012). Analyzing inclusive schooling for students with disabilities in international contexts: Outline of a model. *Journal of International Special Needs Education, 15*(1), 12–23.

Zarembo, A. (2011). Warrior parents fare best in securing autism services. *Los Angeles Times.* Retrieved from http://www.latimes.com/news/local/autism/la-me-autism-day-two-html,0,3900437.htmlstory#axzz2yMUpDrKZ

CHAPTER 5

INCLUSION NEEDS OF YOUTH IN THE FOSTER CARE SYSTEM THROUGH STRATEGIC MENTORING

A Social Justice Perspective

Susanne M. Foulk
University of Southern California

ABSTRACT

This chapter examines current educational disparities for youth in the foster system from a social justice lens. Children and youth in the foster care system across the nation experience perpetual emotional pain, poverty, and displacement. These invisible children are distinguishable by their numerous transitory placements and the issues indicative of their disparity, which include high dropout rates, poor literacy skills, and transition to adulthood with limited independent living skills or social support systems. Foster youth often transition from the system into homelessness and sex trafficking rather than to college and jobs. Underlying the educational experience for foster youth are policies, practices, and trends that serve as exclusionary measures,

Inclusive Practices and Social Justice Leadership for Special Populations in Urban Settings, pages 83–102
Copyright © 2015 by Information Age Publishing
All rights of reproduction in any form reserved.

in which educational the needs of the children are often left unaddressed as overburdened government systems attempt to respond to basic safety needs. Needs of attachment, self-worth, self-efficacy, and self-regulation, which underlie their motivation and expenditure of effort for successful academic pursuits, are left unmet. Examination takes place of the underlying human factor, the substance from which children typically grow up and navigate through the educational system. Recommendations are made for foster youth to be engaged with culturally responsive, trained mentors, who scaffold the children's needs through educational advocacy, educational support, life skills, and social-emotional development. Through mentor engagement, foster youth may more effectively navigate their educational journey, resolve their sense of individual identities as learners, and gain a sense of voice, which assists them in moving beyond their oppression toward successful outcomes and offers hope for their futures.

In 2012, there were an estimated 399,546 children and youth in the foster care system as a result of abuse or neglect in the United States (Children's Bureau, 2013a). These children remained in care for an average of 20.4 months, with 9% remaining five years or more (Children's Bureau, 2013b). Neglect cases make up a majority of the substantiated cases (Children's Bureau, 2013b). Numerous issues are indicative of these children's disparity, which include high drop-out rates, poor literacy skills (Barrat & Berliner, 2013), homelessness, unemployment, substance abuse, transition to adulthood lacking basic independent living skills (Pecora et al., 2006), commercial sexual exploitation, and incarceration (Fong & Berger Cardoso, 2010).

Emerging in research and propelled by policymakers concerned about justice for all children is the unfolding of the educational plight and disparities of children in foster care (Emerson & Lovitt, 2003). These disparities must be viewed with the lens of underlying economic and structural effects, which place this distinct population of vulnerable children and youth in perpetual oppressive conditions of emotional pain, loss, and uncertainty (Unrau, Seita, & Putney, 2008). This chapter addresses the crisis of educating youth in the foster system from a social justice perspective.

This chapter begins with attention to the political and historical underpinnings through which educators can better understand the children and youth's needs. Next, social and economic patterns, trends, and conditions of the children's families are examined, and the social and emotional effects of the children are then reviewed. The final section specifies the means by which strategic mentoring can address the inclusion needs of youth. Questions that guide this discussion are (a) What is the etiology of the effects faced by children in foster care with regard to educational and lifetime achievement outcomes? (b) How does a history of maltreatment for children in the foster system influence their educational experience?

and (c) How can mentoring serve as an important educational intervention to address the inclusion needs of foster youth?

REVIEW OF THE LITERATURE

Agreement exists in both the United States and at the international level regarding the importance of the basic human right of all children to be educated in a context similar to their peers (UNESCO, 2009). Differences have arisen in terms of what inclusion means, who is included, and how to best address inclusive practices, thus rendering conceptualization and implementation of inclusive practice qualitatively different according to context (UNESCO, 2009). A socially just democracy requires that emphasis must be placed on the underlying beliefs and assumptions that guide practices and policies (Lalvani, 2013). The term *inclusion* itself is socially constructed and can carry with it stigmatizing and exclusionary effects that ultimately result in perpetuating oppressive forces on already marginalized individuals (Grum, 2012).

Inclusion of Youth in the System From a Social Justice Perspective

Brofenbrenner (1977) suggested that children are not isolated beings, but are nested within the context of family and community. Ecological forces at the community level, such as poverty, abuse, and violence, have thwarted these children's experience, requiring them to adjust in ways that perpetuate and limit their existence (Garcia-Reid, 2008). Vygotsky (1993) suggested that seemingly adaptive patterns that may be considered abnormal often result in what he considered a secondary disability, which is one that may result from and is embedded in the children's social experience. Thus, one must move away from viewing individuals from a deficit approach and move toward an understanding of individuals within the context of the social and political forces that perpetuate their oppression (Garcia-Reid, 2008; Ginwright & Cammarota, 2011; Lalvani, 2013).

Educational Policies Enacted to Include Youth in the System

Since the passage of PL 94-142, subsequently reauthorized as the Individuals with Disabilities Education Improvement Act or IDEIA (2004), which mandates that children with disabilities be afforded an education in the least restrictive environment, practical implementation has shifted from mainstreaming children with identified disabilities toward offering inclusive education as a basic human right (Lalvani, 2013). Early intervention, an amendment to IDEIA (Part C), ensures that children with disabilities and children with substantiated child abuse cases as young as 0–3 are screened and provided intervention as needed. The most recent revision of the Child Abuse and Treatment Act (P.L. 111-320) (CAPTA) 2010 required further accountability from states to document cases of those children who are eligible for early intervention, but did not receive it. Since the reauthorization of IDEIA, efforts have shifted emphasis from a deficit approach to prevention and intervention through response-to-intervention (RtI), a service delivery model that supports intervention in a multilayered tier model that avoids unnecessarily labeling and stigmatizing children (Froiland, 2011). This model has been widely researched in the academic domain, primarily in early literacy intervention (Grosche & Volpe, 2013). However, RtI can also be implemented to support early identification and intervention in the social-emotional and behavioral domains (Froiland, 2011; Yong & Cheney, 2013).

Many children in the foster care system are in continual transitory out-of-home placements, which results in changing schools, frequently without school records that follow (Noonan et al., 2012). This has largely been recognized as a systemic barrier that prevents youth in the system from receiving the help they need (e.g., special education and related services) in the academic setting and thus limits their academic success. Negative outcomes of school changes and problems transferring records may result in children missing educational services or the necessity to repeat grades or classes (Barrat & Berliner, 2013). Recent legislation focuses on eradicating this structural barrier on behalf of the youth. For example, the Fostering Connections to Success and Increasing Adoptions Act of 2008 (HR 6893) requires that coordinated efforts ensure that the child continue in the same school when placed into the system and that expedient transmission of school records and enrollment take place when it is necessary for a child to transition to a new school. Additional policies, such as the Uninterrupted Scholars Act (P.L. 112-278) amendment to the Family Educational Rights and Privacy Act (FERPA) (U.S.C. § 1232g), facilitates child welfare professionals' access to students' educational records. However, while policies have been enacted, stakeholders may rely on unreliable knowledge and differ in application of these statutes, which makes implementation considerably problematic (Noonan et al., 2012).

Recent data-sharing efforts between the Child Welfare and California Educational systems resulted in baseline empirical evidence of statewide educational trends of students in foster care in California (Barrat & Berliner, 2013). Importantly, this study revealed that children in the system

(N = 43,140) represented a distinct category of children whose educational disparities far exceed any other student category identified as at risk. Additionally, large-scale school finance reform in California recently resulted in the enactment of the Local Control Funding Formula, which recognizes children in foster care as a separate and distinct category of children to receive designated funding and holds districts accountable for their educational progress. From a social justice perspective, this landmark shift of policy and perspective serves to address the disparity in which the children in foster care are educated. Moreover, it is a considerable step in providing needed services to this marginalized population of students.

Educational Placement Practices and Trends

Extant research on the education of children in the foster system is sparse and often characterized by incomplete data and methodological flaws (Trout, Hagaman, Casey, Reid, & Epstein, 2008). Explanations for this problem include educators' unawareness of the foster status of children (Shea, Zetlin, & Weinberg, 2010; Zetlin, Weinberg, & Shea, 2006). Additionally, the transitory nature of the children's experience makes it difficult to maintain necessary academic records (Barrat & Berliner, 2013).

Multiple academic transitions often exacerbate the negative educational experience for foster youth. Courtney, Terao, & Bost (2004) found that more than one-third of foster youth interviewed had experienced five or more school changes. During the 2009–2010 school year in the State of California, one third of the children experienced a school change at least once, and just under 10% attended three or more schools that same year (Barrat & Berliner, 2013). School mobility for these children was reportedly higher than any other subgroup of children. Maintaining stability and increasing the youths' school attendance is important to addressing the educational disparities for those in the system, however, there is evidence that perhaps more is needed (Zorc et al., 2013).

Another specific trend of students in the system includes placement in special education settings at significantly higher rates than the general population of students (Barrat & Berliner, 2013; Courtney et al., 2004; Scherr, 2007; Zetlin, Weinberg, & Kimm, 2004). In a recent meta-analysis, which included international data, an estimated 31% of the 25,692 students in foster care received or qualified for special education services (Scherr, 2007). Across the State of California, students ages 5–17 were identified as having a disability at twice the rate of the general student population (Barrat & Berliner, 2013). Of those students identified, the greatest number were categorized as having an emotional disturbance.

Evidence further suggests that children in foster care are more likely to experience expulsion and grade retention, which places them at risk for dropping out of high school (Barrat & Berliner, 2013). For example, 20% of children in foster care examined in a 2-year longitudinal study had been suspended at least once in their academic careers (Zorc et al., 2013). Thirty-three percent of the 9,950 combined number of students examined through meta-analysis had been retained in a grade at least once (Scherr, 2007). Interestingly, students in foster care experienced grade retention in higher instances at grades 1, 6, and 9 (Courtney et al., 2004), which corresponds with traditional school transitions. Alarmingly, 8% of students in foster care dropped out of California schools in the 2009/2010 school year (Barrat & Berliner, 2013).

The California study, which included a comparison group, revealed other important trends (Barrat & Berliner, 2013). Students in foster care were more likely than the general population of students to be enrolled in the lowest-performing schools. This finding is similar to that identified earlier across the United States (Courtney et al., 2004; Smithgall, Gladden, Howard, Goerge, & Courtney, 2004). Additionally, significant discrepancies in English language arts and mathematics emerged, which revealed similarities to students with disabilities and English language learners (Barrat & Berliner, 2013). According to research conducted of 17-year-old foster alumni, of those who have aged out of the system, almost half had reading skills at the 7th-grade level (Courtney et al., 2004). Finally, students in foster care were more likely to be enrolled in nontraditional schools and were outperformed in general by students identified as low SES, which rendered them the lowest-performing group of all students (Barrat & Berliner, 2013).

Early intervention plays a critical role in the education of children in foster care, yet access itself is seen as a barrier to successful implementation (Aron & Loprest, 2012; Meloy & Phillips, 2012). According to the Children's Bureau (2013b), 26% of children in foster care in 2012 were age three and under, 37% age five and under, and almost half (46%) of children were under seven years old. Pears, Heywood, Kim, and Fisher (2011) found through a small sample (N = 63) of kindergarten-aged (mean age 5.46) students in foster care that only 39% had received early intervention services. Further, they found that 50% of the students were at risk for reading difficulties and 54% revealed prereading skills below the 23rd percentile. These researchers suggest that early intervention may not have typically addressed prereading skills, such as phonological awareness, which should be a targeted area of intervention and screening. Further research is needed in the area of early intervention for children in foster care as only sparse empirical evidence exists.

Entrenched Social and Economic Patterns, Trends, and Conditions From Which Children are Placed Into the Foster Care System

In order to consider the underlying needs of the children placed into the system, it is important to consider the environments from which they come. As indicated earlier, out-of-home placements result predominately from incidences of neglect (Children's Bureau, 2013b). For example, 78% of all cases of children in the State of California who were removed from the home resulted from substantiated cases of neglect. Further, African Americans are significantly overrepresented in child maltreatment cases (Dettlaff et al., 2011; Drake, Lee, & Jonson-Reid, 2009; Knott & Donovan, 2009). From a social justice perspective, immediate and concentrated efforts are needed to understand and eradicate the perpetual victimization faced by these children.

The relationship between economic poverty and risk of maltreatment is well substantiated in the literature, however the process by which maltreatment transpires is less evident (Dettlaff et al., 2011). Environmental stress and social support play an important role in the outcome effects in understanding child maltreatment occurrences (Coulton, Crampton, Irwin, Spilsbury, & Korbin, 2007). Evidence indicates that poor neighborhoods characterized as socially disorganized and unstable co-varied with greater risk of maltreatment (Coulton et al., 2007). Social disorganization and instability are often characterized in the literature by poverty, unemployment, and high mobility. These may in turn contribute to social distress and translate to parent-child interactions (Coulton et al., 2007). There is evidence to suggest, however, that there are differences in how some neighborhoods come together, lending support to individuals, thereby providing needed resources and lowering the risk of maltreatment (Coulton et al., 2007).

The decision to refer a child to out-of-home placement in cases of alleged maltreatment can also differ according to the degree to which a community can be characterized according to social organization (Jantz, Rolock, Leathers, Dettlaff, & Gleeson, 2012). According to an analysis of a 3-year history of out-of-home placement referrals in Illinois, the decision to refer children occurred at higher rates in disorganized communities. These communities were characterized by high impoverishment, child burden, mobility, and crime rates. Analysis revealed that the odds were 130% greater that African American children in the disorganized communities would enter care when compared to White children in organized communities. Overall, African American children across the communities were 57% more likely to enter out-of-home placements than were Whites. An interesting pattern emerged upon researchers' analysis of the referral decisions made in one particular county. This county, which consisted of greater diversity, rendered referral decisions parallel to those of an organized community. Underlying these referral decisions, caseworkers may be making differential assessments of familial access to resources (Dettlaff et al., 2011; Jantz et al., 2012).

Not only do children in foster care represent a largely marginalized population with lower than average socioeconomic status, but their foster parents tend to have lower than the standard level of income in comparison to the general population (Zinn, 2010). According to the National Survey of Child and Adolescent Well Being (OPRE, 2007), foster parents in 1999–2000 had low educational outcomes, with an estimated 60% holding a high school diploma or less. Kinship providers, which are often children's grandparents, tend to have even lower income levels than that of other foster caregivers (Zinn, 2010). According to a study by Zinn (2010), 18% of kinship providers were living below the poverty line. These findings are problematic because the very economic conditions that may have fostered maltreatment, such as disorganized communities and poverty, in particular, may not be considerably different than the conditions in which the children are placed. Further, as discussed earlier, children in foster care are often enrolled in the lowest-performing schools, which further perpetuates the oppression these children face (Barrat & Berliner, 2013).

What Are the Social and Emotional Effects for Children in the Foster Care System?

Investigation into the effects of trauma resulting from maltreatment reveals a significant impact on the brain and development (Ai, Foster, Pecora, Delaney, & Rodriguez, 2013; De Bellis & Zisk, 2014). According to Ai et al. (2013), childhood trauma associated with maltreatment may result in post-traumatic stress disorder (PTSD) or post-traumatic stress syndrome. The mental health functioning of foster care alumni with lifetime PTSD (multiple diagnoses) compared to that of Vietnam War Vets and those with past-year PTSD compared to that of Veterans of Afghanistan and the first U.S.–Iraq conflict (Ai et al., 2013). Additionally, trauma induced complex PTSD, which is characterized by developmental challenges, was determined to be associated with disorganized attachment representations (for a review, see Black, Woodworth, Tremblay, & Carpenter, 2012). Even in cases when PTSD is not formally diagnosed, the opportunity for youth in foster care to form healthy attachments with their parents or caregivers has been disrupted, which places these children at risk for learning and developmental challenges (Britner, Randall, & Ahrens, 2014).

Maltreatment and Trauma Effects

Conclusions rendered from a critical review of the research on PTSD induced from child maltreatment demonstrate that trauma affects multiple regions of the brain and impacts emotional and behavioral regulation and cognitive and executive functioning (De Bellis & Zisk, 2014). Particularly salient is the role of early neglect and prolonged abuse on the brain's development. De Bellis and Zisk (2014) stated that the severe stress experienced by maltreatment of victims results in "detrimental effects on the brain networks that establish an individual's ability to think and regulate their sense of self, motivations, and behaviors" (p. 204). This complex stress is often additive, and intervention may prove problematic because young children who are exposed to trauma may not reveal manifestations of PTSD until adolescence or adulthood (Ai et al., 2013). Importantly, children exposed to trauma may need services even though they may not qualify with a formal diagnosis (Black et al., 2012; De Bellis & Zisk, 2014). Ai and colleagues (2013) suggest that screening and assessment play a critical role in providing child trauma victims with the support needed. These authors caution that proper assessments are not regularly conducted in the child welfare intake system for victims of maltreatment, which is considerably alarming. Interventions that have revealed success include Cognitive-Behavioral Therapy, which targets changes in thought and behavior patterns (Black et al., 2012; De Bellis & Zisk, 2014). In particular, coping self-efficacy mediated the effects of PTSD for adults who had been sexually abused, which lends evidence to the strong role self-efficacy plays in modifying negative cognitions in PTSD victims (Cieslak, Benight, & Lehman, 2008). Further, the role social support has in buffering the biological response to stress is revealed in the research in terms of emotional and behavioral outcomes (De Bellis & Zisk, 2014).

Attachment Effects

Early experiences in caregiving relationships serve as the foundation from which children may establish a secure base needed to learn and develop (Ainsworth & Wittig, 1969; Bowlby, 1969). Children's experiences with their parents and caregivers form working models of attachment, which serve to assist them in developing emotional and behavioral regulation and the sense of self needed to successfully navigate future relationships in their lives (Ainsworth & Wittig, 1969; Cummings & Cummings, 2002). These attachment representations are formed as a result of the availability and responsiveness of the caregiver (Dozier & Rutter, 2008). Children who have experienced trauma as a result of abuse and neglect often develop working models of attachment that are characterized by insecure-attached and disorganized attachment representations (Baer & Martinez, 2006; Carlson, 1998; Dozier & Rutter, 2008). Further, differential effects are evidenced in neglect and abuse maltreatment cases where internal and externalizing problems often emerge (Egeland, Stoufe, & Erickson, 1983). Problems include depression, anxiety, suicide, and severe behavior problems which can in some cases lead to criminal activity later in life. In such cases, problems include difficulties developing trust in relationships (Milan & Pinderhughes, 2000); social and emotional development (Carlson, 1998); and reliance on a negative cognitive style, which is characterized by negative attributions (Hankin, 2005) and may lead to dissociative and externalizing symptomology (Carlson, 1998).

Dozier and Rutter (2008) suggest that it is important to consider that these effects are often additive in nature and quite significant when neglect is experienced in very young children. Also important to understand is that early experience with maltreatment makes many children vulnerable to a disorder later in life (Dozier & Rutter, 2008). Further, Morton and Browne (1998) assert that a pattern of intergenerational transmission exists with insecure attachment symptomology in cases of maltreatment.

Transition Effects

The effects of the multiple transitions (e.g, schools, new homes) encountered by foster youth exacerbate an already vulnerable sense of security children in the foster system experience. According to Ai and colleagues (2013), multiple placements act as a secondary trauma on these children. That is, placement breakdowns promote children's representation of others as untrustworthy and pose challenges to securing a future caregiving placement (Morrison & Mishna, 2006). Pears, Kim, and Leve (2012) found a correlation between multiple placements and poorer self-regulation for middle school girls in foster care. Perceived caregiver support, however, correlated with greater self-regulation and academic competence. Importantly, disrupted length of stay with caregivers and multiple transitions contributes to problems in mental health, socioemotional and behavioral disorders, and educational problems (Pecora, 2012).

Dozier and Lindhiem (2006) identified the importance of caregiver commitment, suggesting that commitment contributes more to the sense of security than does caregiver responsiveness. That is, when commitment is low, placement disruptions are more likely to occur (Dozier & Lindhiem, 2006). Morrison's (2006) research demonstrates the important role a secure relationship has on the development of secure attachment later in children's lives. That is, the emergence of at least one individual who can provide love and support can break the cycle and offer children a sense that they are valuable and worthy individuals. This in turn fosters children's sense of self-worth and provides the foundation for future relationships (Morton & Browne, 1998).

Child Experiences and Effects

Important to this discussion is attention to the experiences of children from their own voice. From a social justice perspective, it is critical that those interested in understanding the realities experienced by youth in foster care amplify the voices of those who have been marginalized (Unrau, 2007). Interviews with youth in care and foster alumni reveal important findings. For example, Unrau and colleagues (2008) identified several themes in foster alumni's recount of their experience. These include feelings of being unwanted, feeling insecure, and a sense of loss of power related to their destiny. Additionally, in spite of these memories of loss, these alumni recalled the protective factor of a caring adult, which served as a source of strength. Drapeau, Saint-Jacques, Lépine, Bégin, and Bernard (2007) found that an increase in perceived self-efficacy was strongly related to adolescents' resilience. Outcomes such as isolation and feelings of abandonment should never be experienced by any child or youth. Clearly, a socially just society requires that each individual member undergird the most vulnerable in society and represent their voice.

Summary

This previous section addressed the social-emotional effects for the children. Following the discussion of the links of maltreatment to poverty, this previous section addressed the link of maltreatment that may result in biological changes to the brain and attachment difficulties that result in reducing self-regulation and executive functioning in the child. Inclusion efforts must therefore address needs of attachment, self-worth, self-efficacy, and self-regulation, which underlie an individual's motivation and expenditure of effort for successful academic pursuits. This section addressed the important protective factor that emerged, that of a caring, committed individual who can assist youth as they navigate their educational experience. Turning our attention to intervention, the next section addresses an emerging tool—human capital—to assist youth toward academic success.

Mentoring as an Inclusion Strategy

Mentoring holds promise for addressing the inequalities that exist for the large number of youth in foster care who become marginalized on their educational journey (Cox, 2013). The mentoring relationship is a meaningful connection established between a young person and a caring and competent individual, which forges the development of trust, empathy, and reciprocity (Rhodes, 2005). This section explains how mentoring can serve as an important educational intervention to address the inclusion needs of these youth.

Why Does Mentoring Matter for Foster Youth?

At the heart of human development is the concept of "the development of identity" (Marcia, 1966). While adolescents in general experience challenges in navigating through the process toward identity commitment, youth in foster care, in particular, may experience challenges as a result of the influx and transitory nature of their experience on their sense of self and identity. The development of identity is a social process of constructing one's self through interaction with others in one's cultural context (Pressley, 1995). Similarly, a goal that is intertwined is the development of self-regulation, which is posited to begin through joint effort (Rogoff, 2003), and which ultimately becomes more autonomous with time and experience (Pressley, 1995). Mentoring provides an important means by which individuals, particularly foster youth, who have experiences of insecurely attached relations may be provided the guidance that allows them to interact in dialog with others in meaningful and purposeful interactions that foster their positive development (Ahrens et al., 2011).

What Are the Attitudes, Qualities, and Characteristics of Effective Mentors?

The issue of trust is central to the establishment of mentoring relationships (Rhodes, 2002), which is grounded in a commitment to address and sustain all that the relationship brings (Dozier & Lindhiem, 2006; Dozier & Rutter, 2008). That is, the basis from which youth may enter into, sustain, and develop successful mentoring relationships is grounded in the experience of having established a trusting relationship, largely through a sense of commitment on the part of the adult. It is therefore important that efforts take place to recruit mentors who have successfully demonstrated competency in the area of sustaining committed relationships (J. E. Rhodes, personal communication, 2013).

Mentors must also be socially responsive. That is, mentors must be capable of responding in ways that not only create a safe context in which trust is established, but that also foster communication, personal development, and exploration (Rhodes, 2002). Included in social responsiveness is the characteristic of empathy, which creates a bridge of understanding and trust in the mentor-protégé relationship (Rhodes, 2002).

Cultural competence is also critical in the mentoring process (Sánchez, Colón-Torres, Feuer, Roundfield, & Berardi, 2014). Mentors must become aware of their own biases, a characteristic similar to effective teaching of urban youth. Mentors must move beyond holding a deficit belief that holds that being a member of the foster youth culture represents that there is something lacking in these individuals that can be better replaced with their own culture (Salzman, 2000). Mentors then must develop a competency in which they become aware of their own attitudes and beliefs, which may serve to either assist or disengage the mentor-protégé relationship. Aware-ness must be gained in order to be sensitive to potential perceived biases that would foster not only a sense of mistrust but would foster a sense that the youth is incapable.

Researchers (Munson et al., 2010) suggest the importance of recognizing natural mentors, those who emerge gradually from youths' social networks. Advocates for natural mentoring relationships suggest the importance of assisting youth in identifying and advocating for themselves in finding a mentor from their current social network. While problematic in many cases for youth in foster care, since they have been removed from their networks, perhaps identifying faith-based and other community-based networks, such as teacher networks, in which children belong is an avenue to explore in identifying a suitable mentor.

What Kind of Mentoring Makes a Difference?

Mentoring needs to be long term and deliberate in fostering important foundational life skills. For youth in the foster system who experience a pre-mature severing of the relationship by the mentor, it is better for the youth that s/he had not entered into the relationship at all (Rhodes, 2002). Men-tors must also be deliberate and purposeful in their interactions with their protégés to foster important skills that are needed in formal and informal learning environments.

Focused on Development of Self-Regulation and Self-Efficacy

Of critical importance is the need for mentors to be deliberate in foster-ing self-regulation. Youth in the foster system must receive strategic assis-tance in learning how to regulate in emotional (Pears et al., 2012) and cog-nitive domains (Taussig & Culhane, 2010). Additionally, in the academic domain, a focus on development of executive functioning through plan-ning, goal setting, and learning strategies are needed for youth in order for them to be successful in school and beyond (Dembo & Eaton, 2000; Zim-merman, 1995). Likewise, self-efficacy (Bandura, 1982), which addresses students' beliefs in their abilities to accomplish a task, can be deliberately fostered through the mentoring relationship. That is, mentors can pro-vide students with alternative explanations for their successes and failures as well as suggest strategies that assist the youth and result in meaningful accomplishments.

Incorporates Academic Tools, Such as Literacy, to Address Structural Inequalities and Promote Development of Social and Academic Identity

As discussed, a specific need for youth foster care is in the area of literacy development. Researchers addressing literacy have found the importance of providing authentic literacy activities in and out of school. Literacy is intertwined with identity development (Moje & Dillon, 2006) and can be effectively fostered in nontraditional contexts such as the mentoring relationship. Cultural tools such as literacy can be deliberately fostered through opportunities that increase access to resources students need in their everyday lives (Moje & Dillon, 2006). Through the use of writing an autoethnography (Camangian, 2010), for example, youth may begin to grapple with their complex identities and come to view writing as a tool that is meaningful to them. Thus, activities surrounding the development of writing for an authentic reason can serve to assist youth in the development of their own identities, while it also assists them in the development of tools that enable their successful academic performance.

Advocacy Roles, Responsibilities, and Training

Mentors need to serve in the role of an advocate (Bruster & Coccoma, 2013; Rhodes, 2002). Youth in the foster system lack a dedicated agent that advocates on their behalf. The mentor can provide this missing component that enables them to navigate successfully through their educational process. This role requires mentors to receive the necessary training that allows them to identify needs, encourage development, and then to advocate on behalf of their student (Rhodes, 2002). Additionally, strategic mentoring needs to serve in the role of advocate and guide youth toward advocating for themselves (Bruster & Coccoma, 2013). Only when these structural edifices are enabled will youth in the foster system have the confidence and ability to move beyond the structural violence (Gaultung, 1969) and inequalities that have been imposed upon them.

Summary

In addressing inclusion for children in foster care, it is important to consider the social, emotional, and cognitive domains of learning (Rhodes, 2002, 2005; Taussig & Culhane, 2010). Particularly beneficial to youth in foster care is strategic encouragement of the development of self-efficacy (Bandura, 1982) and self-regulation in the cognitive, social-emotional (Pears et al., 2012), and academic domains (Dembo & Eaton, 2000; Zimmerman, 1995) in order to support students' attainment of academic and social-emotional success. Importantly, particular attention needs to address the incorporation of life skills (Massinga & Pecora, 2004) and academic tools such as literacy in order to assist youth in addressing the structural inequalities while promoting their social and learner identity (Camangian, 2010). Additionally, mentors need to serve in the role of advocate and guide youth toward advocating for themselves (Bruster & Coccoma, 2013). In this way, a successful mentoring relationship is critical in assisting youth in foster care in navigating their educational journey, developing their sense of identity, and gaining a sense of voice in their own experience through their oppression.

CONCLUSION

The literature regarding the disparities, barriers, effects, and needs of children in the foster system demonstrates that children and youth in foster care need guidance to assist them in their educational journey toward social justice. Amidst a trajectory of loss, disruption, and uncertainty emerged the importance of a caring, stable relationship that will provide the human connection that breaks the children's sense of isolation and disconnection through their transition to adulthood. Ultimately, barriers exist, which often leave the children themselves without guidance, advocacy, and direction in their educational and academic journey. Poor communication among stakeholders, problems with stability of placements, and blurred lines of responsibility on behalf of the children further excludes children in the foster care system (Noonen et al., 2012). Thus, outcome effects must be examined and addressed within the backdrop of the practices that serve to exclude and marginalize children from educational opportunities similar to that of their peers.

Based on the previous discussion, mentoring for inclusion needs to address the following: (a) being committed (Dozier & Lindhiem, 2006) and culturally competent (Sánchez et al., 2014); (b) a deliberate fostering of cognitive and social-emotional development (Rhodes, 2002; Taussig & Culhane, 2010), self-regulation, and self-efficacy (Dembo & Eaton, 2000); (c) incorporation of academic tools, such as literacy, to address structural inequalities and promote development of social and academic identity (Mahiri & Godley, 1998); and (d) serves in the role of advocate (Rhodes, 2002).

As discussed, early intervention is a critical component of the educational success of these children (Aron & Loprest, 2012; Meloy & Phillips, 2012). This requires a committed multidisciplinary approach (A. Tessier, personal communication, August 14, 2014). Research needs to address the development of mentoring for school-aged youth in foster care and education for children in foster care in general. Educational policy must continue to be enacted that serves the needs of youth in foster care. Training needs to be provided to social workers and foster parents to request records, and nationwide implementation is needed of an electronic system that ensures that records follow students. Of critical importance is the need for culturally responsive, trained administrators, teachers, and mentors who will commit to responsively guiding and supporting the children in all domains of development, while serving as an advocate on their behalf. These children deserve a chance to experience satisfying and successful lives. Finally, as children in foster care progress through their education, provision is needed as a means by which they may emerge with a sense of voice, identity, and power to enact agency in their lives.

REFERENCES

Ahrens, K. R., DuBois, D. L., Garrison, M., Spencer, R., Richardson, L. P., & Lozano, P. (2011). Qualitative exploration of relationships with important non-parental adults in the lives of youth in foster care. *Children and Youth Services Review, 33*(6), 1012–1023.

Ai, A. L., Foster, L. J. J., Pecora, P. J., Delaney, N., & Rodriguez, W. (2013). Reshaping child welfare's response to trauma: Assessment, evidence-based intervention, and new research perspectives. *Research on Social Work Practice, 23*(6), 651–668.

Ainsworth, M. D., & Wittig, B. A. (1969). Attachment and exploratory behavior of one-year-olds in a strange situation. In B. M. Foss (Ed.), *Determinants of infant behavior* (Vol. 4, pp.113–136). London, UK: Methuen.

Aron, L., & Loprest, P. (2012). Disability and the education system. *The Future of Children, 22*(1), 97–122.

Baer, J. C., & Martinez, C. D. (2006). Child maltreatment and insecure attachment: A meta-analysis. *Journal of Reproductive and Infant Psychology, 24*(3), 187–197.

Bandura, A. (1982). Self-efficacy mechanism in human agency. *American Psychologist, 37*(2), 122–147.

Barrat, V. X., & Berliner, B. (2013, October 13). The invisible achievement gap report, part 1: Education outcomes of students in foster care in California's public schools. *Stuart Foundation.* Retrieved from http://www.stuartfoundation.org/NewsAndReports/ReportsAndResearch

Black, P. J., Woodworth, M., Tremblay, M., & Carpenter, T. (2012). A review of trauma-informed treatment for adolescents. *Canadian Psychology/Psychologie Canadienne, 53*(3), 192–203.

Bowlby, J. (1969). *Attachment and loss. Vol. I: Attachment.* New York, NY. Basic.

Britner, P. A., Randall, K. G., & Ahrens, K. R. (2014). Youth in foster care. In D. L. DuBois & M. J. Karcher (Eds.), *Handbook of youth mentoring* (2nd ed., pp. 341–354). Los Angeles, CA: Sage.

Brofenbrenner, U. (1977). Toward an experimental ecology of human development. *American Psychologist, 32*, 513–531.

Bruster, B. E., & Coccoma, P. (2013). Mentoring for educational success: Advancing foster care youth incorporating the core competencies. *Journal of Human Behavior in the Social Environment, 23*(3), 388–399.

Camangian, P. (2010). Starting with self: Teaching autoethnography to foster critically caring literacies. *Research in the Teaching of English, 45*(2), 179–204.

CAPTA Reauthorization Act of 2010, P.L. 111-320, 124 Stat. 3459 (2010).

Carlson, E. A. (1998). A prospective longitudinal study of attachment disorganization/disorientation. *Child Development, 69*(4), 1107–1128.

Children's Bureau. (2013a). *Child maltreatment 2012*. Retrieved from http://www. acf.hhs.gov/programs/cb/resource/child-maltreatment-2012

Children's Bureau. (2013b). *The AFCARS report 2012*. Retrieved from http://www. acf.hhs.gov/programs/cb

Cieslak, R., Benight, C. C., & Lehman, V. C. (2008). Coping self-efficacy mediates the effects of negative cognitions on posttraumatic distress. *Behaviour Research and Therapy, 46*(7), 788–798.

Coulton, C. J., Crampton, D. S., Irwin, M., Spilsbury, J. C., & Korbin, J. E. (2007). How neighborhoods influence child maltreatment: A review of the literature and alternative pathways. *Child Abuse & Neglect, 31*(11/12), 1117–1142.

Courtney, M. E., Terao, S., & Bost, N. (2004). Midwest evaluation of the adult functioning of former foster youth: Conditions of youth preparing to leave state care. Chicago, IL: University of Chicago, Chapin Hall Center for Children.

Cox, T. L. (2013). Improving educational outcomes for children and youths in foster care. *Children & Schools, 35*(1), 59–62.

Cummings, E. M., & Cummings, J. S. (2002). Parenting and attachment. In M. H. Bornstein (Ed.), *Handbook of parenting, Vol. IV* (pp. 35–58). Mahwah, NJ: Erlbaum.

De Bellis, M. D., & Zisk, A. (2014). The biological effects of childhood trauma. *Child and Adolescent Psychiatric Clinics of North America, 23*(2), 185–222.

Dembo, M. H., & Eaton, M. J. (2000). Self-regulation of academic learning in middle-level schools. *The Elementary School Journal, 100*(5), 473–490.

Dettlaff, A. J., Rivaux, S. L., Baumann, D. J., Fluke, J. D., Rycraft, J. R., & James, J. (2011). Disentangling substantiation: The influence of race, income, and risk on the substantiation decision in child welfare. *Children and Youth Services Review, 33*(9), 1630–1637.

Dozier, M., & Lindhiem, O. (2006). This is my child: Differences among foster parents in commitment to their young children. *Child Maltreatment, 11,* 338–345.

Dozier, M., & Rutter, M. (2008). Challenges to the development of attachment relationships faced by young children in foster and adoptive care. In J. Cassidy & P. R. Shaver (Eds.), *Handbook of attachment: Theory, research, and clinical applications* (2nd ed., pp. 698–717). New York, NY: Guilford.

Drake, B., Lee, S. M., & Jonson-Reid, M. (2009). Race and child maltreatment reporting: Are Blacks overrepresented? *Children and Youth Services Review, 31*(3), 309–316.

Drapeau, S., Saint-Jacques, M., Lépine, R., Bégin, G., & Bernard, M. (2007). Processes that contribute to resilience among youth in foster care. *Journal of Adolescence, 30*(6), 977–999.

Egeland, B., Sroufe, L. A., & Erickson, M. (1983). The developmental consequence of different patterns of maltreatment. *Child Maltreatment, 7,* 459–469.

Emerson, J., & Lovitt, T. (2003). The educational plight of foster children in schools and what can be done about it. *Remedial and Special Education, 24*(4), 199–203.

Family Educational Rights and Privacy Act (FERPA), 20 U.S.C. § 1232g.

Fong, R., & Berger Cardoso, J. (2010). Child human trafficking victims: Challenges for the child welfare system. *Evaluation and Program Planning, 33*(3), 311–316.

Fostering Connections to Success and Increasing Adoptions Act of 2008, P.L. 110-351, 122 Stat. v3939 (2008).

Froiland, J. M. (2011). Response to intervention as a vehicle for powerful mental health interventions in the schools. *Contemporary School Psychology, 15*, 35–42.

Garcia-Reid, P. (2008). Understanding the effect of structural violence on the educational identities of Hispanic adolescents: A call for social justice. *Children & Schools, 30*(4), 235–241.

Gaultung, J. (1969). Violence, peace, and peace research. *Journal of Peace Research, 6*(3), 167–191.

Ginwright, S., & Cammarota, J. (2002). New terrain in youth development: The promise of a social justice approach. *Social Justice, 29*(4), 82–95.

Grosche, M., & Volpe, R. J. (2013). Response-to-intervention (RTI) as a model to facilitate inclusion for students with learning and behaviour problems. *European Journal of Special Needs Education, 28*(3), 254–269.

Grum, D. K. (2012). Concept of inclusion on the section of Vygotskian socio-cultural theory and neuropsychology. *Solsko Polje, 23*(1), 111–124, 272, 294.

Hankin, B. L. (2005). Childhood maltreatment and psychopathology: Prospective tests of attachment, cognitive vulnerability, and stress as mediating processes. *Cognitive Therapy and Research, 29*(6), 645–671.

Individuals with Disabilities Education Improvement Act (IDEIA) of 2004, P. L.108-446, 20 U.S.C. § 1400 et seq. (2004).

Jantz, I., Rolock, N., Leathers, S. J., Dettlaff, A. J., & Gleeson, J. P. (2012). Substitute care entry: The relationship between race or ethnicity and levels of county organization. *Child Abuse & Neglect, 36*(11/12), 771–781.

Knott, T., & Donovan, K. (2010). Disproportionate representation of African-American children in foster care: Secondary analysis of the national child abuse and neglect data system, 2005. *Children and Youth Services Review, 32*(5), 679–684.

Lalvani, P. (2013) Privilege, compromise, or social justice: Teachers' conceptualizations of inclusive education. *Disability & Society, 28*(1), 14–27.

Mahiri, J. & Godley, A. J. (1998). Rewriting identity: Social meanings of literacy and "revisions" of self. *Reading Research Quarterly, 33*(4), 416–433.

Marcia, J. E. (1966). Development and validation of ego-identity status. *Journal of personality and social psychology, 3*(5), 551–558.

Massinga, R., & Pecora, P. J. (2004). Providing better opportunities for older children in the child welfare system. *The Future of Children, 14*(1), 150–173.

Meloy, M. E., & Phillips, D. A. (2012). Rethinking the role of early care and education in foster care. *Children and Youth Services Review, 34*(5), 882–890.

Milan, S. E., & Pinderhughes, E. E. (2000). Factors influencing maltreated children's early adjustment in foster care. *Development and Psychopathology, 12*(1), 63–81.

Moje, E. B., & Dillon, D. R. (2006). Adolescent identities as demanded by science classroom discourse communities. In D. E Alvermann, D. W. Hinchman, D. W. Moore, S. F. Phelps, & D. R. Waff (Eds.), *Reconceptualizing the literacies in adolescents' lives* (2nd ed., pp. 85–106). Mahwah, NJ: Erlbaum.

Morrison, J., & Mishna, F. (2006). Knowing the child: An ecological approach to the treatment of children in foster care. *Clinical Social Work Journal, 34*(4), 467–481.

Morton, N., & Browne, K. D. (1998). Theory and observation of attachment and its relation to child maltreatment: A review. *Child Abuse & Neglect, 22*(11), 1093–1104.

Munson, M. R., Smalling, S. E., Spencer, R., Scott, L. D., Jr., & Tracy, E. M. (2010). A steady presence in the midst of change: Non-kin natural mentors in the lives of older youth exiting foster care. *Children and Youth Services Review, 32*(4), 527–535.

Noonan, K., Matone, M., Zlotnik, S., Hernandez-Mekonnen, R., Watts, C., Rubin, D., & Mollen, C. (2012). Cross-system barriers to educational success for children in foster care: The front line perspective. *Children and Youth Services Review, 34*(2), 403–408.

Office of Planning, Research & Evaluation (OPRE). (2007, January 15). *NSCAW, no.2: Foster children's caregivers and caregiving environments, research brief, findings from the NSCAW study.* Retrieved from http://www.acf.hhs.gov/programs/opre/resource/national-survey-of-child-and-adolescent-well-being-nscaw-no-2-foster

Pears, K. C., Heywood, C. V., Kim, H. K., & Fisher, P. A. (2011). Prereading deficits in children in foster care. *School Psychology Review, 40*(1), 140–148.

Pears, K. C., Kim, H. K., & Leve, L. D. (2012). Girls in foster care: Risk and promotive factors for school adjustment across the transition to middle school. *Children and Youth Services Review, 34*(1), 234–243.

Pecora, P. J. (2012). Maximizing educational achievement of youth in foster care and alumni: Factors associated with success. *Children and Youth Services Review, 34*(6), 1121–1129.

Pecora, P. J., Kessler, R. C., O'Brien, K., White, C. R., Williams, J., Hiripi, E., . . . Herrick, M. A. (2006). Educational and employment outcomes of adults formerly placed in foster care: Results from the Northwest Foster Care Alumni Study. *Children and Youth Services Review, 28*(12), 1459–1481.

Pressley, M. (1995). More about the development of self-regulation: Complex, long-term, and thoroughly social. *Educational Psychologist, 30*(4), 207–212.

Rhodes, J. E. (2002). *Stand by me: The risks and rewards of mentoring today's youth.* Cambridge, MA: Harvard University Press.

Rhodes, J. E. (2005). *A model of youth mentoring.* Thousand Oaks, CA: Sage.

Rogoff, B. (2003). *The cultural nature of human development.* New York, NY: Oxford University Press.

Salzman, M. (2000). Promoting multicultural competence: A cross-cultural mentorship project. *Journal of Multicultural Counseling and Development, 28*(2), 119–124.

Sánchez, B., Colón-Torres, Y., Feuer, R., Roundfield, K. E., & Berardi, L. (2014). Race, ethnicity, and culture in mentoring relationships. In D. L. DuBois & M. J. Karcher (Eds.), *Handbook of youth mentoring* (2nd ed., pp. 145–158). Los Angele, CA: Sage.

Scherr, T. G. (2007). Educational experiences of children in foster care: Meta-analyses of special education, retention and discipline rates. *School Psychology International, 28*(4), 419–436.

Shea, N. M., Zetlin, A. G., & Weinberg, L. A. (2010). Improving school stability: An exploratory study of the work of the AB 490 liaisons in California. *Children and Youth Services Review, 32*(1), 74–79.

Smithgall, C., Gladden, R. M., Howard, E. Goerge, R. M., & Courtney, M. E. (2004). Educational experience of children in out-of-home care. *Chapin Hall at the University of Chicago.* Retrieved from http://www.chapinhall.org/research/report/educational-experiences-children-out-home-care

Taussig, H. N., & Culhane, S. E. (2010). Impact of a mentoring and skills group program on mental health outcomes for maltreated children in foster care. *Archives of Pediatrics & Adolescent Medicine, 164*(8), 739–746.

Trout, A. L., Hagaman, J., Casey, K., Reid, R., & Epstein, M. H. (2008). The academic status of children and youth in out-of-home care: A review of the literature. *Children and Youth Services Review, 30*(9), 979–994.

UNESCO. (2009). *Policy guidelines on inclusion in education.* Retrieved from http://unesdoc.unesco.org/images/0017/001778/177849e.pdf

Uninterrupted Scholars Act of 2013, P.L. 112-278 (2013).

Unrau, Y. A. (2007). Research on placement moves: Seeking the perspective of foster children. *Children and Youth Services Review, 29*(1), 122–137.

Unrau, Y. A., Seita, J. R., & Putney, K. S. (2008). Former foster youth remember multiple placement moves: A journey of loss and hope. *Children and Youth Services Review, 30*(11), 1256–1266.

Vygotsky, L. S. (1993). Volume 2: The fundamentals of defectology: Abnormal psychology and learning disabilities. In R. W. Rieber & A. S. Carton (Eds.), *The collected works of L. S. Vygotsky.* New York, NY: Plenum.

Yong, M., & Cheney, D. A. (2013). Essential features of tier 2 social–behavioral interventions. *Psychology in the Schools, 50*(8), 844–861.

Zetlin, A. G., Weinberg, L. A., & Shea, N. M. (2006). Seeing the whole picture: Views from diverse participants on barriers to educating foster youths. *Children & Schools, 28*(3), 165–173.

Zetlin, A., Weinberg, L., & Kimm, C. (2004). Improving education outcomes for children in foster care: Intervention by an education liaison. *Journal of Education for Students Placed at Risk, 9*(4), 421–429.

Zimmerman, B. J. (1995). Self-regulation involves more than metacognition: A social cognitive perspective. *Educational Psychologist, 30*(4), 217–221.

Zinn, A. (2010). A typology of kinship foster families: Latent class and exploratory analyses of kinship family structure and household composition. *Children and Youth Services Review, 32*(3), 325–337.

Zorc, C. S., O'Reilly, A. L. R., Matone, M., Long, J., Watts, C. L., & Rubin, D. (2013). The relationship of placement experience to school absenteeism and changing schools in young, school-aged children in foster care. *Children and Youth Services Review, 35*(5), 826–833.

CHAPTER 6

AFFECT AND RESILIENCE IN URBAN FEMALES

An Emerging Paradigm

Theresa Garfield Dorel and Armando Tejeda
Texas A&M University–San Antonio

ABSTRACT

The standards-based reform that has swept the country has served to reach students in the cognitive domain. However, as a result, teaching in the affective domain has been put out of reach for many students, particularly those in high-risk urban centers. In particular, females, who have an inclination toward the affect, are being left out of this effective teaching practice. This chapter attempts to codify why teaching in the affect is so important and what 21st century skills are required for students to succeed in society. Further, this chapter will examine the role of teachers and administrators in cultivating another important characteristic: resilience. Hoerr (2012) suggests one way to achieve this is to have students learn what adversity is in life. The authors of this chapter posit that females in urban settings experience adversity in every-day life, and it is up to teachers and administrators to harness that adversity into a productive character trait, such as resilience.

Inclusive Practices and Social Justice Leadership for Special Populations in Urban Settings, pages 103–121
Copyright © 2015 by Information Age Publishing

An estimated 46,247,000 children live in poverty in the United States, with a majority of those students living in urban environments (NCES, 2013). While there have been many programs to address the diverse needs of students living in urban environments, few have been effective at targeting the needs of females. Single motherhood often perpetuates this cycle of poverty. In order to make a difference in this issue, more attention needs to be paid to affect and to teaching our females to remain resilient and vigilant in their educational attainment. Teachers and administrators must critically examine what we are teaching our females and how we are teaching them. In order to provide equity, our females in urban settings must be equipped with the same 21st century skills that their suburban counterparts are given. In this chapter, the authors will examine the role of teachers and administrators in cultivating resiliency and grit in girls living in urban settings. We posit that girls in urban settings experience adversity in everyday life, and it is up to teachers and administrators to harness that adversity into a productive character trait, such as resilience.

THE FEDERAL RESPONSE TO EQUALIZATION IN EDUCATION: A HISTORICAL PERSPECTIVE

Most educational reform initiatives have given more attention to standards-based cognitive initiatives purported to increase learning outcomes with less attention given to affective reforms, the paradigm of the personal, that address the voices of students and their experiences in schools.

—Friend & Caruthers, 2012, p. 367

The role of the federal government has evolved from one that is driven by funding to one that is driven by accountability. Despite this progression, one role is constant: to provide a funding resource for those local education agencies the government has delineated as being in poverty or at risk. In 1965, the Elementary and Secondary Education Act (ESEA) was passed to serve as an impetus to exert federal control in the states' rights of educating our nation's youth. The intent of Title I of the ESEA was to provide financial assistance to local education agencies (LEAs), which were serving children from poverty (Boyce, 2012). Title I in particular was aimed toward assisting schools that educated students identified as living in poverty. Yet, according to Cohen, Moffitt, and Goldin (2007),

> Everyone was poorly informed; there was little knowledge of how to improve schools, teaching and learning were weakly understood, and state and federal intervention had been rare. Practitioners at all levels of the federal system faced large new tasks with small capabilities. (p. 529)

The response of the federal government was, and continues to be, to provide extra funding to meet the needs of these students. However, even though teachers and schools were funded with these monies, the way the funds were used, and how teachers were trained to work with students from low income areas, was largely left up to individual local education agencies. Oftentimes, the funding is spent on pullout programs or class size reduction (Henry, Fortner, & Thompson, 2010).

Another central occurrence in the federal government's role in education was the creation of the U.S. Department of Education in 1980. Many federal programs are meant to supplement those at the state level, and the Department of Education was partly formed as a response to provide equality in education (Stephens, 1984). This solidified the role of the government in the delivery of educational opportunities for students. This move was not without concern. Radin and Hawley (1988) report that the Department of Education was really created as a way for the National Education Association (NEA) to get its stronghold in public policy. It wasn't until 2001, with the reauthorization of ESEA, that the role of the government really developed its stronghold over the LEAs.

The enactment of the No Child Left Behind Act of 2001 (NCLB), the latest iteration of the ESEA, served to appoint the federal government as gatekeepers of federal funding. The goals purported by the intent of the act were lofty to say the least. No child should be left behind in their education. All children should be reading on grade level and show literacy and math proficiency on grade level by the fourth grade (NCLB, 2001). All students, regardless of income, ethnicity, ability, and background, should be academically proficient by the year 2014.

Companies which provided materials and programs to schools scrambled to provide evidence of their worthiness to be funded through title monies. Textbook publishers, which must align to state standards, responded by including multistate standards that led to many topics being superficially addressed (Reys & Lappan, 2007). Schools were held accountable for the adequate yearly progress (AYP) of each student. Accountability was technically left up to each state, but the federal government held each state accountable to report back to the government. Local control was once again destructured.

Standards-Based Reforms: A Reactive Approach

The National Council for Teachers of English (NCTE) was founded in 1911. The National Council for Teachers of Mathematics (NCTM) was created in 1920. The National Science Teacher Association (NSTA) was created in 1944. Each of these organizations developed standards for educating our nation's youth in core areas. However, it wasn't until the 1950s that standards-based reform began as a response to the space race (Tenam-Zemach & Flynn, 2011). Schools were told they were not producing students that were competitive in the sciences and math. As a result, sweeping reforms were discussed. It wasn't until the 1990s that "standards-based reform" really became the battle cry of education (Thurlow, 2000). States were strongly encouraged to follow these standards, and the push for national standards became part of the national agenda. In 2009, this development became a reality when 44 out of 50 states, and the District of Columbia, adopted a common core of standards in the United States.

The development of these standards was largely politically driven by the passage of NCLB. Thus, they were reactionary and not proactive in the educational arena. Again, the needs of our struggling students were being pushed aside as states tried to adjust their curriculum to align with these standards. Five years later, teachers are becoming more vocal about the common core, which is becoming akin to a four letter word. According to Tenam-Zemach and Flynn (2011),

> Once again, it is worth questioning whether the development of these standards meets the overarching purposes of education in the United States, or whether the standards are reconstructing those purposes to meet specific agendas of those who desire to maintain an hegemonic position. (p. 119)

Regarding the common core standards, McDonnell and Weatherford (2013) write that there is a lack of prior field testing of the standards, a cookie-cutter approach to education, and a lack of public debate about their adoption and lack of transparency about the financial support behind the common core.

Race to the Top is President Obama's response to No Child Left Behind. Race to the Top (RTT) altered how the federal government is involved in public education through the most influential avenue: funding. Callahan and Sadeghi (2013) asserted that in order to secure the funding,

> states were expected to implement legislative changes to education policy and design a blueprint for change with a focus on four reform goals: 1. Adopting standards and assessment; 2. building data systems to store student data longitudinally; 3. recruiting, rewarding, and retaining effective teachers and principals; 4. turning around the lowest achieving schools. (p. 69)

This oversight of the federal government has redefined how we approach funding for schools that may be at risk. According to Montes (2012), RTT has been successful in promoting substantive change in the adoption of national standards. However, it is not without criticism. Gottlieb (2013) comments that RTT perpetuates a deficit model for teachers because the problem concerning teacher quality is constructed at the policy level as one of inadequate knowledge. Some may misconstrue this "inadequate knowledge" as being aimed at females, since they largely compose the teaching profession. Alternatively, the policymakers are largely male. Historically, little has been done to provide females adequate opportunity to achieve adequate knowledge.

History of Educational Opportunity for Females

The education of females has not always been a priority of the state and federal governments. It wasn't until the passage of acts such as the Smith-Hughes Act of 1917 and the subsequent George Reed Act of 1929 that women's education was really brought to the forefront. These acts, and other "George" Acts, essentially provided equal funding for vocational education; specifically home economics and agriculture (Walters, 1986). Although public education was supposed to be accessible for most students regardless of gender, the type of educational opportunity was largely dictated by gender. Females were directed into home economics, secretary training, and fields that were gender biased, such as teaching and nursing. In 1972, the passage of Title IX attempted to level the playing field.

Essentially, Title IX of the Education Amendments of 1972 bans sex discrimination in any federally funded education program. Touted as a title that brought some semblance of equity to sports in college and high school, it has done much more than that. The U.S. Department of Justice reported in June 2012 that Title IX, by providing girls and women equal access to education, has dramatically expanded women's access to athletic programs and increased their educational attainment (Sandberg & Verbalis, 2013). Since Title IX, little has been passed by way of legislation for females in education.

GENDER EQUITIES AND INEQUITIES

There have been several programs that focus on the equity of education for males. Most of these programs have been targeted toward narrowing the achievement gap and keeping males out of the criminal justice system. One study by Steinmayr and Spinath (2008) looks specifically at the achievement gap of boys in light of the gains that females have made in education. They examine the impact that personality and motivation play in achievement. O'Neil, Challenger, Renzulli, Crasper and Webster (2013) strongly suggested the need for more programs for middle school boys. Even though urban females are also at risk, little has been done to narrow the achievement gap for females and keep females out of the criminal justice system. While urban Black females are doing better than urban Black males, this is misleading. They are still achieving well below their White female counterparts (Rollock, 2007).

There are some programs that focus directly on females, such as inner city youth development organizations (Loder & Hirsch, 2003). These programs provide evidence that community youth clubs can provide a powerful pathway to motivation for girls. Broussard, Mosely-Howard, and Roychoudhury (2006) examine the fidelity of mentors for students to help foster resilient behaviors. They found that on average, students who participated in the mentorship program reported that their mentor helped keep them off the streets and out of trouble. Students also said their mentor kept them on the right track. School attendance was positively impacted, and there was affective change in the students.

Although delinquency risk factors affect both genders, specific factors such as maltreatment, depression, and anxiety greatly enhance a female's chance of delinquency, while school connectedness and success offer protections against these risk factors (Bloom, Owens, Dechenes, & Rosenbaum, 2002). Trillo and Redondo (2013) observe that females who engage in antisocial behavior tend to be less attached to the conventional settings of feminine traits and more attached to those who are deviant themselves. Delinquency rates are higher for urban females as opposed to their suburban counterparts. Females compose approximately 30% of the delinquents in the system (Chesney-Lind & Pasko, 2012). The same qualities that can be attributed to success, such as assertiveness, independence, emotional resilience, and free expression, are also seen as going against the mainstream and leads to more office referrals that impact the school-to-prison pipeline (Blake, Butler, Lewis, & Darensbourg, 2011).

Unresolved Issues in Educating Urban Females

Despite continuous waves of reform, inequitable resources and poor outcomes are still typical of urban schooling.
—Taines, 2011, p. 59

Massey (2007) reports that at the bottom of a stratified education system stand urban schools, with fewer resources allocated to student populations with a lower socioeconomic status. Urban schools are espousing change for their youth, but in reality the students look in the face of poverty, unemployed parents, and daily discrimination (MacLeod, 2009). One response to this disconnect has been to employ a culturally relevant and responsive approach to education. Oftentimes, this approach is regarded in university settings, where students are "exposed" to diverse populations through in-service, practica, and field experiences (Nuby, 2010). This "Ivory Tower" approach broadens the chasm between the need of truly implementing culturally relevant pedagogy and the practice of such a methodology. "Culturally relevant teachers know when to introduce relevant examples from their students' backgrounds and experiences to make learning more meaningful" (Ladson-Billings, 1998, p. 261). Another issue facing administrators when applying a culturally responsive approach is that administrators must face their own biases and recognize their own values and be culturally competent themselves (Weinstein, Curran, & Tomlinson-Clarke, 2003).However-er, even if the university setting can reach preservice teachers and provide culturally relevant teachers, it doesn't mean the receiving urban schools will be able to embrace such an approach.

According to Sleeter (2012), culturally responsive approaches have been usurped by standardized curricula. Based on the work by Darling-Hammond (2012a), "The truth is that the competitive market approach leaves the most vulnerable children behind" (p. 14). One suggestion is to organize teaching around the core curriculum that focuses on higher-order thinking, inquiry, and problem solving (Darling-Hammond, 2012b). In other words, teach in the affect.

The Educational Leadership Response

The main issue facing administrators in the face of the standards-based reform is that they are accountable on some level for the "achievement" of all students. Because of the stress on accountability, the current foci remain on those curricula that are standards based in nature and that are easily addressed in classrooms and produce results on standardized tests. Thus, many of the curricular approaches are those that give the most "bang for the buck" and are largely based in the cognitive domain (Harris, 2011). Standardization ultimately leads to substandard educational opportunities because funding is based on school failure and risk. Any resources that are used are going to the quick fix to raise test scores and not on programs focused on the affect (Baker, 2011).

Out of standards-based reforms have emerged a school of thought related to providing evidence-based practices and models such as Response to Intervention (RTI). RTI is a tiered approach to intervention. All students should be receiving Tier 1, or universal interventions. Those students that don't progress in Tier 1 will move into more intense interventions in Tier 2 or 3 (Fuchs, Fuchs, & Vaughn, 2014). Artiles, Bal, and King Thorius (2010) suggest that RTI may be a social justice approach in itself. In other words, does RTI remove some of the bias that is inherent in the disproportionate representation of students of color in special-education and at-risk programs?

Wealthier districts have more resources and opportunity for affective teaching and learning thus widening the gap between promoting citizenry that can problem solve and create (affect) and those who can answer a question on a standardized test. Consequently, the lens through which we must impact the future of our females in urban settings must be one of equity and accessibility. It is not enough to allocate additional resources and funding to urban schools and females in urban settings, such as pregnancy prevention and dropout prevention, but to provide actual internal approaches such as programs focusing on resiliency and affect. A further call must be made for equity in providing adequate preparation in those skills necessary for current students to become successful in the 21st century.

SOCIAL JUSTICE FRAMEWORK REVISITED

It would be easy to say what is wrong with the system and attempt to fix it. However, that in itself continues to marginalize our youth in urban settings and particularly females. This "Ivory Tower" approach has led to perpetuating the system of dysfunction in the urban setting. Given the current demographics of a typical college professor—privileged White male—it is no surprise that little has been done to actually address the issues of the disproportionality of females living in extreme poverty in urban centers. In some areas, the teacher community may also have norms and values that are incongruent with the students' cultural backgrounds (Tozer, Senese, & Violas, 2009). Paris (2012) asserts that current policies and teaching practices are explicitly seeking to create a monocultural society based on the White, middle-class norms of cultural being. He further emphasizes that unless we embrace cultural pluralism, students will continue to lose their sense of self. Ehrmann (2007) asserted that "attention centered on the 'achievement gap' does not typically focus on the interaction between gender and the characteristics of segregated environments as an important additional influence on academic performance" and "by failing to consider how males and females may respond to their environmental contexts differently, most studies neglect how gender identity may mitigate and channel long-term effects of racial isolation on academic achievement" (p. 1392).

Social justice is interpreted in many ways. However, most interpretations of social justice refer to egalitarian societies that are based on the principles of equality, human rights, and dignity (Zajda, Majhanovich, & Rust, 2006). Social justice also emphasizes consciousness and activism to struggle for equity (Christopher & Taylor, 2011). There are inherent differences between equity and equality. Equity is defined as fairness and equality is to make things the same. Both definitions lend themselves to a sense of social justice. The questions remain: What effect has the barrage of social justice programs really had on this at-risk population? Are these programs really targeting the real issue at hand?

SOCIAL JUSTICE, AFFECT, AND RESILIENCE

While awareness of societal inequalities does not guarantee action, knowledge around existing societal inequalities is a necessary step toward engaging in social justice.
—Torres-Harding, Steele, Schulz, Taha, & Pico, 2014, p. 56

Teaching for social justice requires an intentional pedagogy. Mthethwa-Sommers (2013) studied social justice educators and found that

> social justice educators are educators who unveil oppressive structures and practices and work toward achieving social change. They persuade and motivate prospective and practicing teachers to critically analyze and evaluate dominant racist, sexist, classist, and xenophobic ideology and its manifestations; and urge them to challenge and reject the oppressive dominant ideology in their public school classrooms. (p. 220)

It is not enough to say one is for social justice; instead, one must become part of the social justice pedagogy (Schoorman, 2011) and demonstrate what social justice looks like in practice.

Affect

Much of the Eurocentric curriculum present in schools has been biased and fails to appeal to females in an urban setting (Meier, 2002). In a study of 35 gifted females from an urban district, researchers found that affective characteristics such as motivation, independence, problem solving, and a heightened sensitivity to each other all served to drive the students into achievement (Reis & Diaz, 1999). Females have a strong propensity toward social justice itself. However, females are not being reached in the domain that is most intuitive to them: affect.

Affect, as defined by the Merriam-Webster's Dictionary (n.d.), is a *set of observable manifestations of a subjectively experienced emotion* or *the conscious subjective aspect of an emotion.* It first came into the realm of the educational setting in 1956 when Bloom published his taxonomy of learning. The affective domain is related to a person's attitudes and values, and historically little attention has been paid to it in education because of the focus on assessment and accountability. According to Savackiene (2010), this is partly due to the impression that it is difficult to assess this domain, and therefore knowledge and skills are more highly valued. School leaders want to know that curricular approaches are focusing on the skills being assessed at state levels.

The five stages of the affective domain include receiving, responding, valuing, organizing, and characterization by a value (Stenzel, 2006). Too often, teachers expect students to be able to value learning that is approached at the cognitive level. To truly impact affect, students need to challenge their thinking, which potentially shifts their subjectivities. According to Dorel (2014), "Subjectivities are those judgments that are modified or affected by personal views, experience, or background. They are perceived realities as opposed to factual accounts. They are based in belief structures and manifest themselves in behavior" (p. 29). In a study by Kang, Heo, Jo, Shin, and Seo (2010), the affective domain is identified as four factors: self-identity, self-value, self-directedness, and self-accountability. Each of these factors, when used in the educational context, addresses affective variables, such as a sense of confidence, and are considered critical factors for successful learning.

Learning experiences border on bland and neutral, and rarely focus on a child's affective domain (Dunn & Stinson, 2012). If it does become part of the curriculum, it is often focused on the positive emotions. Little is being done to acknowledge personal strife and teach females in an urban setting to capitalize on realistic emotions as a catalyst for change.

One such approach to this disconnect is to teach in a way that bridges the affective and cognitive domains. Bolin, Khramtsova, and Saarnio (2005) suggest the way to achieve this balance is through authenticity in assignments. In other words, craft assignments that establish a clear connection between the classroom content and the world in which students live. Student are eager to learn in an authentic environment and are hungry for school experiences that are personally meaningful (Steiner-Adair, 2013). Affect must be cultivated in the same way teachers cultivate and build knowledge—it must be taught (Cammarota, 2011).

Another approach toward effectively teaching affect is to create an environment in the classroom that evokes creativity (Tomlinson, 2013). Friend and Caruthers (2012) state that improving academic achievement for students in an urban setting can be done by including students' voices in the educational process itself. In other words, connecting the students to the affective domain will produce students who want to learn. It isn't just enough to teach *affectively*, we must also appeal to the female's sense of resiliency.

Resilience

Resilience is defined many ways. It is a way to overcome obstacles and adjust easily to change. In educational literature, it is used to define kids who are at risk and thrive regardless of their environment (Perkins-Gough, 2013). Teaching students to rethink their limitations and to require students to work in areas that are unfamiliar and less comfortable can help develop this sense of resiliency (Hoerr, 2012). The capacity to respond and adapt to extreme stress is also referred to as resilience (Maddi, 2006). Resilience is not a single phenomenon, but rather outcomes and behaviors in distinct circumstances (McMurray, Connolly, Preston-Shoot, & Wigley, 2008). Schultz (1999) reports that urban females resist the examples they see in their everyday lives—teen pregnancy and violence—and focus on how their life can be different. This resilience is profound in the minds of our urban females. Resilience is also seen as one half of the grit construct.

Grit

Duckworth, Peterson, Matthews, and Kelly (2007) define a construct of grit as perseverance and passion for a long-term goal. Further, grit entails working strenuously toward challenges and maintaining effort despite adversity. Duckworth et al. suggest that grit is akin to a marathon runner's stamina; anyone can sprint for a short distance, but those with grit will cross the finish line of a marathon. In a female without this grit characteristic, disappointment or boredom leads to changing the course. A female with this characteristic will plow forward and trudge through the issue. According to Goodwin and Miller (2013), grit comprises traits such as goal-directedness, motivation, self-control, and positive mindset. How students perceive their abilities in relation to a task can shape the outcome of such a task (Pappano, 2013). Pappano (2013) further explains that teaching grit may be a small intervention, but a small change may bring about a big effect.

These concepts—grit and resilience—are intrapersonal traits found in the *21st Century Skills* (NRC, 2012). The NRC emphasizes "Success in work and life in the 21st century is associated with cognitive, intrapersonal, and interpersonal competencies that allow individuals to adapt effectively to changing situations rather than to rely solely on well-worn procedures" (p. 70). As a result, success in the 21st century also calls for the students to have the ability to make authentic interdisciplinary connections (Farahani, 2005). Also necessary to the ability to make these connections is to be skilled in the affective domain.

INCLUSIVE PRACTICES FOR AFFECT AND RESILIENCY

Programs that promote affective learning and resiliency are not as widely researched as is necessary to meet the call for research-based practices for students. Castro-Olivo et al. (2013) examined a comprehensive model for promoting resiliency in schools. In their study, a new model emerged. This model included such factors as self-efficacy, peer relationships, family relationships, family belonging, community relationships and belonging, and school relationships and belonging. Each of these individual characteristics is used to teach resilience to students in urban settings.

Steese et al. (2006) piloted Girls' Circle, which specifically trained girls in resiliency practices. These gender-specific approaches to girls living in an urban environment boost the girls' healthy development in a positive way. Srsic and Rice (2012) took the idea of a gender-specific approach to resilience and used it to work with females with emotional behavioral disorders. It was found that these at-risk females were also looking for trust and loyalty and an element of dedication and self-sacrifice. Cannon, Hammer, Reicherzer, and Gilliam (2012) examine a framework referred to as relational cultural theory, in which aggressive females are provided an intervention. This intervention emphasizes social justice as a way to give the adolescent females a voice, and ultimately, power.

According to Yeager and Dweck (2012), students' mindsets can be changed and in turn can promote resilience. Essentially, students can be taught how to apply resiliency techniques in their lives. The application of teaching a growth mindset has been shown to significantly boost student motivation and achievement (Dweck, 2012). Barnett (2011) writes that teaching in the affect requires a certain amount of trust. Barnett further writes, "In the development of affective skills, like listening to and negotiating social differences, we might begin by asking students to reveal relatively neutral information about the self, gradually asking for more revelation on more difficult, potentially controversial, questions" (p. 677). Teaching in the affect has been shown to decrease misbehaviors and increase the number of insightful expressions by students as well as the type of expressions that were grounded in cognitive and emotional understanding (Shechtman & Leichtentritt, 2004).

A study conducted by Cokley, McClain, Jones, and Johnson (2011) of African American females in an urban setting found,

> As expected, academic self-concept had a large effect size and was significantly predictive of GPA. The relationship between academic self-concept and GPA is well-established, with academic self-concept being a consistently strong correlate and predictor of GPA. Students who feel confident about their academic abilities should be expected to have higher GPAs than students who feel less confident. (p. 64)

It appears that reaching the students at their affective core will impact grade attainment.

CONCLUSIONS, IMPLICATIONS, AND RECOMMENDATIONS

The lack of connection between the standards-based movement, teaching the urban female resilience, and the affective domain needs to be intersected for the success of our students. Stiff-Williams (2010) suggests that in order to do this, we must fuse the standards approach and character education. This is outlined in five steps:

- Identify the values and character emphases that reflect community consensus and show how good decision-making is at the basis of all these values;
- Guide teachers in analyzing state standards to determine teaching targets and identify character education emphases, such as decision making, that relate to the targets;
- Provide staff training and planning time for teachers to design unit plans that meld state standards and character education teaching;
- Support teachers in the implementation of lesson activities that emphasize state standards and character development learning experiences;
- Promote the use of performance-based assessments, such as observation instruments and scoring rubrics that can effectively evaluate aspects of character development (p. 116).

In order to reach the urban youth, particularly females, emerging pedagogies must develop. The quality of the teaching can far outweigh any disadvantage of gender, school effects, socioeconomic status, family, or ability (Lovat & Clement, 2008). Even though children typically perpetuate the inequalities they observe (Olson, Dweck, Spelke, & Banaji, 2011), teachers can level the playing field by teaching in the affect, focusing on resilience, and demonstrating true inclusive practices. According to Sapon-Shevin (2008), "Inclusion is about creating a society in which all children and their families feel welcomed and valued" (p. 50).

Urban school leaders must also answer the call to provide cultural competence and address social justice. No longer can cognitive domains be taught in isolation. There must be a connection between affect and cognition. Although the cognitive domains are heavily assessed at the state levels, pause must be given to integrate affective learning into the classrooms. Affect in urban settings cannot focus on the detrimental effects of high-stakes testing or symptoms of posttraumatic stress disorder that many of our urban youth face, but instead on how to capture the affect with effect (Schutz & Pekrun, 2007). In order to stop the marginalization of urban females, school leaders need to step out from behind their desks and become actively engaged in the instruction of the students. This is achieved by providing an inclusive environment for all students (Crow, 2007). School leaders need to help the teachers overcome the deficit mentality many teachers have when working with diverse populations (Gainer & Lorratta, 2010). Addressing and eliminating the marginalization in schools is essential when defining a school leader that is grounded in social justice (Theoharis, 2008). This defining of leadership starts with the principal as an instructional leader.

Making the students' identities part of a principal's leadership practice leads to a pedagogy in which students find their own realities represented in school curriculum, which leads to greater success (Mansfield, 2014). This is particularly true of females. Since principals both directly and indirectly influence what is offered as professional development, they directly influence the focus of the development itself (Kose, 2009).

Overall, much needs to be done in order to reach females in urban settings in the affect and to teach them resiliency. However, it is not a cost-prohibitive approach at all. It is an approach that can be addressed with a simple reallocation of existing resources toward teacher preparation and administrative preparation that leads to an understanding of the affect. Further understanding the way to teach resilience to our females is also a direct approach. Both require a new pedagogical framework, but one that can be attained with the right perspective and in the right context.

REFERENCES

Artiles, A. J., Bal, A., & King Thorius, K. (2010). Back to the future: A critique of response to intervention's social justice views. *Theory into Practice, 49,* 250–257.

Baker, K. (2011). High test scores: The wrong road to national economic success. *Kappa Delta Pi Record, 47*(3), 116–120.

Barnett, P. E. (2011). Discussions across difference: Addressing the affective dimensions of teaching diverse students about diversity. *Teaching in Higher Education, 16*(6), 669–679.

Blake, J. J., Butler, B. R., Lewis, C. W., & Darensbourg, A. (2011). Unmasking the inequitable discipline experiences of urban Black girls: Implications for urban educational stakeholders. *Urban Review, 43,* 90–106.

Bloom, B., Owens, B., Deschenes, E., & Rosenbaum, J. (2002). Moving toward justice for female juvenile offenders in the new millennium: Modeling gender-specific policies and programs. *Journal of Contemporary Criminal Justice, 18,* 37–56.

Bolin, A. U., Khramtsova, I., & Saarnio, D. (2005). Using student journals to stimulate authentic learning: Balancing Bloom's cognitive and affective domains. *Teaching of Psychology, 32*(3), 154–159.

Boyce, S. G. (2012). The obsolescence of San Antonio v. Rodriguez in the wake of the federal government's quest to leave no child behind. *Duke Law Journal, 61*(5), 1025–1066.

Broussard, C. A., Mosely-Howard, S., & Roychoudhury, A. (2006). Using youth advocates for mentoring at-risk students in urban settings. *Children and Schools, 28*(2), 122–127.

Callahan, K., & Sadeghi, L. (2013). A blueprint for change: Lessons in educational reform. *Public Manager, 42*(2), 68–70.

Cammarota, J. (2011). From hopelessness to hope: Social justice pedagogy in urban education and youth development. *Urban Education, 46*(4), 828–844.

Cannon, K. B., Hammer, T. R., Reicherzer, S., & Gilliam, B. J. (2012). Relational-cultural theory: A framework for relational competencies and movements in group work with female adolescents. *Journal of Creativity in Mental Health, 7,* 2–16.

Castro-Olivo, S. M., Tran, O. K., Begum, G. F., Arellano, E. M., Garcia, N. M., & Tung, C. Y. (2013). A comprehensive model for promoting resiliency and preventing violence in schools. *Contemporary School Psychology, 17*(1), 23–34.

Chesney-Lind, M., & Pasko, L. (2012). *The female offender: Girls, women, and crime.* Thousand Oaks, CA: Sage.

Christoper, D. H., & Taylor, M. J. (2011). Social justice and critical peace education: Common ideals guiding student teacher transformation. *Journal of Peace Education, 8*(3), 295–313.

Cohen, D. K., Moffitt, S. L., & Goldin, S. (2007). Policy and practice: The dilemma. *American Journal of Education, 113,* p. 515–548.

Cokley, K. McClain, S., Jones, M., & Johnson, S. (2011). A preliminary investigation of academic disidentification, racial identity, and academic achievement among African American adolescents. *The High School Journal, 95*(2), 54–68.

Crow, G. M. (2007). The complex landscape of successful principal practices: An international perspective. *International Studies in Educational Administration, 35*(3), 67–74.

Darling-Hammond, L. (2012a). Redlining our schools. *Nation, 294*(5), 11–15.

Darling-Hammond, L. (2012b). Soaring systems. *Education Review, 24*(1), 24–33.

Dorel, T. (2014). Impacting the way we teach: Exploring subjectivities among preservice teachers. *The National Forum of Teacher Education Journal, 24*(1/2), 29–36.

Duckworth, A., Peterson, C., Matthews, M. D., & Kelly, D. R. (2007). Grit: Perseverance and passion for long-term goals. *Journal of Personality and Social Psychology, 92*(6), 1087–1101.

Dunn, J., & Stinson, M. (2012). Learning through emotion: Moving the affective in from the margins. *International Journal of Early Childhood, 44,* 203–218.

Dweck, C. S. (2012). Mindsets and human nature: Promoting change in the Middle East, the schoolyard, the racial divide, and willpower. *American Psychologist, 67*(8), 614–622.

Ehrmann, N. (2007). From the ghetto to the ivory tower: Gendered effects of segregation on elite-college completion. *Social Science Quarterly, 88*(5), 1392–1413.

Farahani, A. J. (2005). The shifting paradigm: Who is the intellectual of the 21st century? *International Education Journal, 6*(4), 512–515.

Friend, J., & Caruthers, L. (2012). Reconstructing the cultural context of urban schools: Listening to the voices of high school students. *Educational Studies, 48,* 366–388.

Fuchs, D., Fuchs, L., & Vaughn, S. (2014). What is intensive instruction and why is it important? *Teaching Exceptional Children, 46*(4), 13–18.

Gainer, J. S., & Larrotta, C. (2010). Reproducing and interrupting subtractive schooling in teacher education. *Multicultural Education, 17*(3), 41–47.

Goodwin, B., & Miller, K. (2013). Grit + talent = student success. *Educational Leadership, 71*(1), 74–76.

Gottlieb, D. (2013). Eisner's evaluation in the age of race to the top. *Curriculum and Teaching Dialogue, 15*(1/2), 11–25.

Harris, D. M. (2011). Curriculum differentiation and comprehensive school reform: Challenges in providing educational opportunity. *Educational Policy, 25*(5), 844–884.

Henry, G. T., Fortner, C. K., & Thompson, C. L. (2010). Targeted funding for educationally disadvantaged students: A regression discontinuity estimate of the impact on high school achievement. *Educational Evaluation and Policy Analysis, 32*, 183–204.

Hoerr, T. R. (2012). Got grit? *Educational Leadership, 69*(6), 84–86.

Kang, M., Heo, H., Jo, I., Shin, J., & Seo, J. (2010). Developing an educational performance indicator for new millennium leaders. *Journal of Research on Technology in Education, 43*(2), 157–170.

Kose, B. W. (2009). The principal's role in professional development for social justice. *Urban Education, 44*(6), 628–663.

Ladson-Billings, G. (1998). Teaching in dangerous times: Culturally relevant approaches to teacher assessment. *The Journal of Negro Education, 67*(3), 255–267.

Loder, T. L., & Hirsch, B. J. (2003). Inner-city youth development organizations: The salience of peer ties among early adolescent girls. *Applied Developmental Science, 7*(1), 2–12.

Lovat, T., & Clement, N. (2008). Quality teaching and values education: Coalescing for effective learning. *Journal of Moral Education, 37*(1), 1–16.

MacLeod, J. (2009). *Ain't no makin' it: Aspirations and attainment in a low-income neighborhood* (3rd ed.). Boulder, CO: Westview.

Maddi, S. R. (2006). Hardiness: The courage to grow from stresses. *Journal of Positive Psychology, 1*(3), 160–168.

Mansfield, K. C. (2014). How listening to student voices informs and strengthens social justice research and practice. *Educational Administration Quarterly, 50*(3), 392–430.

Massey, D. (2007). *Categorically unequal: The American stratification system.* Thousand Oaks, CA: Sage.

McDonnell, L. M., & Weatherford, M. S. (2013). Organized interests and the common core. *Educational Researcher, 42*(9), 488–497.

McMurray, I., Connolly, H., Preston-Shoot, M., & Wigley, V. (2008). Constructing resilience: Social workers' understandings and practice. *Health & Social Care in the Community, 16*(3), 299–309.

Meier, D. (2002). A view from the schoolhouse. *Daedalus, 131*(3), 41–44.

Merriam-Webster. (n.d.) *Affect.* Retrieved from http://www.merriam-webster.com/dictionary/affect

Montes, G. (2012). Race to the Top, value-added models, and the Catholic view of education. *Catholic Social Science Review, 17*, 337–344.

Mthethwa-Sommers, S. (2013). Pedagogical possibilities: Lessons from social justice educators. *Journal of Transformative Education, 10*(4), 219–235.

National Center for Educational Statistics (NCES). (2013). *The condition of education 2013.* U.S. Department of Education, NCES 2013-037.

National Research Council (NRC). (2012). *Education for life and work: Developing transferable knowledge and skills in the 21st century* (J. W. Pellegrino & M. L. Hilton, Eds.). National Academies Press.

No Child Left Behind (NCLB) Act of 2001. P. L. No. 107-110 § 115, Stat. 1425.

Nuby, J. (2010). An awakening through an inner-city immersion experience. *Multicultural Perspectives, 12*(1), 42–49.

Olson, K. R., Dweck, C. S., Spelke, E. S., & Banaji, M. R. (2011). Children's response to group-based inequities: Perpetuation and ratification. *Social Cognition, 29*(2), 270–287.

O'Neil, J. M., Challenger, C., Renzulli, S., Crasper, B., & Webster, E. (2013). The Boy's Forum: An evaluation of a brief intervention to empower middle-school urban boys. *The Journal of Men's Studies, 21*(2), 191–205.

Pappano, L. (2013). 'Grit' and the new character education. *Education Digest, 78*(9), 4–9.

Paris, D. (2012). Culturally sustaining pedagogy: A needed change in stance, terminology, and practice. *Educational Researcher, 41*(3), 93–97.

Perkins-Gough, D. (2013). A conversation with Angela Lee Duckworth. *Educational Leadership, 71*(1), 14–20.

Radin, B. A., & Hawley, W. D. (1988). *The politics of federal reorganization: Creating the U.S. Department of Education.* New York, NY: Pergamon.

Reis, S. M., & Diaz, E. (1999). Economically disadvantaged urban female students who achieve in schools. *The Urban Review, 31*(1), 31–54.

Reys, B., & Lappan, G. (2007). Consensus or confusion? *Phi Delta Kappan, 88*(9), 676–680.

Rollock, N. (2007). Why Black girls don't matter: Exploring how race and gender shape academic success in an inner city school. *Support for Learning, 22*(4), 197–202.

Sandberg, K., & Verbalis, J. G. (2013). Sex and the basic scientist: Is it time to embrace Title IX? *Biology of Sex Differences, 4*(1), 1–4.

Sapon-Shevin, M. (2008). Learning in an inclusive community. *Educational Leadership, 66*(1), 49–53.

Savickiene, I. (2010). Conception of learning outcomes in the Bloom's taxonomy affective domain. *The Quality of Higher Education, 7,* 37–57.

Schoorman, D. (2011). Reconceptualizing teacher education as a social justice undertaking: Underscoring the urgency for critical multiculturalism in early childhood education. *Childhood Education, 87*(5), 341–344.

Schultz, K. (1999), Identity narratives: Stories from the lives of urban adolescent females. *The Urban Review, 31*(1), 79–106.

Schutz, P., & Pekrun, R. (2007). Introduction to emotion in education. In P. Schutz & R. Pekrun (Eds.), *Emotion in education* (pp. 3–10). Amsterdam, The Netherlands: Academic.

Shechtman, Z., & Leichtentritt, J. (2004). Affective teaching: A method to enhance classroom management. *European Journal of Teacher Education, 27*(3), 323–333.

Sleeter, C. E. (2012). Confronting the marginalization of culturally responsive pedagogy. *Urban Education, 47*(3), 562–584.

Srsic, A., & Rice, E. H. (2012). Understanding the experience of girls with EBD in a gender-responsive support group. *Education and the Treatment of Children, 35*(4), 623–646.

Steese, S., Dollette, M., Phillips, W., Hossfeld, E., Matthews, G., & Taormina, G. (2006). Understanding Girls' Circle as an intervention on perceived social support, body image, self-efficacy, locus of control, and self-esteem. *Adolescence, 41*(161), 55–74.

Steiner-Adair, C. (2013). Got grit? The call to educate smart, savvy, and socially intelligent students. *Independent Schools, 72*(2), 28–32.

Steinmayr, R., & Spinath, B. (2008). Sex differences in school achievement: What are the roles of personality and achievement motivation? *European Journal of Personality, 22*, 185–209.

Stenzel, E. J. (2006). A rubric for assessing the affective domain for retention purposes. *Assessment Update, 18*(3), 9–11.

Stephens, D. (1984). President Carter, the Congress, and NEA: Creating the Department of Education. *Political Science Quarterly, 98*(4), 641–663.

Stiff-Williams, H. R. (2010). Widening the lens to teach character education alongside standards curriculum. *The Clearing House, 83*, 115–120.

Taines, C. (2011). Intervening in alienation: The outcomes for urban youth of participating in school activism. *American Educational Research Journal, 49*(1), 53–86.

Tenam-Zemach, M., & Flynn, J. (2011). America's race to the top, our fall from grace. *Curriculum and Teaching Dialogue, 13*(1/2), 113–124.

Theoharis, G. (2008). Woven in deeply: Identity and leadership of urban social justice principals. *Education and Urban Society, 41*(3), 3–25.

Thurlow, M. L. (2000). Standards-based reform and students with disabilities: Reflections on a decade of change. *Focus on Exceptional Children, 33*(3), 1–16.

Tomlinson, C. A. (2013). Fairy dust and grit. *Educational Leadership, 70*(5), 85–86.

Torres-Harding, S. R., Steele, C., Schulz, E., Taha, F., & Pico, C. (2014). Student perceptions of social justice and social justice activities. *Education, Citizenship, and Social Justice, 9*(1), 55–66.

Tozer, S., Senese, G., & Violas, P. (2009). *School and society: Historical and contemporary perspectives* (6th ed.). New York, NY: McGraw-Hill.

Trillo, V. M., & Redondo, L. M. (2013). The role of gender identity in adolescents' antisocial behavior. *Psicothema, 25*(4), 507–513.

U.S. Department of Justice. (2012, June 23). *Equal access to education: Forty years of Title IX*. Retrieved from http://www.justice.gov/crt/about/edu/documents/titleixreport.pdf

Walters, N. J. (1986). *The definitions, purposes, and objectives of federal funded vocational education through the various Vocational Acts 1917-1976*. ERIC Document number ED267298. Retrieved April 13, 2014, from http://eric.ed.gov/?id=ED267298

Weinstein, C., Curran, M., & Tomlison-Clarke, S. (2003). Culturally responsive classroom management: Awareness into action. *Theory into Practice, 42*(4), 269–276.

Yeager, D. S., & Dweck, C. S. (2012). Mindsets that promote resilience: When students believe that personal characteristics can be developed. *Educational Psychologist, 47*(4), 302–312.

Zajda, J., Majhanovich, S., & Rust, V. (2006). Introduction: Education and social justice. *Review of Education, 52,* 9–22.

CHAPTER 7

EDUCATING THE INCARCERATED THROUGH A COMMUNITY JAILING MODEL

A Social Justice Leadership Perspective

Brantley R. Choate Sr.
California Department of Corrections and Rehabilitation

Anthony H. Normore
California State University–Dominguez Hills

ABSTRACT

Today's reality television provides only a glimpse into the reality of prison or jail life. Television sensationalizes the experience by focusing on only the worst events and the most disruptive inmates. In truth, most of the 2.2 million inmates in today's jails and prisons will eventually be released. Is it possible to rehabilitate such a large number of men and women who have been institutionalized for such a long period of time? This chapter examines models of cultural, restorative, and social justice leadership centered on the idea of "Community Jailing"—a direct supervision technique allowing for greater and meaningful officer/inmate interaction (Petteruti & Walsh, 2008). Even

Inclusive Practices and Social Justice Leadership for Special Populations in Urban Settings, pages 123–142
Copyright © 2015 by Information Age Publishing
All rights of reproduction in any form reserved.

though the direct supervision model has been used in hundreds of jails and prisons for the past 30 years, ironically, the U.S. inmate population has grown 500% (Maguire & Pastore, 2006). While many states are experiencing a slowing of the rate of growth of their prison population, and some even a small decline, the federal prison population continues its rapid expansion. This chapter begins with an review of extant literature, which served as the framework to determine why the current practices of direct jail supervision have failed. Subsequently, the authors offer suggestions for making positive change, including prison-based/education-based incarceration programs. A new "community jailing" supervision model is suggested as a social justice response coupled with evidence to corroborate lower incidents of jail violence, a reduction in recidivism, and improved public safety.

Research indicates that 97% of those now incarcerated in U.S. prisons will eventually be released and return to the community (Serin & Crime and Justice Institute, 2005). What is the purpose of incarceration? Should our society attempt to rehabilitate offenders or should we incapacitate criminals through long sentences. The rehabilitate versus incapacitate argument continues today, even though both options have been tried over the past 400 years. Based on the names of many prisons in the country, corrections and rehabilitation appear to be a major focus. For example, in California, the state system is named the California Department of Corrections and Rehabilitation. Ohio refers to their state prison system as the Ohio Department of Rehabilitation and Corrections. Louisiana is called the Louisiana Department of Public Safety and Corrections. Are these titles misnomers or do they portray the institution's true mission? T. Don Hutto, a well-known prison reformer from Arkansas, stated "The [corrections] terminology itself has changed far more rapidly than have the actual practices. As too often happens in other endeavors, when we don't know exactly what we ought to be doing or how, we simply change the names" (Seiter, 2006, p. 27). This chapter will discuss how the ideas from leaders can shape and influence public policy for generations and, in this case, influence the current system of mass incarceration. We begin by providing a brief overview of the literature from social justice leadership to help set the context for a community-jailing model for educating incarcerated populations—a marginalized population that if educated properly may help reduce rates of recidivism and lessen the school-to-prison pipeline. We then discuss how leaders have used a direct supervision technique we will call "community jailing" to reduce inmate violence and reduce recidivism.

LEADERSHIP FOR SOCIAL JUSTICE

Recent scholars have paid considerable attention to practices and policies that have marginalized students and pose challenging questions to school leaders, educational scholars, and the broader community to engage in discussions about leadership for social justice (Boske & Diem, 2012; Normore & Brooks, 2014). A shift is needed to provide leverage for changes in bureaucratic systems that exist to serve the status quo. Although leadership has been widely studied, there is a persistent lack of agreement about what constitutes the most effective leadership styles in educational settings. What is clear, however, from research is that serving marginalized populations such as prison inmates and alternative community schools requires a unique set of leadership skills and knowledge reflective of and responsive to the cultural and linguistic diversity of those populations (Sanchez & Stuckey, 1999; Seidl, 2007).

According to Marshall and Oliva (2006), social justice "has generated a great deal of scholarship over the last decade, which in essence capitalizes on the relevance of such a discourse" (p. 5). However, the notion of social justice is hard to capture. Dantley and Tillman (2006) assert, "It is demanding, fraught with controversy, and highly contextualized...most people believe it is important but far fewer take the time or energy to actively pursue it" (p. 261). They further claim that discussions about social justice in the field of education have typically framed the concept around several issues, including race, diversity, marginalization, morality, ability, gender, sexual orientation, and spirituality (p. 17). Other researchers (e.g., Bogotch, 2005) zero in on a key component by stating that "social justice, like education, is a deliberate intervention that requires the moral use of power" and concludes that it is "both much more than what we currently call democratic schooling and community education, and much less than what we hold out as the ideals of progressing toward a just and democratic society and a new humanity worldwide" (pp. 7–8). In practice, individuals for social justice seek to challenge political, economic, and social structures that privilege some and disadvantage others. They challenge unequal power relationships based on systems of oppression and educational context. Among the education contexts are correction facilities, prisons, and jails.

HISTORICAL PERSPECTIVE OF INCARCERATION

Origin of Incarceration: 18th and 19th Century

Punishment by imprisonment did not exist in Europe or the European colonies prior to the 1780s. Jails were only a means of detention until acquittal, fines, corporal, or capital punishment. Punishment was typically reserved for the lower classes since the rich could pay fines for redemption. Some of the earliest known forms of punishment are known as retributive justice. The most well-known phrase used to describe retributive punishment is "an eye for and eye," signifying that when one has injured another, the perpetrator is penalized to a similar degree. In other words, the punishment is proportionate to the crime. Punishments included "torture, beating, branding, and mutilations" (Seiter, 2011, p. 18). Liars had their tongues removed, and thieves had fingers or hands cut off, and adulterers had a scarlet A branded on their foreheads to reduce their attractiveness and discourage any further adultery (Seiter, 2011).

The Puritans were some of the earliest settlers on the American continent and usually conducted punishment in public. Capital and corporal punishment and whippings were carried out in the town center. Other forms of punishment such as the use of stocks and pillories were used where offenders sat with their hands, head, and feet secured to a wooden frame. This form of punishment provided cause for public humiliation and ridicule. Capital punishment was for repeat offenders and first-degree murder. Capital crimes increased with the industrial revolution, where manufacturing took away many working-class trade jobs, thus increasing the crime rate (see Seiter, 2011).

In the 1680s, William Penn, Governor of Pennsylvania, abolished capital punishment and corporal punishment. Instead, he provided free food and lodging for prisoners, and the replacement of stocks and pillories with houses of detention. Opposition to capital and corporal punishment by Penn and the Quakers generated the argument to create a system of long-term imprisonment. In 1773, John Howard, Sheriff of Bedfordshire, England, coined the term "penitentiary" as an idea for offenders to do penance for their sins rather than receiving brutal punishment. These ideas led to the development of two distinct systems in the United States: the Pennsylvania and Auburn systems (see Seiter, 2011).

Pennsylvania System

In 1790, the first prison was established in the United States by converting a wing of the Walnut Street Jail in Philadelphia. The Walnut Street Jail was established to house sentenced offenders where the primary objective was reformation of the offender. Reading the Bible and personal reflection was part of the penance process. Inmates were forced to be silent and were kept in individual cells. Moral contamination was feared by the guards. Prisoners worked on handicrafts in their cell during the day and read the Bible in the evenings.

Auburn System

In Auburn, New York, a similar system was created. Inmates were still kept in individual cells at night, but worked together during the day in factories to help pay for the costs to run the prison.

The Auburn system was known as the "congregate and silent" system. Even though inmates worked together during they day, they were still forced to remain silent and not speak to anyone. The Auburn system consisted of hard labor, silence, and individual cells at night (Seiter, 2011). According to Mauer (2006), "What is important in the long run was not the differences between these models but their similarities, which still exemplify prisons today: the emphasis on isolation (with prisons being organized on the cell model), labor and surveillance" (p. 5).

Indeterminate Sentencing

In 1840, Captain Alexander Maconochie and Sir Walter Crofton of Scotland developed the idea of indeterminate sentencing, preparing offenders for release. Inmates could work their way to a less restrictive environment and be released on a conditional basis. This system led to the development of the parole system as we know it today (Seiter, 2011).

Criticisms

Even though most Europeans considered the U.S. system as the world standard, some were skeptical in their analysis. As early as the 1840s,

> studies in France decided that prisons do not reduce crime; rather detention causes recidivism. Many felt that prisons were only factories for free labor provided by the poor. Charles Dickens felt the...daily tampering with the mysteries of the brain to be immeasurably worse than any torture of the body. (Mauer, 2006, p. 5)

Marx wrote,

> If a man is shaped by his environment, his environment must be made human. If man is social by nature, he will develop his true nature only in society, and the power of his nature must be measured not by the power of the separate individual but the power of society. (as cited in Mauer, 2006, p. 7)

Did our penal system become nothing short of slave labor provided by the poor, void of training and rehabilitation?

Period of Transition: 1910–1960

According to Seiter (2011), the Reformatory Era led to increased vocational training and the production and sale of prison-made goods. These practices were soon challenged by organized labor as the country entered the Great Depression. With the passage of the Hawes-Cooper Act in 1929 and the Ashurst-Sumners Act in 1935, open-market sales of inmate goods became limited. Suddenly there was no marketplace for prison-made goods therefore inmates became idle and prison administrators lost a key revenue stream. From 1935 until 1960, prisons became overcrowded, resulting in prison riots. In the 1964 *Cooper v. Pate* decision, the United States established the "Hands Off" doctrine, allowing inmates the right to file complaints against correctional officers for cruel and inhumane punishment. Toward the end of this period, the term "penology" was replaced by the term "corrections."

Rehabilitation Era:1960–1980

In the early 1960s, the medical model became the dominant theory influencing prison and other correctional practices. According to Seiter (2006),

> Under the medical model, offenders were believed to be "sick," inflicted with problems that caused their criminality; they needed to be diagnosed and treated, and rehabilitative programs would resolve their problems and prepare them for release as "well" into the community, able to be productive and crime-free. (p. 24)

In the 1970s, the rehabilitation and medical model came under attack in publication titled, *What Works?—Questions and Answers About Prison Reform.* by Robert Martinson (1974). This publication reviewed more than 200 studies and found no consistent findings indicating that any single treatment program significantly reduced recidivism. The study provided statistical support for politicians pressured to be tough on crime to reduce funding for rehabilitative programs. During this period, programs lost funding, and parole was eliminated in several states.

Retributive Era: 1980–2000

These two decades marked the resurgence of the Retributive Era, where political leaders were forced to be tough on crime, thus creating tough sentencing laws. Rehabilitative programing was removed in most prisons, and public safety was the primary concern. While this retributive period may not be as harsh as the 17th century design, there was a return to the classical school of criminality, where tough punishments were believed to deter and prevent crime. In many ways, our country has come full circle.

The greatest increase in incarceration occurred during the Reagan administration in the 1980s. Even though the 500% increase in incarceration is partly due to economics, it was primarily precipitated by the political war on drugs. This period of incarceration was not intended to rehabilitate offenders, but to "incapacitate criminals through more severe punishment, including longer sentences, thereby bringing down the crime rate" (Mauer, 2006, p. 15).

THE ORIGINS OF DIRECT SUPERVISION

Ironically, as the new retributive period began, so did the concept of "direct supervision." Popularized in 1974, direct supervision began when the New York and Chicago Metropolitan Correctional Centers accepted their first inmates. The open architecture of these facilities provided greater and direct contact between inmates and staff. According to Wener (2006), today direct supervision is "found in hundreds of settings and accepted by the American Correctional Association and American Jail Association, the U.S. Bureau of Prisons, and many states and local corrections departments" (p. 21). Facilities specifically designed for direct supervision allow for residential-style décor and furnishings, and open units where officers walk and work together with inmates. Based on Wener's research, there are five key historical factors leading to the proliferation of direct supervision:

> the change in the role of the officer; the placement of the officer within the living unit, in contact with inmates; the decentralization of functions to the living units; the decision to apply "soft architecture" to inmate units; and the development of a formal set of principles for managing these systems" (p. 22)

Many jails and prisons built within the last 30 years contain elements of direct supervision, but most are not fully functional with "direct" supervision programs. This is in part due to political influences dictating public policy as well as the mindset of those running penal institutions. During the past 30 years, incapacitation has been the sentiment of the public and therefore the politicians. Public policy during this time has created overcrowding in the jails and prisons, many which are forced to release individuals early and unprepared for community reentry. Since most correctional officers were born, raised, and trained with the incapacitation model, how do we change a multigenerational mindset? Given the proper political environment, is it possible that the people within the system can provide the necessary leadership to make a change? As in the past, this is an opportunity for leaders to emerge to steer the correctional system on a different path. It is the authors' belief that the path should include a community-jailing model led by individuals who are invested in rehabilitation. By borrowing ideas from the community-oriented policing model, a new community-jailing model can emerge to better prepare individuals for successful community reentry, reduce recidivism, and improve public safety. First we need to explore the philosophical underpinnings of community-oriented policing.

COMMUNITY-ORIENTED POLICING PHILOSOPHY

The community-policing model requires policing agencies to reach out to key community stakeholders to participate in law enforcement efforts. Maintaining collaborative relationships with other governmental agencies, community and faith-based organizations, nonprofits, and for-profit companies helps share the burden of law enforcement, improves information sharing, and enhances public safety. Key to successful programs is proper officer recruitment and training, positive labor relations, and longer-term assignments. According to the U.S. Department of Justice (n.d., pp. 1–14), "Job descriptions should recognize community policing and problem-solving responsibilities and encourage the recruitment of officers who have a 'spirit of service,' instead of only a 'spirit of adventure'" (p. 9).

Leadership for Community-Oriented Policing

Encouraging community partnerships and engagement via frontline law enforcement leadership requires a fundamental shift in the sociocultural nuances of police officers who have remained driven by performance during the community policing era. In support of research (see Ellis & Normore, 2014a, 2014b), we argue this shift requires creative approaches to leadership throughout the police hierarchy and a challenge to the hierarchical model of policy implementation that sometimes conflicts with community policing. We further assert that collaboration between police leaders, correctional facilities, and a community through community-oriented policing is worth examining. Collaboration oftentimes is associated with empowerment, engagement, and building rapport and relationships. It is universally agreed that well-executed collaborative efforts can transform leadership, communities, and modern organizations into successful entities and can have resounding positive impact on job satisfaction, including healthy behaviors and attitudes in the workplace. Researchers have concluded that personnel in police departments who participate in community-oriented policing report higher job satisfaction (e.g., Winfree & Newbold, 1999).

While public safety and criminal justice systems in general are in constant transition, the components of community-oriented policing are also transforming. Communities seek myriad opportunities to connect to their police departments. In turn, police organizations want to reciprocate by seeking more trust and transparency to assist in fighting crime. As departments search for the best plans that unite the public and police, we fail to remember a basic concept. It is not plans, systems, or structures that dictate organizational success or failure; it is our people (Senge, 1990). Therefore, we must look for new ways of working with people, and new ways of encouraging leadership. Leading is about the relationships. The stronger the relationships, the more people are willing to challenge their assumptions while stretching their capacities. Such a statement begs the question: Might trust and transparency come from fostering better collaboration platforms between the police and public? If so, it stands to reason that all constituents with a vested interest in the service and protection of communities must deliberately and intentionally build rapport, model empathy, and build trust. It is relationships which bring true collaboration and connection.

In order to improve collaboration, law enforcement and correctional education leaders must first look at the group-development process to properly engage both employees and the community. From there, leaders are better primed to understand how small group settings provide opportunities to build rapport and create connection through empowerment, group dynamics, and building and sustaining rapport. In turn, more effective communication and community engagement are likely to result. In conjunction with earlier work on police leadership (see Ellis & Normore, 2014b), law enforcement agencies are primed to connect with their communities. While there has been much progress in establishing robust networks to exchange information, police leaders and officers in general can be effective at building effective and enduring relationships with the public. We believe community-oriented policing and networking coupled with reciprocity is the ultimate form of public safety for reducing crime and rates of recidivism. The network of collaboration a leader has is a marker of his/her influence that goes to the heart of the definition of leadership (see Ellis & Normore, 2014b).

TABLE 7.1 Similarities Between Direct Supervision and Community Policing

Direct Supervision Model	Community Policing
Direct contact between inmate and staff	Law enforcement reaching out and working collaboratively with community stakeholders
Officers work together with inmates	Recruitment of officers with a spirit of service instead of adventure
Decentralization of functions to living units	Providing more local control to local neighborhoods
Staff training	Staff training

If community policing has been so successful on the outside, why can't some of the key ideas be used inside penal institutions? Table 7.1 shows the similarities between direct supervision and community policing. Important to the success of these models are the people who run them. After all, the systems or structures do not dictate the success or failure of an organization; it is the people (Senge, 1990). Contact, collaboration, spirit of service, and local control are ideas that make both models successful.

COMMUNITY JAILING AND EDUCATION

Just like the community policing model, the local correctional officer is in control over his precinct (yard, dormitory, pod, or cell block). Remember Reed and Malloy from the *Adam 12* television series? They were the epitome of community policing. They knew every business owner, drug dealer, and prostitute. They knew their "beat" and for the most part, their community respected them. The Reed/Malloy team knew exactly who to go to get critical information and worked directly with the community they served. Likewise, the community jailer should know every inmate they supervise. Supervision is more than being available at count time—the correctional officer should serve as a case manager. He/she should know things such as the inmate's mental health needs, educational level, reentry goals, addiction issues, family issues, physical abuse issues, homelessness, and so on. The correctional officer needs to be actively engaged. Changing from a traditional correctional officer to a case manager is a difficult transition and not in the mindset of many entering the career.

Creating such a change needs to come from leaders willing to take a risk as well as officers willing to make a sacrifice. Fullan (1999) stated, "Top-down mandates and bottom-up energies need each other" (p. 19). The most successful rehabilitation programs in the jails and prisons are found where the staff buy into the process and take ownership of their educational area (see Choate & Normore, 2013; Choate, Normore, & Bates, 2012). In fact, they have a greater impact on reducing jail violence through positive interactions with inmates. Research on treatment in general has indicated that the working relationship between staff and the inmate accounts for almost one third of the change that occurs (Lambert, 1992). Officers are most successful when they "strike a balance between an enforcement and intervention role; clarify their role with the client; model pro-social behaviors, show empathy without diminishing accountability; and focus interactions on problem solving and addressing criminogenic needs" (Crime and Justice Institute at Community Resources for Justice, 2009, p. ix). Criminogenic refers to "producing or leading to crime or criminality" (www.merriam-webster.com/dictionary/criminogenic). Therefore, staff participation in teaching drug education, parenting, and relationship classes helps the inmate trust the system. In fact, a correctional officer who demonstrates the inclination and ability to address offender responsivity (ability to respond to programs) through nonjudgmental communication may well be the impetus for an offender to contemplate behavioral change (Christensen & Crime and Justice Institute, 2008, p. 17).

Providing a supportive environment through educational programs is not always part of the vision or psyche of the rookie or veteran staff. To a certain degree, it is not "cool" to participate in the deliverance of supportive programs such as education inside the jails and prisons. Christiansen and the Crime and Justice Institute (2008) assert "professionals within criminal justice systems seldom find agreement on correctional strategy and, therefore, often oppose one another in deed as well as perspective...As such, our system of criminal justice tends to be a system in name rather than practice" (p. 1). Hence, while the United States attempts substantial integration in particular areas (e.g., the midwestern U.S.), oftentimes the two systems of education and law enforcement inherently struggle to coexist (Normore & Fitch, 2011). Furthermore, "The biggest challenge in adopting better interventions is not identifying the interventions with the best evidence so much as it is changing our existing systems to appropriately support the new innovations" (Crime and Justice Institute at Community Resources for Justice, 2009, p. 1).

Christensen and the Crime and Justice Institute (2008) conducted research with the U.S. National Institute of Corrections to determine whether jails play a role in improving offender outcomes. Findings indicated that those who act in a "manner contrary to effective treatment will counter the effects of otherwise sound correctional treatment" (p. 7). Staff rotations can also be a barrier, not allowing correctional officers enough time to understand the needs of the inmates in their area. Furthermore, often night-shift staff is not fully aware of programs occurring in the day, therefore, creating friction between inmates and staff. Sometimes the old system of incapacitation interferes with rehabilitation. For example, an inmate might be studying all day diligently under the supervision of an officer working with the mindset of rehabilitation. An evening shift officer who believes in incapacitation might throw away the inmates work under the guise of "contraband." These inconsistencies are counterproductive and create confusion and sometimes violence.

EFFECTIVE EDUCATION PROGRAM COMPONENTS

Effective programs are behavior based and target as many criminogenic needs as possible (Latessa, 2006). According to Latessa (2006), behavioral programs might include "Structured social-learning programs where new skills are taught, and behaviors and attitudes are consistently reinforced; cognitive behavioral programs that target attitudes, values and beliefs, peers, substance abuse, anger, etc.; and family-based interventions that train family members appropriate behavioral techniques" (p. 524). Furthermore, effective education programs should prepare people for successful community reentry and employment.

A recent RAND Corporation study indicated that inmates participating in the most successful prison education programs had 43% lower odds of recidivating than inmates who did not. This translates into a reduction in the risk of recidivating of 13 percentage points (Davis, Bozick, Steele, Saunder, & Miles, 2013). These authors reiterate that the odds of obtaining employment postrelease among inmates who participated in correctional education (either academic or vocational programs) were 13% higher than the odds for those who had not participated. A recent L.A. County recidivism study conducted by Austin, Green, Harris, and Allen (2013) on those involved in rehabilitative programs revealed an average reconviction rate of 24% after 12 months of their release date—a substantial 12-point decrease from those who did not participate in programs.

Despite all efforts to program inmates in custody, barriers to successful reentry for offenders are many. Some barriers include difficulty in obtaining employment, acquiring housing, medical needs, and active substance abuse (Gunnison & Helfgott, 2010). A 5-year follow-up study of Indiana inmates provides clear evidence that employment and education levels are the significant predictors for recidivism (Lockwood, Nally, Ho, & Knutson, 2012). Gunnison and Helfgott (2010) found that the association with criminal peers is also a hindrance to successful reentry. Therefore, effective programs need to teach people "to become self-sufficient and help them to acquire the necessary and appropriate skills" (Schwartz & Levitas, 2011, para. 46). For many, reentry barriers are created or increased by substance abuse and addiction. The most recent California Department of Corrections recidivism report indicates "the combination of in-prison substance abuse programming and [completion of] aftercare results in the best outcome" (California Department of Corrections and Rehabilitation, 2011, p. 48).

The challenges to successful reentry create a need for proper management and follow-through with inmate case-management plans. Case-management plans should guide the inmate toward successful reentry, hence the need of committed officers on the inside. The inmate should work closely with staff and volunteers to ensure their basic reentry needs are met. Basic needs include housing, identification and social security cards, transportation, employment, further treatment, continuing education, and social services. In preparation for reentry, it is incumbent upon education program personnel to develop authentic education programs for improving teaching and learning for diverse learners from an interdisciplinary perspective. Such a program ought to be offered through substantive partnerships and engage with inmates in search of appropriate goals for improving educational outcomes that will strengthen the quality, accessibility, and cultural relevance of education programs for these potential students.

The program must develop incarcerated learners and leaders with knowledge and understanding, and who acknowledge and are sensitive to social and equity issues, culture, history, and economic challenges of the communities into which they reenter. These learners will need experiences to create lifelong learning opportunities that encourage and support the efforts of the incarcerated members to improve their quality of life and to meet their responsibilities through meaningful contributions to the communities in which they live and interact. The greatest educational challenge for many is to build learning environments that allow each of their members to obtain an education that creates good people that are knowledgeable and wise. For example, research indicates that within marginalized populations, high achievement in learning and motivation depend on the spiritual well-being of students, early attention to cognitive development, sense of identity, and social/cultural maturity (Sanchez & Stuckey, 1999). This belief incorporates the position that improved academic performance will not occur until other factors identified above are included as part of a comprehensive approach for nurturing and educating the whole human being.

WHY COMMUNITY JAILING?

Often those who advocate for rehabilitative programs are viewed as being "soft on crime" or called names such as "inmate lover" or "hug a thug." Even though the authors are not sworn officers, they have spent extended periods of time inside both county jails and state prisons. These experiences provided opportunities to work in a training capacity with both officers and inmates. It is the authors' opinion that providing rehabilitative programs is the best response to the current public safety issue. As stated in the beginning, 97% of the country's 2.2 million prisoners will get out. History has already taught us that punishment through retributive methods does not work—rehabilitation is the only alternative. There are three compelling reasons to provide rehabilitative programming: improved public safety, reduce jail/prison violence, and cost savings. Improved Public Safety

According to Mentor and Wilkinson (2005), "Research consistently demonstrate[s] that quality education is one of the most effective forms of crime prevention" (p. 1). Reduced recidivism leads to reduced criminality on the streets and better public safety. Reduced criminality equates to fewer victims in our communities.

Lower Inmate Violence

Serin (2005) explains, "Correctional programming is not a 'getting soft' approach to crime rather it is holding inmates accountable for their criminal behavior and providing ways for them to become pro-social" (p. 4). Correctional programming "reduces recidivism by rates of 20-40%, but it must adhere to strict criteria in order to be effective" (p. 15). For example, "offenders who participate in certain types of institutional or community-based treatment programs are less likely to be repeat offenders than the nonparticipants" (Dilulio, 1991). If we were to learn from our past, it seems that we would embrace a practice of offender rehabilitation designed to teach new cognitive skills— methods that provide alternative courses to steer offenders away from poor decisions that have resulted in their repeat offending (Christensen & Crime and Justice Institute, 2008, p. 5). Jail violence and "use of force" has also been impacted by providing educational programs. In fact, in the year 2012, inmate versus staff assaults were reduced from 171 the prior year to 57 in 2012 (Los Angeles County Sheriff's Department, 2013, p. 2). Since staff force is usually used in response to inmate violence, staff force has also declined.

A recent study of data regarding inmate violence inside the Los Angeles County jails indicates that during the 2012/2013 fiscal year, the overall rate of inmate-on-inmate assaults was 12.8% in the jail system. In areas where extensive rehabilitative programming occurs, jail violence percentages dropped to 3% (Austin et al., 2013). It is evident throughout the system that wherever there is rehabilitative programming, there is less violence inside the jails. Safer jails also provide a more conducive learning environment for rehabilitative education.

Cost Savings

Although this may seem like a costly endeavor, "the return on investment for education programs more than justifies the modest expense devoted to them" (Austin et al., 2013). A recent RAND Corporation report states that for correctional education programs to break even, they need to reduce the 3-year reincarceration rate by about two percentage points (Davis et. al., 2013). Interestingly, the RAND findings show that participation in correctional education programs reduces the risk of recidivism by 13 percentage points three years after release from prison.

SOCIAL JUSTICE LEADERSHIP: EMPIRICAL OBSERVATIONS

As stated earlier, the authors have had extensive experience working inside correctional facilities. The following observations help ground our theory that correctional programming is more effective if the officers on duty are part of the process, hence creating a community jailing environment. In 2013, the authors published a study conducted using inmate focus groups inside the Los Angeles County Jail system (Choate & Normore, 2013). In conducting this research, they examined jail violence, recidivism, and leadership from the perspective of the inmate leader. Two focus groups of programmed inmates were interviewed to gain a deeper understanding of the social phenomenon of the role of leadership in jail transformation. Two male inmate focus group interviews were conducted, scribed, and coded. Each group contained six inmates and lasted approximately 60 minutes. Staff leadership was one of the central themes that emerged from this study.

During the interview, interesting phenomena occurred. The inmates thanked the jail leadership for replacing the custody staff with "nicer" people. Since the custody staff was the same rank and file as usual, we wondered why they thought the staff was different and even replaced. It was not the jail leadership that changed the custody staff, but the inmate themselves who changed the "heart" of the custody staff, thus changing the staff's attitudes and behaviors. This change of heart and attitude could only take place through experiencing the success of the program over a period. Yes, most of the staff who started out as nonbelievers are now participating and making a difference in the lives of the inmates. Perhaps the staff was changing their "moral purpose" and providing "empathy and relationships across diverse groups" (Fullan, 1999, p. 2)

Common characteristics of leadership found amongst the staff were trust and genuine concern. Thomas Aquinas said, "One who is trusted cannot sustain a reciprocal relationship with others. Without reciprocity of purpose, leadership itself will not exist" (Zoller, Normore, & Harrison, 2013, p. 3). The greatest trust and unconditional love was found with those staff members who sacrificed their personal time to help the inmates. Some quotes from the inmates were as follows: "What about the guy who hobbles in with a cane at 7:30 Sunday mornings to teach us?" "Officer D. changed his work schedule just to be able to help us." "Officer A. comes in on his Saturdays so we can see our kids." "Chaplain J. has cancer and he still comes in to help us." "Our teacher's son was in the hospital and he still came to work." "Ms. C's brother was missing and she showed up to help us." "Officer M. cried in front of me and said she prays for us." "Officers say goodnight to us."

One can surmise from the above statements that custody leadership is more about showing care through actions. The building of trust is critical as it pertains to how the inmate interacts with custody. This not only impacts the inmate's ability to progress in their education but also reduces unnecessary use of force incidents. Another LASD Deputy provides a perfect example. He states, "Use of force has never been an issue with me because I talk to the people."

While all California prisons provide some form of rehabilitative programming, a few are taking a leadership role to break the tide of incapacitation. For example, Ironwood State Prison in Blyth, California, recently celebrated their success with the production of a TEDx event. In touring this facility, the enthusiasm for rehabilitative programming was palpable from all levels of staff. Inmates helped create the first state prison with an online Associates of Arts degree through video conferencing where hundreds have completed their schooling. Warden Dave Long provided the ultimate example of leadership by enrolling in college with the inmates to receive his own degree. This is community jailing at its finest. San Quentin State Prison has taken advantage of the plentiful volunteer force in the San Francisco Bay Area by providing college preparation and Associates of Arts degree programs through Patton University.

FINAL REFLECTIONS

Recognition that the role of leaders in any organization is at least in part to advocate on behalf of traditionally marginalized and poorly served citizens carries a corollary contention that leaders must increase their awareness of various explicit and implicit forms of oppression, develop an intent to subvert the dominant paradigm, and finally, act as a committed advocate for educational change that makes a meaningful and positive change in the education and lives of traditionally marginalized and oppressed populations (Jean-Marie, Normore, & Brooks, 2009). From a traditional standpoint, education researchers have introduced the concept of critical pedagogy. Critical pedagogy includes practices that are designed to raise learners' critical consciousness about oppressive social conditions (Freire, 1998). Freire argues that critical pedagogy focuses on personal "liberatory education" through the development of critical consciousness. Serving as a catalyst to the commitment to social justice liberatory education attempts to empower all learners to engage in critical dialog that critiques and challenges oppressive social conditions and to envision and work toward a more just society. Such strategies can help current and future correctional leaders to confront transformative and changing social conditions and historical contexts for leading jails. Further, it provides the opportunity to analyze and reexamine federal policies and practices that have caused a loss of dignity and ability for many incarcerated to adapt to the demands of modern society, partly because of the failure of prison systems to prepare inmates for successful reentry.

Concepts about knowledge and learning support critical pedagogy and a more social constructivist approach to teaching for social justice. Understanding how knowledge is constructed is critical. Based on the work of Jean-Marie et al. (2009), knowledge is not something that exists outside of language and the social subjects who use it. It is a socially constructed process and one that cannot be divorced from the learners' social context. It is constructed by "doing" and from social-development experience. An effective instructor of the incarcerated makes sure she understands the students' preexisting conceptions and guides activities to address and build on them, thereby preparing students to make social changes; create space and spaces for trust; and nurture participatory, equitable, and just relationships rather than simply managing programs and services (Winfree & Newbold, 1999). Such strategies facilitate the opportunity for empowerment rather than simply trying to "deliver it." Researchers argue that critical pedagogy also has a more collective political component, in that critical consciousness is positioned as the necessary first step of a larger collective political struggle to challenge and (Giroux, 1996) transform oppressive social conditions and to create a more egalitarian society.

Within a culture of social and cultural oppression, inmates learn about competition, unequal self-worth, and psychological warfare. They also learn that covert relational aggression is a viable and useful strategy to take with them into the outside world. For example, bullying is part of a curriculum of dominance and oppression in which some inmates, both perpetrators and witnesses, have learned that aggression is an acceptable form of dehumanization, while other inmates, both victims and witnesses, have learned docility and silence as strategies for survival (Apple, 1990). A profoundly personal exploration of a reentry approach ought to be fully aligned with, and driven by, deeply held values where meaningful curriculum allows for understanding of deeply personal core of their own leadership and how well they can adapt to change once released.

We have an aging and culturally biased correctional education discourse. Evidence suggests our antiquated styles and methods of jailing are creating hindrances in successfully preparing inmates for reentry. The ultimate goal is to reduce crime in general and completely close the school-to-prison pipeline. However, this challenge will take time and collaboration on part of myriad constituents, including state legislatures, schools, communities, and an abundance of resources. Research indicates that prison-based education, education-based incarceration, and correctional education take a penetrating look at the needs and challenges of society's disenfranchised— the denizens of our streets, the emotionally and physically incarcerated, our children in juvenile halls and in unsettled homes. From a social justice perspective, we believe it is incumbent to encourage public awareness of the causes that underlie the destructive cycles plaguing these populations, including the abuse and neglect that cycle through generations (Choate et al., 2012). It therefore stands to reason that when effectively addressed through education, the economic burden on society is lightened and an advocacy to increase understanding engenders a moral and humane response. Instilling the premise of providing education through community jailing within correctional facilities and jails is a positive response which focuses on providing inmates the skills necessary to live productive, crime-free lives outside of custody. In turn, we contend that this can lead to a reduction in crime, a reduction in recidivism rates, and a possible response to reducing the school-to-prison pipeline.

REFERENCES

Apple, M. W. (1990). *The hidden curriculum and the nature of conflict in ideology and curriculum.* New York, NY: Routledge.

Austin, J., Green, J., Harris, R., & Allen, R. (2013). Evaluation of education-based incarceration programs. Los Angeles County Sheriff. In J. Austin, R. Ocker, & R. Allen (Eds.),.*Alternatives to incarceration plan for Los Angeles County: A safer and smaller jail system* (pp. 1–41). Denver, CO: JFA Institute.

Bogotch, I. E. (2005, November). *Social justice as an educational construct: Problems and possibilities.* Paper presented at the annual meeting of the University Council of Educational Administration, Nashville, TN.

Boske, C., & Diem, S. (Eds.). (2012). *Global leadership for social justice: Taking it from the field to practice.* Bingley, UK: Emerald.

California Department of Corrections and Rehabilitation. (2011, November 23). *2011 adult institutions outcome evaluation report.* Retrieved from http://www.cdcr.ca.gov/Adult_Research_Branch/Research_Documents/ARB_FY_0607_Recidivism_Report_(11-23-11).pdf

Choate, B., & Normore, A. H. (2013). Leadership's role in reducing jail violence and recidivism. In A. H. Normore & N. Erbe (Eds.), *Collective efficacy as a multidisciplinary approach to leadership development: International perspectives* (pp. 163–182). Bingley, UK: Emerald.

Choate, B., Normore, A. H., & Bates, D. (2012). Maximizing Education Reaching Individual Transformation (M.E.R.I.T.): A groundbreaking leadership development program for inmates in Los Angeles County Sheriff's Department. *Law Enforcement Today.* Retrieved from http://lawenforcementtoday.com/2012/10/17/maximizing-education-reaching-individual-transformation-merit/#comment-2487

Christensen, G. E., & Crime and Justice Institute. (2008). *Our system of corrections: Do jails play a role in improving offender outcomes?* Washington, DC: U.S. Department of Justice, National Institute of Corrections.

Cooper v. Pate, 378 U.S. 546 (1964). Retrieved from http://en.wikipedia.org/wiki/Cooper_v._Pate

Crime and Justice Institute at Community Resources for Justice. (2009). *Implementing evidence-based policy and practice in community corrections* (2nd ed.). Washington, DC: National Institute of Corrections.

Dantley, M. E., & Tillman, L. C. (2006). Social justice and moral transformative leadership. In C. Marshall & M. Oliva (Eds.), *Leadership for social justice: Making revolutions in education* (pp. 16–30). Boston, MA: Pearson.

Davis, L., Bozick, R., Steele, J., Saunders, J., & Miles, J. RAND Corporation. (2013). *Evaluating the effectiveness of correctional education.* Washington, DC: U.S. Department of Justice, Bureau of Justice Assistance.

Dilulio, J. J. (1991). No escape: The future of American corrections. New York, NY: Basic.

Ellis, B., & Normore, A. H. (2014a, May). Police leadership: Connecting with communities through a partnership initiative. *Peace Officers Research Association of California Law Enforcement.* Retrieved from http://porac.org/

Ellis, B., & Normore, A. H. (2014b). Community-oriented policing: The power of collaboration. *Law Enforcement Today.* Retrieved from http://www.lawenforcementtoday.com/2014/03/09/community-oriented-policing-the-power-of-collaboration/

Freire, P. (1998). *Pedagogy of freedom: Ethics, democracy and civic courage.* Lanham, MD: Rowman & Littlefield.

Fullan, M. (1999). *Change forces the sequel* (2nd ed.). Bridgeport, CT: Buchanan.

Giroux, H. A. (1996). *Fugitive cultures: Race, violence and youth.* New York, NY: Routledge.

Gunnison, E., & Helfgott, J. (2010, March 12). Factors that hinder offender reentry success: A view from community corrections officers. *International Journal of Offender Therapy and Offender Comparative Criminology, 55*(2), 287–304. Retrieved from http://www.ncbi.nlm.nih.gov/pubmed/20228319

Jean-Marie, G., Normore, A. H., & Brooks, J. (2009). Leadership for social justice. *Leadership Education, 4*(1). Retrieved from http://www.ucea.org/current-issues/

Lambert, M. J. (1992). Psychotherapy outcome research: Implications for integrative and eclectical therapists. In J. C. Norcross & M. R. Goldfried (Ed.), *Handbook of psychotherapy integration* (pp. 94–129). New York, NY: Basic.

Latessa, E. J. (2006). What works in reducing recidivism? *University of St. Thomas Law Journal, 3*(3), article 7. Retrieved from http://ir.stthomas.edu/cgi/viewcontent.cgi?article=1095&context=ustlj

Lockwood, S., Nally, J., Ho, T., & Knutson, K. (2012). The effect of correctional education on post release and recidivism: A 5-year follow-up study in the state of Indiana. *Crime and Delinquency, 58*(3), 380–396.

Los Angeles County Sheriff's Department. (2013, February). *Education based incarceration: Creating a life worth living.* Retrieved from http://shq.lasdnews.net/content/uoa/EBU/March2013-EBI_CreatingALifeWorthLiving.pdf

Maguire, K., & Pastore, A. (2006). *Sourcebook of criminal justices statistics.* Retrieved from www.albany.edu/sourcebook/pdf/t657.pdf

Marshall, C., & Oliva, M. (2006). *Leadership for social justice: Making revolutions in education,* Boston, MA: Pearson.

Martinson, R. (1974). What works?—Questions and answers about prison reform. *The Public Interest, 35,* 22–54.

Mauer, M. (2006). *Race to incarcerate: The sentencing project* (2nd ed.). New York, NY: New York Press.

Mentor, K., & Wilkinson, M. (2005). Literacy. In M. Bosworth (Ed.), *Encyclopedia of prisons and correctional facilities* (pp. 555–558). Thousand Oaks, CA: Sage.

Normore, A. H., & Brooks, J. S. (2014). *Educational leadership for social justice: Views from the social sciences.* Chapel Hill, NC, Information Age.

Normore, A. H., & Fitch, B. D. (2011). *Leadership in education, corrections, and law enforcement: A commitment to ethics, equity, and excellence.* Bingley, UK: Emerald.

Petteruti, A., & Walsh, N. (2008, April 1). Jailing communities: The impact of jail expansion and effective public safety strategies. *Justice Policy Institute.* Retrieved from http://www.justicepolicy.org/research/1946

Sanchez, J., & Stuckey, M. E. (1999, Summer). From boarding schools to the multicultural classroom: The intercultural politics of education, assimilation, and American Indians. *Teacher Education Quarterly, 26*(3). Retrieved from http://www.teqjournal.org/sample_issue/article_5.htm

Schwartz, S., & Levitas, L. (2011, March, 22). Restorative justice for veterans: The San Francisco Sheriff's Department's Community of Veterans Engaged in Restoration (COVER). *The Free Library.* Retrieved from http://www.thefreelibrary.com/'Restorative justice for veterans: the San Francisco Sheriff's...-a0275849594

Seidl, B. (2007). Working with communities to explore and personalize culturally relevant pedagogies: Push, double images, and raced talk. *Journal of Teacher Education, 6*(2), 168–183.

Seiter, R. (2011). *Corrections: An introduction* (3rd ed.). New York, NY: Pearson.

Senge, P. (1990). *The fifth discipline: The art and practice of the learning organization.* New York, NY: Doubleday.

Serin, R., & Crime and Justice Institute. (2005). *Evidence-based practice: Principles for enhancing correctional results in prisons.* Washington, DC: U.S. Department of Justice, National Institute of Correction.

U.S. Department of Justice, Office of Community Oriented Policing Services. (n.d.). *Community policing defined.* Retrieved from http://www.cops.usdoj.gov/pdf/vets-to-cops/e030917193-CP-Defined.pdf

Wener, R. (2006, March/April,). Direct supervision: Evolution and revolution. *American Jails,* 21–24.

Winfree L., & Newbold, G. (1999). Community policing and the New Zealand Police: Correlates of attitudes toward the work world in a community-oriented national police organization. *Policing: An International Journal of Police Strategies & Management, 22*(4), 589–618

Zoller, K., Normore, A., & Harrison, B. (2013). Leadership thinking: A discipline of the mind for the effective law enforcement supervisor. *Journal of Authentic Leadership in Education, 2*(4), 1–10.

CHAPTER 8

A CULTURALLY RESPONSIVE FRAMEWORK FOR SOCIAL JUSTICE

Mere Berryman
The University of Waikato

Ann Nevin
Arizona State University

Suzanne SooHoo
Chapman University

Therese Ford
The University of Waikato

ABSTRACT

A pressing challenge in education, which has been driven by and in turn continues to drive the ongoing and seemingly immutable educational disparities, can be associated with the power imbalances in classrooms and schools as a result of increasing ethnic, cultural, and language diversity disrupting the composition of the dominant mainstream. As our education systems become more culturally, ethnically, and linguistically diverse, rather than benefiting

Inclusive Practices and Social Justice Leadership for Special Populations in Urban Settings, pages 143–164
Copyright © 2015 by Information Age Publishing

and learning from each other, we still expect all students to be represented within the same curriculum, pedagogy, and testing regimen, or we form separate enclaves and the divide becomes even wider. When diverse students have physical and/or learning disabilities, these situations are further exacerbated and problematized. In this chapter, the authors theorize within an alternative framework that we have termed "culturally responsive inclusion." Based on key understandings derived from Kaupapa Māori and Freirean philosophies as delineated in *Culturally Responsive Methodologies* (Berryman, SooHoo, & Nevin, 2013), we encourage a framework where establishing respectful relationships of interdependence with people is central to both human dignity and praxis. A culturally responsive framework such as this challenges traditional notions of the professional expert working with objectivity; instead it opens up spaces that call for engagement through the establishment of relational and interdependent discourses.

For populations viewed as diverse, education can often result in belittlement and marginalization. In this chapter, the authors consider research from both New Zealand and the United States in an attempt to better understand some of the issues related to inclusion that continue to be misunderstood and unresolved. We discuss how a more responsive and relational response to the wide spectrum of student differences and diversity might mediate more socially just and inclusive classroom environments. Our findings suggest a more critical and indigenous, relational response for inclusion, which, in line with our recent work on research methodologies, we have termed "relational and culturally responsive" (Berryman et al., 2013).

HISTORICAL PERSPECTIVES ON INCLUSIVE PRACTICES

We are an international team of scholars from New Zealand and the United States who have long been concerned about a pressing challenge in education that has been driven by and in turn continues to drive the ongoing and seemingly immutable educational disparities for marginalized students in both our countries. These disparities can be associated with the power imbalances, often perpetuated in classrooms and schools as a result of increasing ethnic, cultural, and language diversity, that disrupt the composition of the dominant mainstream. As our education community's systems become more culturally, ethnically, and linguistically diverse, rather than benefiting and learning from each other, the systems still expect all students to be represented within the same curriculum, pedagogy, and testing regimen or educators form separate enclaves and the divide among groups becomes even wider (Berryman, 2008). When diverse students have physical and/or learning disabilities, these situations are further exacerbated and problematized. Within their schools, communities, and society, this rift is the reality for many diverse populations in the countries that we each represent (e.g., Klinger et al., 2005; Sullivan, 2011).

In New Zealand, social justice and inclusion are often framed within the Treaty of Waitangi (Ballard, 2007). This treaty document, signed in 1840, promised power sharing and self-determination for the indigenous Māori tribes and for all other peoples who came to reside in this country. Today, like many indigenous peoples across the world, social justice is far from the reality for Māori. For example, the educational experience of many Māori continues to result in participation and achievement disparities between themselves and non-Māori students, many of whom are of European descent (known as Pākehā).

In the United States, the need for more socially just and inclusive schooling is evident in the continued labeling, tracking, and segregated instruction for students of color, students with disabilities, students from indigenous cultures, students whose families have recently immigrated, students who speak languages other than English, and students who come from impoverished families (Banks, 2002). Sixty years ago in 1954, U.S. courts ruled that separating children on the basis of race was unconstitutional (Brown vs. Board of Education, 1954) and the ensuing Civil Rights Movement encouraged parents of children with disabilities to seek equal educational treatment for their children, culminating in the Education for All Handicapped Children Act of 1975 (P.L.94-142)—subsequently reauthorized as the Individuals with Disabilities Act (IDEA, 1990, 1997). Currently, national legislation such as the Individuals with Disabilities Education Improvement Act (IDEIA, 2004) and its subsequent amendments mandate that students with disabilities be granted access to the curriculum and instruction of their nondisabled peers. Nevertheless, the most compelling evidence comes from school enrolment data that shows that students of color (e.g., Black, Hispanic, Asian) and students from culturally and linguistically diverse families continue to be overrepresented in special-education classrooms and underrepresented in classrooms for the gifted and talented (Sullivan, 2011). Collier (2012) raises the same concern for students from indigenous families, that is, Native American, Alaskan and Hawaiian native populations. Citing data reported by the Alliance for Excellent Education (2004), there continues to be "a great deal of disproportionality remaining in the placement of culturally and linguistically diverse students in special education" (p. 9).

CURRENT PERSPECTIVES ON INCLUSIVE EDUCATION

These educational inequities, which are mirrored by the experiences of the Māori people in New Zealand, contribute to the increasing division between many indigenous and nonindigenous groups in wider society.

Disparities such as these are often embedded in historical discourses of *pathology* and *deficit* (Bishop & Glynn, 1999; Shields, Bishop, & Mazawi, 2005). While recognizing the strong influence of deficit discourses such as these, this chapter focuses mainly on what can be achieved when educators focus on discourses of their own personal and professional *agency* (Bishop, Berryman, Tiakiwai, & Richardson, 2003).

In New Zealand, the period from 1980 to 1990 saw major economic reform from the neoliberal program of deregulation and commercialization of state activities in the health, education, and welfare systems (Butterworth, & Butterworth, 1998). One result of these reforms was that schools began to operate as businesses (Peters, Marshall, & Massey, 1994). However, it also became clear in this period that the educational disparities identified between Māori and non-Māori had not been improved (Walker, 2004). Despite Walker (2004) and others linking Māori educational disparity to the unjust social order that had arisen from the colonial experience, deficit discourses of Māori student's inability to learn continued to be linked to low socioeconomic status (SES) and renewed calls by mainstream educators and politicians to close the achievement gap.

During this period, researchers continued to assert that a close link existed between SES and students' ability to learn and achieve (Chapple, Jefferies, & Walker, 1997; Harker & Nash, 1990; Nash, 1993). For example, Harker and Nash (1990) found that "Maori children under-achieve when compared with Pākehā children because of quantitative differences in the cultural, that is literary, resources possessed by their families" (p. 39). The third report on Progress toward Closing Social and Economic Gaps between Māori and non-Māori (Te Pūni Kōkiri, 1998) confirmed that educational disparities were still present on most of the social, health, and educational indicators. The then-Prime Minister, Helen Clark, chaired the Cabinet gaps committee herself, seeing the need to close the gaps as a social equity priority . The opposition party leader argued that equity for Māori, while neglecting non-Māori underachievers, was divisive. The media joined in the argument with discourses of "endless handouts to Māori," and discussion regarding closing the gaps was dropped. The focus turned to Treaty settlements and the negotiation of Iwi (tribal) education partnerships (Berryman, 2008). The Labour-led government argued for Treaty settlements and devolution of funds to Māori groups as capacity building, thus enabling Māori to close the gaps themselves (Walker, 2004).

At the same time, Māori aspirations for economic and educational agency and self-determination, as defined by the Treaty of Waitangi, resulted in the founding of a kaupapa Māori system of education that grew from outside of the state system. G. H. Smith (1997) suggested that, "Māori communities armed with the new critical understandings of the shortcomings of the state and structural analyses began to assert transformative actions to deal with the twin crisis of language demise and educational under achievement themselves" (p. 171). Te Wānanga o Raukura (an iwi tertiary setting) and Te Kōhanga Reo (Māori language, Early Childhood settings), for example, were kaupapa Māori educational settings, developed as a response to the loss of Māori language and cultural identity. The Waipa Kōkiri Centre (a Māori tertiary setting), also recognized the need to enhance employment opportunities for Māori who had left school with no formal qualifications (Walker, 2004). In other words, Māori are leaving school with no formal qualifications and thus they needed help to get jobs. Māori at all levels of education had begun to exercise their agency and determination in a purposeful and strategic way.

ALTERNATIVE PERSPECTIVES

In this section, the authors raise two alternative perspectives that can provide insight into inclusive education practice: the influence of well-prepared teachers and the influence of the hidden curriculum. In strong contrast to researchers who traditionally argued that low SES and resource and cultural deprivation will almost certainly result in poor educational achievement (Chapple et al., 1997; Harker & Nash, 1990; Nash, 1993), Ministry of Education research undertaken by Hattie (1999, 2003a, 2003b) and Alton-Lee (2003, 2006) demonstrated that the most important systemic influence on student's educational achievement was the effectiveness of their teachers. While both Hattie and Alton-Lee had also considered the traditionally perceived influences on learning and achievement, such as whānau (families), home community, pedagogy, teachers, school systems, and the students themselves, their analysis showed that with effective teachers, low socioeconomic settings were not immutable in terms of Māori students' achievement. Similarly, in the United States, researchers such as Linda Darling-Hammond and others argued for better preparation and higher standards for teachers (e.g., Darling-Hammond, 2001) as a way to close the achievement gap.

One of the ways education systems marginalize and minoritize children and youth is through what has become known as the hidden curriculum. The hidden curriculum, defined as "the unintended outcomes of the schooling process" (p. 183) by McLaren in 1989, continues to persist 24 years later, making one wonder how *unintended* this curriculum is. Stealthy and strong, the hidden curriculum maintains an invisible and powerful presence in schooling as it runs alongside the official curriculum. Although it is not officially named, one witnesses its existence by the damage it does to students and families, in particular those who are from minority populations. The features of the hidden curriculum are domination and marginalization. It is the force and conditions that can push students to the edge of survival and/or out of schools completely. The hidden curriculum includes codes of conduct, classroom organization, grouping practices, teaching and learning styles, and what is intentionally omitted in curriculum—essentially everything outside of the official course materials—policies, structures, and practices that alienate students from their own authentic ways of knowing, being, and becoming. It is the curriculum that "no teacher explicitly teaches but that all students learn" (Banks, 2002, p. 20).

The hidden curriculum can perpetuate situations where some benefit while others are disenfranchised. The hidden curriculum is where we learn that "some of you are better than others" (Bigelow, 1995, p.165). Durkheim (1965) and Bourdieu (1977) maintain that schools reproduce the existing social order rather than change or reduce class-based discrepancies. Oakes (1985) attributes social reproduction of social class to the tracking, sorting, and streaming of students into ability groups. Although tracking was originally meant to equalize educational opportunity (Deschenes, Cuban, & Tyack, 2001), we are not surprised that students labeled as "at risk" as kindergarteners are also "at risk" as high school seniors (if they are still in school), thus debunking the meritocracy myth. Deil-Amen and DeLuca (2010) accuse school systems of perpetuating an educational underclass by providing a "structured lack of opportunities" (p. 29) to minority students.

SooHoo (2006) notes that school bullying is not a part of the official curriculum, yet generation after generation of school children learn who counts and who does not through their encounters with bullying—both from the bullying itself and how it is prioritized and dealt with by adults. Some students are left with lifetime "hidden curriculum" scars from the lessons they learned from bullies on the playground, in the halls, on the buses, and behind the locker room doors (SooHoo, 2006). Scholars and practitioners have a responsibility to ask what social, political, or economic forces sustain the hidden curriculum and what can be done to expose this malignancy in schools.

In New Zealand Indigenous Māori researchers such as Bishop and Berryman (2006) and L. T. Smith (1999) and non-Māori, Pākehā researchers such as Ballard (2007, 2008) argue schools were not built with Māori students' education success as Māori in mind (Ministry of Education, 2013). Rather, Consedine and Consedine (2005) suggest that the education system in New Zealand began as a means of preparing the Indigenous Māori (savage other) to take their rightful place in New Zealand society as second-class citizens. Thus, education aimed to assimilate and prepare Māori students for the lower socioeconomic classes of colonial society (Berryman, 2008). Today, assessment-based streaming of students, as measured by a narrow band of tests, a practice common in many New Zealand secondary schools, continues to perpetuate a situation that is well recognized of upper-stream classes that are disproportionally full of White students and lower-stream classes that are disproportionately full of brown students.

In place of the word Māori, one could replace different words in the U.S. context: Blacks, Latinos, Muslim, sexual minority youth, or immigrants. Across these populations, children with identified special needs are likely to be assigned to the lowest-stream classrooms, with many schools providing special segregated classrooms to separate them even further (e.g., Klingner et al., 2005; Sullivan, 2011). Again, one is left to wonder, who then were schools built for? As noted by Blankenship and Lilly (1981), "Throughout history, education has been for the elite and educational practices have reflected an elitist orientation" (p. 18). Underscoring this situation, Deschenes et al. (2001) assert "that schools as currently organized are much better calibrated to serve privileged groups than groups placed on the margin" (p. 527).

EDUCATIONAL LEADERSHIP

Derived from the above discussion, we have identified some of the issues that continue to go unresolved for meeting the needs of marginalized populations either within school or community settings. First, school leadership and staff often choose "treating all children the same" often in the name of egalitarianism and being fair to all instead of addressing diversity. Second, school personnel tend to remain ignorant of skin color and culture. Third, there exists a lack of understanding about personal identity and how it is intertwined with language of origin, color/race, ethnicity, and culture. Fourth, there is a prevailing belief that some groups of students are less prepared or less able to fully participate and succeed in the range of curriculum activities in contrast to the belief that all children have special needs.

We argue that school leaders must disrupt and change the status quo that all too often perpetuates student marginalization and underachievement. In order to do this, leaders need to understand that schools have traditionally had a role in reproducing the fabric of the society in which they are located, that leaders are part of the power base, and that, under the school's mandated policies and within their own spheres of influence, school leaders have the power and the responsibility to make more of a difference for all marginalized students.

How leadership is undertaken and evolves in schools can accelerate or hinder the social change required to address these disparities. In considering different theories of leadership, the notion that an individual leader might work largely from one model or style has led to descriptions of leadership practice according to types (e.g., Devecchi & Nevin, 2010). It may be more useful however to think of leadership from different perspectives as leaders work within different contexts. While acknowledging that the role of leaders in pursuing inclusion is complex, in this chapter we are proposing leadership from two different perspectives—culturally responsive leadership and transformative leadership.

CULTURALLY RESPONSIVE LEADERSHIP

In Culturally Responsive Methodologies (Berryman et al., 2013), the authors drew from explanations of critical theory and kaupapa Māori theory to position research methodology within notions of freedom from domination, self-determination, and relationships. Critical pedagogy (Freire, 1998; McLaren, 2015) asks us to address power differentials and unlearn our hegemonized notions of power. This process means questioning rather than accepting the concept of the few having power and privilege over the masses. It also means believing that through individual and community development, empowerment, and self-determination, we can confront social injustices (Griffiths, 1998). If an idea (and resulting conditions) has been socially constructed, it can be socially deconstructed, that is, concepts that have dehumanized individuals such as racism, can be analyzed and replaced with anti-oppressive theories (e.g, Berryman et al., 2013) of hope. One can identify a new liberatory free space—a symbolic space without mental shackles that prevent us from humanizing our previous existence. One can envision possibility and thus reverse hegemony. With this new-found clarity of social and spiritual self-determination, we can forge new pathways with others by engaging in dialog and praxis toward social good, equity, and the reduction of hegemonic control by the privileged.

Similarly, kaupapa Māori theory (G. H. Smith, 1999) emerged as a simultaneous grassroots movement of resistance to the dominant colonial stance and a movement of revitalization of Māori cultural processes and practices. Forging new relationships in a Kaupapa Māori cultural context requires participants to undergo formal rituals of encounter and to respect these new relationships and the cultural preservation of Māori autonomy, or the autonomy of any other cultural group with whom one seeks to engage. Rather than imposing ourselves upon the hosts, we must call upon traditional rituals of encounter—act as visitors by respecting and adhering to the cultural protocols and language of the hosts. In this way, one is more likely to broker, more appropriately, a new and acceptable role in that space.

While the key difference between kaupapa Māori theory and critical theory lies in the epistemologies from which each emerged and subsequently the primacy and degree of emphasis of relationships and power, there are many similarities. Both theoretical traditions value human dignity and strive for reciprocity of voice; both honor the necessity of relationships and dialog; both desire multicultural revitalization; both cultivate conditions for a social and political consciousness necessary for reform; both resist hierarchical power structures; both strive for epistemological pluralism; and both envision power (agency) over one's own destiny, especially for those who are marginalized. Relational, dialogical, and narrative principles provide the means to engage within these two theoretical frameworks. Finally, both theories are based on interlocking experiences and understandings of oppression and loss. However great the similarities in ideologies and principles, they defy essentialism and transcend separate categories through contextual intersectionalities.

Therefore culturally responsive leaders involve themselves in coming to know each other in ways that are dialogical and relational. Culturally responsive leaders might consider coming to know and developing a new cultural praxis. Developing a new cultural praxis requires leaders to name and understand how we are complicit in practices that exclude, similar to Danforth's notion of viewing, "ourselves as inseparable from the dynamics that create injustice and suffering" (Danforth, 1997, p. 4). Leaders who disrupt traditional discourses of segregation and marginalization also engage in relational and dialogical consciousness and interactions, are willing to understand and attest to both sides of an issue, and understand that praxis that supports marginalization and exclusion must be resisted and replaced with praxis to promote an identity of becoming, belonging, and inclusion, if they are to promote epistemological pluralism (Berryman et al., 2013). These tenets are supported by Paulo Freire's (1998) work on conscientization, dialog, and transformative praxis. "Conscientization is the active process through which a critical understanding of the social-political-economical circumstances is gained that enables one to actively change oppressive circumstances" (Cruz, 2013, p. 173). Conscientization is maintained through a dialectic relationship between action and reflection as well as dialog.

TRANSFORMATIVE LEADERSHIP

Transformative leadership is advanced within a culturally responsive leadership approach. Shields (2010) identifies three different perspectives of leadership for change: transactional, transformational, and transformative. She suggests that these three leadership types are underpinned by some similar and some quite different principles, and that leaders will quite often move from one leadership type to another in an almost unconscious manner. In this chapter, we are focusing on transformative leadership. Like culturally responsive leadership, transformative leadership begins by understanding inappropriate uses of power and privilege and then seeks to challenge and change these situations through the practice of leadership

(Shields, 2010). This perspective on leadership takes seriously the personal and the public responsibility to use power, privilege, and position to promote social justice and enlightenment for the benefit, not only of individuals, but also of society as a whole (Shields, 2010). Such leadership practice requires attending to the needs and aspirations of the wider community in which one serves. Change comes from the result of a deeper understanding of the differing power relations within which we all live.

How will we recognize transformative leadership? Shields (2010) posits key activities that signal transformative leadership. Transformative leaders commit to equitable change; deconstruct and reconstruct knowledge frameworks that perpetuate inequity and injustice; focus on emancipation, democracy, equity, and justice; address the inequitable distribution of power; emphasize both individual and collective good; emphasize interdependence, interconnectedness, and global awareness; balance critique with promise; and demonstrate moral courage. In the next section, we describe several applications in which we believe transformative leadership can be identified.

APPLICATIONS OF A CULTURALLY RESPONSIVE AND SOCIALLY JUST FRAMEWORK

A number of research programs that have sought to address injustices and academic marginalization experienced by the special populations within society, communities, schools, and individual homes and families. Specifically, we describe Te Kotahitanga (Unity of Purpose), the Incredible Years, School Renewal, the Influence of Cultural Capital, Home-School Partnerships, and a teenager learning English as a second language.

TE KOTAHITANGA

Te Kotahitanga (Unity of Purpose), a research and development reform program in New Zealand secondary schools, commenced in 2001 and was aimed at reducing the achievement disparities between Indigenous Māori and non-Māori students. By talking with groups of people, including Māori students, family members, and educators, about what would engage Māori students in education (Bishop & Berryman, 2006), researchers found from Māori students themselves that their achievement was linked to the quality of their relationships and interactions with teachers. Drawing from these combined narratives of experience, a series of interdependent pedagogical principles termed a "culturally responsive pedagogy of relations" (Bishop, Berryman, Cavanagh, & Teddy, 2007, p. 15) were developed. This pedagogical approach emphasizes the importance of teachers developing learning and teaching relationships where power is shared so that learners can be more self-determining; cultural location and knowledge counts, so that both students and teachers can safely bring "who they are" to the learning context; knowledge is co-created so that learning is interactive, dialogic, and spiraling; and teachers and students can be connected and committed to one another through the establishment of a vision for what constitutes educational excellence.

The impact of implementing Te Kotahitanga in Phase 3 and 4 schools is reported by Bishop, Berryman and Wearmouth, (2014). When this pedagogical response is implemented effectively, the schooling experiences of Māori students improve dramatically, with attendance, retention, engagement, and achievement all showing positive gains in relation to a comparison group of schools. This evidence empirically demonstrates that responsive and relational pedagogies such as these, when implemented, can indeed result in learning contexts where Māori students feel that they belong and where they are more able to enjoy and achieve educational success as Māori (Ministry of Education, 2013). In Phase 5, national qualification results for Māori students also showed year-to-year improvements, with evidence from a number of individual schools clearly showing that the achievement gap between indigenous Māori students and their non-Māori peers can be closed (Alton-Lee, 2014).

THE INCREDIBLE YEARS

The Incredible Years (Webster-Stratton, 2009) is a systematic and comprehensive curriculum that promotes social competence and prevents or reduces conduct problems through parent, teacher, and child (0–5 years) training. Webster-Stratton attests that the program has been tested for effectiveness across groups of diverse populations and the program has been replicated or adapted in Native American context (Dionne, 2008, Dionne, Davis, Sheeber, & Madrigal, 2009) and proven effective in these settings as well. In New Zealand, Berryman, Woller, and Glynn (2009) sought to understand the Incredible Years program first from the literature and then from the experiences of groups of Māori people who had either facilitated the program or learned from participating in the program. Māori facilitators and parents alike reported that the program was

> responsive to the cultural location of the whānau, used interactive dialogic and reciprocal interactions emerging from strong relationships and connectedness, reinforced a common vision of supporting parents to work more effectively with their children, and promoted the sharing of power and whānau self determination. (Berryman et al., 2009, p. 56)

It was also clear that staff, parents, and the community collectively experienced benefits.

> Māori facilitators talked about the new skills and understandings that whānau took from the conversations they had within the Incredible Years programme.... Whānau agreed that the programme had enhanced their self esteem as parents as well as improving their relationships with their children and they discussed the positive changes the Incredible Years programme had made to their lives and the lives of their children [and their extended families] through dialog. (Berryman et al., 2009, p. 58)

SCHOOL RENEWAL

In a school renewal study, SooHoo (1990), as the elementary school principal and as a researcher, found students designated as "high risk" and evaluated as having special needs also suffered from a discontinuous learning program at her school. Students with individual education programs who often shuttled from place to place to access special resources within the school day were unable to synthesize the constellation of resources, and no one seemed to notice. Picture the student who qualifies for speech therapy, asthma therapy, adaptive physical education, and a resource teacher. This scenario was characterized by the saying, "The hurrier I go, the behinder I get." Not only did these students lag behind academically, but there was no time to develop social relationships with their teachers or peers (SooHoo, 1990).

A research team of teachers decided to shadow "at risk" students, allowing the faculty to name and identify the problems that ultimately led to the restructuring of the students' school day. Alongside this inquiry project, SooHoo (1990) worked with her teachers to reform the roles of teachers and facilitated their move from disciplinarians to empowered problem solvers. This multiyear effort of building a culture of dialog and relationships resulted in a transformation of both the school environment and students' learning situations. Moreover, after teachers constructed programs that provided academic and social continuity for students with special needs, they continued toward a whole-school-reform effort, inviting community members to think about a year-round school calendar designed around the literature on how children learn best.

THE INFLUENCE OF CULTURAL CAPITAL

Hanreddy (2013) interviewed Latino and White families whose children with disabilities attended a school that practiced inclusive education. She found that Latino and White families drew upon distinctly different cultural traditions and practices to navigate school systems. For Latino families, the knowledge of their children, community connections, and vision for their children's futures did not assist in securing high-quality placements for their children due to mismatches with the school district. Latino families tried to communicate their expectations for inclusive education for their children but felt uncomfortable expressing their concerns about segregated settings.

Informal networks and strategies resolved day-to-day issues for the Latino families as well as the White families but did not lead to substantive changes in educational program decisions for Latino families. White families were included in decision-making processes and were more likely to secure their desired educational placement. Hanreddy (2014) reported that expectations for children with significant disabilities were shaped in part by schooling experiences. Specifically, when their children were young, most families had few models of an educational setting that would serve as an inclusive environment for their children. Following 7 to 9 years in an environment in which both families and children experienced full membership and belonging, practices that served to exclude became visible to the Latino families, who began to understand that their children could be disabled by their educational settings.

HOME-SCHOOL PARTNERSHIP

Traditionally, in mainstream schools, students and families have been understood and responded to from two contrasting perspectives. One perspective suggests that any deficits reside in the students, their families, and/or their cultural groups (e.g., Bishop et al., 2003. Sullivan, 2011). Viewing differences as deviance promotes divisions and frequently serves to exclude students and their families from experiencing education success. In contrast, sociocultural theories of human development (e.g., Vygotsky, 1987) emphasize the importance of understanding the relationships and interactions between students, teachers, and between schools and home communities. This theoretical framework, which we term "culturally responsive inclusion," recognizes and values the role families have in shaping each learner's cultural toolkit (Bruner, 1996) and seeks to work in partnership with home communities so that families are better placed to feel a sense of belonging and able to contribute more authentically to their child's formal learning.

Research undertaken by Glynn, Berryman and Glynn (2000) and Berryman (2001) demonstrated that when schools engage with the skills and expertise of Māori families to collaboratively operationalize the reading tutoring procedure in the Pause Prompt Praise program (Glynn, McNaughton, Robinson, & Quinn, 1979), the achievement of these students could be considerably accelerated. Creating relational, sociocultural contexts that enabled families to learn to use this literacy strategy meant that schools in some instances allowed families to determine the time and location of community training sessions. Within these training sessions, providing an opportunity for families to share their experiences and understandings of literacy acquisition created an interactive and dialogic means by which participants could learn from and with each other. The process of providing ongoing feedback, feed-forward and support around participants' tutoring practices and their children's progress, enabled schools to affirm the contribution families were making to learning and reinforced the school's commitment to both the partnership and the shared vision of accelerating the students' education success.

A TEENAGER LEARNING ENGLISH AS A SECOND LANGUAGE

Nancy Kane (as cited in Beckett et al., 2002) worked in a career development classroom at a high school located in a school district in a metropolitan area of the southwest United States, where 60%–70% of the community were from families with bilingual Spanish/English speakers. Ariadi (Ari), an 18-year-old senior female with a learning disability, was bilingual in Spanish and English. Her special education goals and objectives focused on direct instruction in pragmatic English language, social problem solving, and the development of social insight. Ari's goals were directly related to using English to achieve academically in all content areas. Nancy and Ari agreed that Ari would negotiate and manage interactions to accomplish a task within a small group of classmates with progress indicators such as (a) asking a peer to confirm her understanding of directions to complete an assignment, (b) modifying a statement made by a peer, and (c) negotiating cooperative roles as she accomplished the assignments. Nancy created a series of four structured lessons to help Ari and classmates practice her oral expression in English within a class discussion format. This allowed all the students to cognitively rehearse and practice their skills and knowledge in preparation for taking a state examination to qualify as food service workers. Students wanted to earn a food handler's certificate as a way to qualify for summer jobs.

Nancy and her cooperating teacher relied on sheltered English techniques (Walter, 1996) to develop both metacognitive and social competence. For example, as a review technique, Nancy created a study guide using the Cloze technique (Lovitt, 1995, p. 57), in which the students, working independently, had to find the correct English word or phrase to complete the sentence. This provided a guided opportunity to reread the food handlers manual. Then, the students worked in small groups to generate key vocabulary and concepts described in the manual. They turned the words into questions that were likely to be on the food handler's test. They printed the questions on 3×5 cards on one side, and on the other side, they printed the answers. Nancy used these cards to generate a Food Handler's Game Show, wherein two teams of students competed to orally express the correct answers to the questions. The students had to collaborate and rehearse the answers with each other before stating their answer to the class. Techniques for sheltered content instruction (Faltis, 1993; Walter, 1996) included demonstrations and modeling, interactive means of checking for understanding, organizing instruction around a theme, engaging students in active participation, and sensitive error correction. As an example of sensitive error correction, Nancy analyzed the error patterns shown in the first pretest review of vocabulary words. She had the students make their own word cards to take home and place in conspicuous places so as to study more frequently. She interviewed Ari to ask how Ari approached the task of a "Cloze" test question. Nancy then used prompts to guide her through a systematic process of crossing out the used vocabulary words and comparing the sentence to the sentence in the manual. The simple monitoring technique to keep track of academic progress was percentages correct on pre- and posttests for each lesson. The final assessment was the state-controlled health department test for issuing a food handlers' certificate.

The teacher successfully obtained a copy of the manual in Spanish. Ari was asked in what language she would prefer to take the food handler's test. She decided to take it in Spanish, even though she had completed all in-class discussions and written work successfully in English. Ari and 100% of her classmates passed the state food handler's test, an occasion for great celebration! An unexpected outcome of this series of lessons was that Ari encouraged the members of her family to study for and take the test.

ANALYSIS OF APPLICATIONS

In writing this chapter, we intended to provide readers with some examples that show how the relational and culturally responsive interactions we advocate can lead naturally to multiple ways of honoring cultural pluralism. What can we learn from the applications described above? We believe these applications illustrate how diverse ways of knowing and understanding the world can bring different knowledge bases inside the school and classroom and from which to learn. We discuss themes common to the applications, and then describe a social justice framework for leadership that is responsive to the cultural contexts of special populations.

THEMES

To facilitate understandings of how classrooms and schools can provide opportunities for even their most *diverse* students to belong, be accepted and to learn, we articulate the following themes:

1. When people can determine their own questions and sense-making processes, we may all be better placed to learn (e.g., Bishop & Berryman, 2006).
2. Within relationships of interdependence, students, their families, teachers, and school leaders are connected to one another through relationships of mutual trust and respect (e.g., Bishop & Glynn, 1999).
3. Interdependence and a common vision of success for all people provide a focus for collective action and collaborative solution seeking (e.g., Bishop et al., 2014).
4. Learning (Change) is dialogic, active, problem based, holistic, and spiraling (Bishop et al, 2007) when learners raise their own questions and evaluate answers and when knowledge is collaboratively co-created through relationships and interactions of reciprocity.
5. People's prior knowledge and experience—their cultural toolkit (Bruner, 1996)—is incorporated into the learning context and regarded as valid and legitimate.

Understanding and putting the themes into action are essential to achieving a social justice framework for leadership that is responsive to the cultural contexts of special populations.

A SOCIAL JUSTICE FRAMEWORK FOR LEADERSHIP THAT IS RESPONSIVE TO SPECIAL POPULATIONS

"Learning is not only an intellectual exercise; it also involves a sense of 'becoming' a member of a community or a sense of being excluded from it" (Wearmouth & Berryman, 2009, p. 7). We suggest that culturally responsive leadership requires us to consider not only what happens in schools but also society at-large and to question how we ourselves may be contributing to a status quo where some groups are successful and others continue to be less so. In so doing, other questions may be raised:

1. Who decides what inclusivity/exclusivity or belonging/being included looks like/feels like, and how do leaders perpetuate or disrupt the status quo in order to better facilitate the needs of others?

2. Why should leaders negotiate relations of trust and respect with students and families, and how should they do this?

When we ourselves are prepared to hold the mirror up to our own conscientization and praxis, the essential characteristics of school leaders who employ a culturally responsive approach to social justice may become clearer. There is increased diversity in schools worldwide and increased marginalization of those who are different from the dominant societal view (Sleeter, 2011). The culturally responsive and relational interactions we advocate lead naturally to multiple ways of honoring cultural and epistemological pluralism, because different ways of knowing and understanding bring diversity inside the classroom and school as authentic and legitimate. When schools reach out to multiple and diverse communities, they are more able to bring these knowledge bases back into the school. In this chapter, we argue that a sense of belonging and inclusion can be fostered when all participants learn each other's ways of seeing the world and when each person experiences respect for his/her views.

Schools are places where identities are developed, and they are places that bring teachers and learners together through their essential "unfinishedness" (Freire, 2001). As such, they are places where we are all developing—we can all learn from each other. Likewise, as school leaders, teachers, parents, and students engage in dialog and come to know each other in respectful ways, we are better able to name the problems and identify potential solutions. From the act of respectfully posing questions and alternatives from all participants, possible pathways to serve children and families from diverse communities are more likely to emerge.

Differential power relations are renegotiated through dialog; this requires an ongoing commitment of respect to those who enter those relational spaces and respect for the process itself. It is in this dialog, like good teaching, that we may "become." Over time, we may even "belong." We have come to realize that belonging and feeling included is not a geographic or physical place; it is a state of mind linked to trust, faith, humanity, community, and social justice.

We argue that as educational professionals, we must go beyond a moral imperative to embrace dialog and relationships. Our examples bring together the importance of the relationships that are formed at a personal level and how the different cultural groups are actually able to design interventions that reflect their own cultural location. Based on key understandings derived from kaupapa Māori (Bishop, 2005; G. H. Smith, 1999) and Freire (1986, 2001), and as delineated in *Culturally Responsive Methodologies* (Berryman et al., 2013), we encourage a framework where establishing respectful relationships of interdependence with people is central to both human dignity and praxis. A culturally responsive framework such as this challenges traditional notions of the professional expert working within an objective context; instead, it opens up spaces that call for engagement through the establishment of relational and interdependent discourses that encourage us to co-create an interdependent, socially just reality.

REFERENCES

Alliance for Excellent Education. (2004, June 23). *Tapping the potential: Retaining and developing high-quality new teachers* [Report]. Washington, DC. Retrieved from http://www.all4ed.org/publications/TappingThePotential/Tapping-ThePotential.pdf

Alton-Lee, A. (2006). How teaching influences learning: Implications for educational researchers, teachers, teacher educators and policy makers. *Teaching and Teacher Education, 22*(5), 612–626.

Alton-Lee, A. (2014). *Ka Hikitia Demonstration Report: Effectiveness of Te Kotahitanga Phase 5 2010–12.* Manuscript in preparation.

Alton-Lee, A., & New Zealand Ministry of Education (2003). *Quality teaching for diverse students in schooling: Best evidence synthesis.* Wellington, New Zealand: Ministry of Education.

Ballard, K. (2007). *Education and imagination: Strategies for social justice.* Keynote address to the National Conference of New Zealand Association for Research in Education. Christchurch, NZ: University of Canterbury.

Ballard, K. (2008, November). *Teaching in context: Some implications of a racialised social order.* Keynote address presented at the inaugural Te Kotahitanga conference, University of Waikato, Hamilton, New Zealand.

Banks, J. (2002). *An introduction to multicultural education.* Boston, MA: Allyn & Bacon.

Beckett, C., Diel, A., Comella, S., Kane, N., Romero, P., & Bergquist, G. (2002). Meeting the special needs of dual language learners with disabilities: Integrating data-based instruction and the standards for teaching English for speakers of other languages *Resources in Education.* (ERIC Document Reproduction Service No. ED464429)

Berryman, M. (2001). *Toitū te whānau, toitū te iwi: A community approach to English transition.* (Unpublished master's thesis). University of Waikato, Hamilton, New Zealand.

Berryman, M. (2008). *Repositioning within indigenous discourses of transformation and self-determination.* (Unpublished doctoral thesis). University of Waikato, Hamilton, New Zealand.

Berryman, M., SooHoo, S., & Nevin, A. (2013). *Culturally responsive methodology.* Bingley, UK: Emerald.

Berryman, M., Woller, P., & Glynn, T. (2009). *The incredible years: Learning from the experiences of Māori Whānau and Māori staff in special education.* Hamilton, New Zealand: Ministry of Education.

Bigelow, B. (1995). Getting off the track: Stories from an untracked classroom. In D. Levine, R. Lowe, B. Peterson, & R. Tenorio (Eds.), *Rethinking schools* (pp.155–168). New York, NY: New Press.

Bishop, R. (2005). Freeing ourselves from neo-colonial domination in research: A kaupapa Maori approach to creating knowledge. In N. K. Denzin & Y. S. Lincoln (Eds.), *The Sage handbook of qualitative research* (3rd ed., pp. 109–138). Thousand Oaks, CA: Sage.

Bishop, R., & Berryman, M. (2006). *Culture speaks: Cultural relationships and classroom learning.* Wellington, New Zealand: Huia.

Bishop, R., Berryman, M., Cavanagh, T., & Teddy, L. (2007). *Te Kotahitanga Phase 3 Whanaungatanga: Establishing a culturally responsive pedagogy of relations in mainstream secondary school classrooms.* Wellington, New Zealand: Ministry of Education.

Bishop, R., Berryman, M., Tiakiwai, S., & Richardson, C. (2003). *Te Kotahitanga: Experiences of Year 9 and 10 Maori students in mainstream classrooms.* Wellington, New Zealand: Ministry of Education.

Bishop, R., Berryman, M., & Wearmouth, J. (2014). *Te Kotahitanga: Towards effective education reform for indigenous and other minoritised students.* Wellington, New Zealand: New Zealand Council for Educational Research Press.

Bishop, R., & Glynn, T. (1999). *Culture counts: Changing power relations in education.* Palmerston North, New Zealand: Dunmore.

Blankenship, C., & Lilly, M. S. (1981). *Mainstreaming students with learning and behavior problems.* New York, NY: Holt, Rinehart and Winston.

Bourdieu, P. (1977). *Reproduction in education, society and culture.* London, UK: Sage.

Brown v. Board of Education of Topeka, Kansas (1954). Retrieved from http://www.ourdocuments.gov/doc.php?flash=true&doc=87

Bruner, J. (1996). *The culture of education.* Boston, MA: Harvard University Press.

Butterworth. G., & Butterworth, S. (1998). *Reforming education the New Zealand experience 1984–1996.* Palmerston North, New Zealand: Dunmore.

Chapple, S., Jeffries, R., & Walker, R. (1997). *Maori participation and performance in education. A literature review & research programme.* Report for the Ministry of Education, Wellington, New Zealand.

Collier, C. (2012, May/June). Special education for indigenous students. *National Association for Bilingual Education Perspectives,* 9-10. Retrieved from http://jan.ucc.nau.edu/~jar/NABE/Collier%20SE.pdf

Consedine, R., & Consedine, J. (2005). *Healing our history: The challenge of the Treaty of Waitangi.* London, UK: Penguin.

Cruz, A. L. (2013). Paulo Freire's concept of conscientizacao. In R. Lake & T. Kress (Eds), *Paulo Freire's intellectual roots: Toward historicity in praxis* (pp. 169–182). London, UK: Bloomsbury.

Danforth, S. (1997). Autobiography as critical pedagogy: Locating myself in class-based oppression. *Teaching Education, 9*(1), 3–14.

Darling-Hammond, L. (2001). New standards and old inequalities: School reform and the education of African-American students. *Journal of Negro Education, 69*(4), 263–287.

Deil-Amen, R., & DeLuca, S. (2010). *The underserved third: How our educational structures populate an educational underclass.* Tucson, AZ: Routledge.

Deschenes, S., Cuban, L., & Tyack, D. (2001). Mismatch: Historical perspectives on schools and students who don't fit them. *Teachers College Record, 103*(4), 525–547.

Devecchi, C., & Nevin, A. (2010). Leadership for inclusive schools. In A. H. Normore (Ed). *Global perspectives on educational leadership reform: The development and preparation of leaders of learning and learners of leadership* (pp. 211–243). Bingley, UK: Emerald.

Dionne, R. (2008, June 4). *Evidence-based programs in American Indian communities.* Prevention Webinar presented by the Federal Interagency Work Group on Child Abuse and Neglect. Retrieved November 2, 2014, from http://vimeo.com/13811467

Dionne, R., Davis, B., Sheeber, L., & Madrigal, L. (2009). Initial evaluation of a cultural approach to implementation of evidence-based parenting interventions in American Indian communities. *Journal of Community Psychology, 37*(7), 911–921.

Durkheim, E. (1965). *The elementary forms of the religious life* (J. W. Swain, Trans.). New York, NY: Free Press.

Education of All Handicapped Children Act (EHA, 1975) *Public Law No. 94-142.* Washington, DC: The Congressional Record.

Faltis, C. (1993). Critical issues in the use of sheltered content teaching in high school bilingual programs. *Peabody Journal of Education, 69* (1), 136–151.

Freire, P. (1986). *Pedagogy of the oppressed* (11th ed.). Middlesex, UK: Penguin.

Freire, P. (1998). *Teachers as cultural workers: Letters to those who dare teach.* Boulder, CO: Westview.

Freire, P. (2001). *Pedagogy of freedom: Ethics, democracy, and civic courage.* Lanham, MD: Rowman & Littlefield.

Glynn, T., Berryman, M., & Glynn, V. (2000, April). *Reading and writing gains for Maori students in mainstream schools: Effective partnerships in the Rotorua home and school literacy project.* Paper presented at the World Congress on Reading, Auckland, New Zealand.

Glynn, T., McNaughton, S., Robinson, V., & Quinn, M. (1979). *Remedial reading at home: Helping you to help your child.* Wellington: New Zealand Council for Educational Research.

Griffiths, M. (1998). *Educational research for social justice: Getting off the fence.* London, UK: Open University Press.

Hanreddy, A. (2013). *Forced choices and limited options: Parent perspectives on high school for their children with significant disabilities* (Dissertation). Chapman University, College of Educational Services, Orange, CA

Hanreddy, A. (2014, November). *How do legal-bureaucratic school systems serve to impede access and reproduce disparity?* Presentation for National Association for Multicultural Education, Oakland CA.

Harker, R., & Nash, R. (1990). Cultural reproduction and school achievement: A case for kura kaupapa Maori. *ACCESS, 9*(2), 26–39.

Hattie, J. (1999, August 2). *Influences on student learning.* Inaugural Lecture, University of Auckland, Auckland, NZ. Retrieved from http://projectlearning.org/blog/wp-content/uploads/2014/02/Influences-on-Student-Learning-John-Hattie.pdf

Hattie, J. (2003a). *Teachers make a difference: What is the research evidence?* Paper presented at the Australian Council for Educational Research Annual Conference.

Hattie, J. (2003b). *New Zealand education snapshot: With specific reference to the years 1–13.* Paper presented at the Knowledge Wave 2003, The Leadership Forum, Auckland, NZ.

Individuals with Disabilities Education Act (IDEA). (1990). *Public Law 99-457.* Washington, DC: Congressional Record.

Individuals with Disabilities Education Act (IDEA). (1997). *Public Law 105-17.* Washington, DC: Congressional Record.

Individuals with Disabilities Education Improvement Act (IDEIA). (2004). *Public Law No. 108–446.* Washington DC: Congressional Record.

Klingner, J., Artiles, A., Kozleski, E., Harry, B., Zion, S., Tate, W., Duran, G., & Riley, D. (2005). Addressing the disproportionate representation of culturally and linguistically diverse students in special education through culturally responsive educational systems. *Education Policy Analysis Archives, 13*(38). Retrieved November 2, 2014, from http://www.nccrest.org/PDFs/core_principles_EPAA.pdf

Lovitt, T. (1995). *Tactics for teaching.* Englewood Cliffs, NJ: Prentice Hall.

McLaren, P. (2015). *Life in schools: An introduction to critical pedagogy in the foundations of education.* Boulder, CO: Paradigm.

Ministry of Education. (2013). *Ka Hikitia—Accelerating success 2013–2017.* Wellington, New Zealand: Ministry of Education.

Nash, R. (1993). *Succeeding generations: Family resources and access to education in New Zealand.* Auckland, New Zealand: Oxford University Press.

Oakes, J. (1985). *Keeping track: How schools structure inequality.* New Haven, CT: Yale University Press.

Peters, M., Marshall, J., & Massey, L. (1994). Recent educational reforms in Aotearoa. In E. Coxon, K. Jenkins, J. Marshall, & L. Massey, (Eds.), *The politics of learning and teaching in Aotearoa—New Zealand* (pp. 251–272). Palmerston North, New Zealand: Dunmore.

Public Law 94-142. (1975, November 29). *Education of All Handicapped Children Act of 1975.* Retrieved November 2, 2014, from http://www.gpo.gov/fdsys/pkg/STATUTE-89/pdf/STATUTE-89-Pg773.pdf

Shields, C. (2010). Transformative leadership: Working for equity in diverse contexts. *Educational Administration Quarterly, 46*(4), 558–589.

Shields, C., Bishop, R., & Mazawi, A. E. (2005). *Pathologizing practices: The impact of deficit thinking on education.* New York, NY: Lang.

Sleeter, C. (Ed.). (2011). *Professional development for culturally responsive and relationship-based pedagogy* (1st ed.). New York, NY: Lang.

SooHoo, S. (1990). School renewal: Taking responsibility for providing an education of value. In J. Goodland & P. Keating (Eds.), *Access to knowledge: An agenda for our nation's schools* (pp. 206–221). New York, NY: College Entrance Examination Board.

SooHoo, S. (2006). *Talking leaves: Narratives of otherness.* Cresskill, NJ: Hampton.

Smith, G. H. (1997). *Kaupapa Māori as transformative praxis.* A thesis in fulfilment of the requirements of the degree of Doctor of Philosophy in Education. University of Auckland, New Zealand.

Smith, L. T. (1999). *Decolonizing methodologies: Research and indigenous peoples.* London, UK: Zed.

Sullivan, A. (2011). Disproportionality in special education identification and placement of English language learners. *Exceptional Children, 77*(3), 317–334.

Te Pūni Kōkiri. (1998). *Progress towards closing social and economic gaps between Māori and non-Māori.* A report to the Minister of Māori Affairs, Te Puni Kōkiri, Wellington, New Zealand.

Vygotsky, L. (1987). *The collected works of L. S. Vygotsky* (R. W. Rieber & A. S. Carton, Trans.). New York, NY: Plenum. (Original works published in 1934, 1960)

Walker, R. (2004). *Ka whawhai tonu matou struggle without end* (Rev. ed.). Auckland, New Zealand: Penguin.

Walter, T. (1996). *Amazing English!* New York, NY: Addison-Wesley.

Wearmouth, J., & Berryman, M. (2009). *Inclusion through participation in communities of practice in schools.* Wellington, New Zealand: Dunmore.

Webster-Stratton, C. (2009). Affirming diversity: Multicultural collaboration to deliver the incredible years parent programs. *International Journal of Child Health and Human Development, 2*(1), 17–32.

CHAPTER 9

OUR FORGOTTEN SONS

The Underachievement of Boys of Color in America's Urban Centers

Nicole Limperopulos
Teachers College, Columbia University

ABSTRACT

In the 1954 landmark Supreme Court case *Brown v. Board of Education*, the Court struck down race-based segregation in schools throughout the nation. However, 59 years after the monumental Supreme Court decision, we stand at a precipice that threatens to undermine the success of our democracy: enduring exclusionary practices that perpetuate the chronic underachievement of boys of color in our nation's urban centers. The central purpose of this chapter is to catalyze educational leaders to eradicate the exclusionary processes that contribute to the cycle of inferiority and underachievement by adopting best practices that address the discreet needs of this unique population. Calling upon a corpus of literature in urban studies, psychology, adolescent development, and educational leadership, this chapter deconstructs the factors that contribute to the underachievement of boys of color, including historic attitudes of racism and classism, the effects of chronic violence exposure, misdiagnosis and disproportionate classification as special-education students,

Inclusive Practices and Social Justice Leadership for Special Populations in Urban Settings, pages 165–187
Copyright © 2015 by Information Age Publishing

and application of harsh discipline policies that lead to increased rates of entry into the criminal justice system. Finally, this chapter implores educational leaders to implement inclusive practices that eradicate the marginalization of boys of color, thereby enabling them to reach their full academic and personal potential as valued members of the school community.

A review of quality of life indicators for males of color living in the United States reveals a grim picture. Males of color, ages 15–19, have a homicide rate nine times higher than White males in the same category, making homicide the leading cause of death for Black and Latino males under the age of 25 in urban environments (DuRant, Pendergrast, & Cadenhead, 1994; Skolnick & Currie, 1994). African American males represent only 12% of the U.S. population, however, they contract HIV at a rate seven times higher than White men and account for an estimated 44% of all new HIV infections (Centers for Disease Control, 2013). According to a 2000 Bureau of Justice Report, African American males compose the largest segment of the prison population in the United States and are incarcerated at a rate that is five times higher than White males. Howard (2008) cited Elsner (2004) when noting that "one in every eight African American men in their 20s and 30s were behind bars in 2003," and projections based on current demographics indicated that "one in every three African American men can expect to spend time either incarcerated, on probation, or under some type of jurisdiction of the penal system during his lifetime" (p. 958).

Statistics on the educational attainment of urban males of color reveal a chronic state of underachievement and the presence of exclusionary practices. In 2000, the Department of Education's Office of Civil Rights (OCR) collected data from 72,000 schools in 7,000 districts, which serve approximately 85% of students in the United States (Department of Education, 2000). The findings of the study revealed that although boys of color only composed 18% of the sample, they represented 35% of those suspended once, 46% of students suspended more than once, and 39% of all expulsions (Department of Education, 2000). Further, over 70% of students involved in school-related arrests were boys of color. Boys of color are disproportionally referred to special-education classes, remedial classes, and alternative schools (Department of Education, 2000). Although boys of color compose 21% of students in special education, they represent 44% of those with disabilities subject to mechanical restrains and 42% of those who are placed in seclusion (Department of Education, 2000).

Other data drawn from the OCR report (Department of Education, 2000) reveals various racial discrepancies in schools throughout the nation—discrepancies that amount to educational malpractice. While 55% of high schools with low minority enrollment offered calculus, only 29% of schools with high African American and Latino populations offered advanced math courses (Department of Education, 2000). As Jackson (2008) noted, boys of color represented only 4% of students placed in honors classes or gifted and talented programs. Finally, data collected from the Department of Education's Office of Civil Rights (2000) demonstrated that schools with high minority student populations were more likely to have inexperienced, low-paid educators and a high teacher turnover rate. According to Lewin (2012), "On average, teachers in high-minority schools were paid $2,251 less per year than their colleagues elsewhere. In New York high schools, though, the discrepancy was more than $8000, and in Philadelphia, more than $14,000" (p. 2).

This chapter seeks to catalyze educational leaders to eradicate the enduring exclusionary practices that perpetuate the chronic underachievement of boys of color in our nation's urban centers. In order to do so, this chapter is organized in the following way. First, we examine the historical purpose and structure of our nation's educational system and the role that racism and classism played in shaping the birth of our current educational institutions. Next, readers are provided with an introduction to a multitude of factors, which when ignored, are contributing to the underachievement of boys of color in our nation's urban centers. Such factors include academic tracking, the rejection of "outsider" cultures, and application of harsh disciplinary policies that lead to increased rates of entry into the criminal justice system. Finally, readers explore inclusive practices that serve to eradicate the marginalization of boys of color, thereby enabling them to reach their full academic and personal potential as valued members of the school community and democratic society.

AN EARLY EVOLUTIONARY PATH

Our urban schools are *not* failing our boys of color. Despite the preponderance of evidence documenting the underachievement of boys of color, our urban schools are *not* failing our African American and Latino boys. Although a review of published research and anecdotal evidence that substantiate claims of underachievement among boys of color led Diane Abbott, a member of the British Parliament, to declare the issue a "silent catastrophe" (Graham & Robinson, 2004, p. 654), our urban schools are *not* failing our boys of color. In fact, our schools are succeeding at exactly what they were designed to do: prepare a select group of privileged students to ascend into the ranks of the learned class. In order to develop a robust understanding of how we, as a nation (United States) arrived at a precipice that holds adverse implications for boys of color, Black communities, and our democratic society, it is important to trace the historical purpose, structure, and evolution of our nation's education system.

In the early days of the Republic, Thomas Jefferson emerged as a strong proponent of a two-track education system; one for the laboring and one for the learned (Jefferson, 1814). Jefferson envisioned that the aforementioned tracks would enable the young nation to rake the geniuses from the rubbish by "providing that every citizen receive an education proportioned to the condition and pursuits of his life" (1784, p. 2).

Although schools in the early colonial period were established to disseminate the tenets of Calvinism, the institutions quickly evolved into an exclusionary system that was designed to cater to the children of Anglo-Protestants. Throughout the 19th century, the most affluent Anglo-Protestants attended Latin grammar schools, private institutions that offered a classical curriculum and prepared students for higher education (Oakes, 1985). The children of middle-class Anglo-Protestants attended public academies, which delivered a curriculum that fused classical and modern subjects in an attempt to prepare students for life, good citizenship, and higher education (Oakes, 1985). Since recently arrived immigrants, minority groups, and the urban poor attended neither the Latin grammar schools nor the academies, student grouping proved unnecessary at these early educational institutions.

A NEW MODEL OF SCHOOLING

At the end of the 19th century, a third type of secondary school emerged; one that would be publically financed and controlled. Public schools were founded on the Lancasterian model, where one instructor taught hundreds of students in a single room. Rote instruction was delivered to older children, who in turn passed the information down to younger students. Public schools emphasized discipline and obedience, which were qualities factory owners sought out in their employees.

Despite the advent of the public secondary school system, less than 10% of the nation's high school–aged students attended public or private school in 1890 (Oakes, 1985). Prior to the turn of the 20th century, most citizens considered secondary schooling an institution designed for the children of wealthy Anglo-Protestants. Since students enrolled in secondary schooling were a homogenous group, "individual differences were not an educational concern, and grouping was not an educational practice" (Oakes, 1985, p. 17).

Waves of new immigrants flooded America in record numbers, resulting in a population explosion during the early decades of the 20th century. Many immigrant families arrived on America's soil poor and uneducated, and it quickly became apparent that the nation's newest members were not the elite, light-skinned Anglo-Protestants who had settled this land. The rapid influx of immigrants—15 million in total—coincided with newly enforced compulsory education and child labor laws (Oakes, 1985). As a result, student enrollment in secondary schools throughout the nation between 1890 and 1918 ballooned from approximately 200,000 to 1.5 million students; an increase of over 700% (Oakes, 1985). Interestingly, during this period, a dramatic shift occurred in the type of students who began enrolling in public secondary schools, particularly those schools located in urban areas. No longer was the study body composed of a homogenous grouping of affluent Anglo-Protestants. Instead, nearly 58% of students in the nation's metropolitan areas were first-generation Americans (Oakes, 1985).

Given the rapid changes occurring in 20th century America, a variety of competing groups emerged, eager to determine the purpose and direction of secondary schooling.

> Colleges and universities wanted a more standardized pre-collegiate education. Many of the middle class called for free public education available to all youth. Poor and immigrant families were eager for the economic benefits they believed schooling would provide their children. Businessmen were interested in acquiring a more productive and literate workforce. Organized labor was concerned about who should control the training of workers. Progressive reformers sought humane solutions to the immense social problems confronting the burgeoning population of poor and immigrant youth. But most of the population increasingly feared the potential dangers that could result from what was seen as unrestrained hordes of urban immigrants. (Oakes, 1985, p. 20)

In order to satisfy the various interest groups, a new institution was created—the comprehensive high school. The new model of secondary schooling assuaged the concerns of the masses by promising something for everyone, but not the same thing for everyone (Oakes, 1985). Rather than a common curriculum designed to prepare students for higher education, the comprehensive high school introduced tracking and ability grouping, which provided wildly disparate academic preparation for students from different backgrounds.

The newly formed comprehensive high school brought together, for the first time in America's history, a heterogeneous grouping of students across lines of race, ethnicity, and class. However, once together, students were immediately delineated into various tracks that corresponded with their racial, ethnic, and economic backgrounds. Concurrently, the U.S. Supreme Court handed down a ruling that "upheld the constitutionality of racial segregation in public facilities under the doctrine of separate but equal" (Groves, 1951, p. 68). The Court's ruling officially recognized segregation as legal, thereby enabling southern states to pass laws requiring racial segregation in public schools.

THE SURVIVAL OF THE FITTEST (OR WEALTHIEST)

Tracking and academic grouping, which came to define school reform in the early 20th century, emanated from the proliferation of Social Darwinism. Social Darwinism posited that humans' survival depends not only on their physical traits but also their psychological attributes—attributes that played a fundamental role in their morality and ability to reason (Hawkins, 1997). Therefore, in an epoch that prized science and industry, Social Darwinism provided scientific evidence that "biological, not social, forces accounted for the inferiority of certain groups," which was evidenced through the presence of "poverty, crime, and moral depravity" (Oakes, 1985, p. 23). As a member of the Boston school committee noted, "Many of these children come from homes of vice and crime. In their blood are generations of inequity... They hate restraint or obedience to law" (Oakes, 1985, p. 23).

Perhaps most damning was the fact that school administrators and teachers, who hailed from the middle and upper classes, saw the educational potential of poor and immigrant children as different from those of the affluent Anglo-Protestant classes. Ability grouping was therefore an outgrowth of Social Darwinist ideas held primarily by those who had successfully benefited from their class, race, privilege, and access to education. In fact, countless educators perpetuated the idea that "children of the affluent were considered to be abstract thinkers," while those of the lower classes and racial minorities were considered to be "laggards, socially inefficient, and ignorant" (Oakes, 1985, p. 35). As one educator noted,

> We can picture the educational system as having a very important function as a selecting agency, a means of selecting the men of best intelligence from the deficient and mediocre. All are poured into the system at the bottom; the incapable are soon rejected to drop out after repeating various grades and pass into the ranks of unskilled labor. The more intelligent who are to be clerical workers pass into the high school; the most intelligent enter the universities whence they are selected for the professions. (Oakes, 1985, p. 35)

Initially, students were placed into various academic tracks based on their racial, ethnic, and economic backgrounds. However, Edward Thorndike's development of IQ tests provided an objective measure by which achievement groupings were substantiated. Thorndike's research demonstrated that intelligence was a fixed trait that remained constant over time, thereby enabling him to link intelligence to heredity. Low scores derived from the poor and immigrant classes simply confirmed the prevailing views set forth by the Social Darwinists. Thorndike heralded his intelligence tests as a metric that could objectively separate the affluent from the poor within a common school, thereby cementing his popular credibility within society's existing power structure by rooting the test's standards deeply in Anglo-Protestant middle-class values.

Thorndike drew support for his findings from the writings of Lewis Terman, an early pioneer in the field of intelligence testing, who determined that 80% of the poor and immigrant populations tested were determined to be "feeble-minded." According to Terman (1923),

> Their dullness seems to be racial, or at least in the family stocks from which they come. The fact that one meets this type with such extraordinary frequency among Indians, Mexicans, and Negros suggests quite forcibly that the whole question of racial differences in mental traits will have to be taken up anew... there will be discovered significant racial differences. Children of this group should be segregated in special classes. They cannot master abstractions, but they can often be made efficient workers. (p. 28)

With the support of the Anglo-Protestant middle class solidified, intelligence testing became a meritocratic basis for assigning students to different curricula based on ability grouping. A 1932 survey of 150 public secondary schools revealed that 75% of the sample were students placed in different academic tracks based on the results of intelligence tests (Race Forward, 2006). Oaks (1985) stated, "The wildly believed link between inherited social and economic status and ability—as supported by test scores—was seen as a scientific, efficient, and fair method for predicting the probable future for students" (p. 38).

A SYSTEM CANNOT FAIL THOSE IT WAS NEVER DESIGNED TO PROTECT

With the passage of the landmark case *Brown v. Board of Education of Topeka, Kansas* in 1954, the U.S. Supreme Court determined that de jure segregation violated the Equal Protection Clause of the Fourteenth Amendment, and therefore declared "separate educational facilities to be inherently unequal." The Court's ruling effectively struck down the exclusionary practices that had been officially sanctioned by schools districts throughout the nation since the 1896 ruling in *Plessy v. Ferguson* and subsequently ushered in a period of integration in America's schools.

While, in theory, *Brown v. Board of Education of Topeka* provided equal access to education for students of all races, the Court's decision was inherently flawed. Without explicit provisions designed to dismantle the centuries-old exclusionary model upon which our educational system was founded, de facto segregation would continue to suffocate the nation's schools and marginalize our boys of color.

In the wake of the *Brown* decision, schools throughout the nation summarily resisted the integration of students of color in the school community. However, boys of color in particular were perceived as the great outsiders—those who were seeking access to the very system that feared them and rejected their membership. Established and entrenched Anglo-Protestant norms and values that came to dominate America's educational system immediately labeled boys of color as "socio-culturally dislocated, dysfunctional, and deviant" (Solomon & Palmer, 2004, p. 2). Further, the characterization of boys of color as "aggressive, violent, disruptive, and deviant grew out of a discourse of fear" (Solomon & Palmer, 2004, p. 2).

Boys of color, more than any other student population in America, are most negatively impacted by "distorted constructions of race and gender" (Howard, 2008, p. 962). As a result, boys of color became the "victims of detrimental racial politics which play out" in schools throughout the United States (Howard, 2008, p. 962). Throughout American history, boys of color have been "caught in a web of stereo-typed notions of race and gender that place them at considerable disadvantages in schools" (Howard, 2008, p. 966). Howard further asserted,

> The mere exploration of the social construction of the Black male image in the U.S. over the last four centuries reveals a highly problematic depiction ranging from the docile or the bewildered slave, to the hyper-sexed brute, to the gregarious Sambo, the exploitative pimp or slickster, to the super athlete and entertainer. (p. 966)

Howard (2008) cites Hutchinson (1994) when noting that such perceptions of boys of color contribute to the "assassination of the Black male image." Such perceptions dominate the racial politics that are deeply embedded in our nation's explicit and implicit attitudes toward boys of color (Howard, 2008).

A significant tension developed as our educational institutions wrestled with the tension of preserving Anglo-centric values and norms while concurrently incorporating boys of color into the school community. Historic attitudes of racism and classism converged with the exclusionary principles that guide our educational system to perpetuate a system that served as the second generation of segregation, which sought to (a) maintain the existing model through a multitrack curricula, (2) preserve Anglo-Protestant middle-class norms through the rejection of "outsider" cultures, and (c) stress obedience and harsh discipline as a way to control marginalized groups.

SECOND GENERATION OF SEGREGATION:
TRACKING IN THE 21ST CENTURY

Two centuries after Jefferson's proposed two-track educational system, the "deep structure of tracking remains uncannily robust" (Oakes, 1985, p. xi). This type of educational malpractice continues to disadvantage students assigned to lower tracks, and results in outcome gaps in achievement, graduation rates, and entry into higher education (Oakes, 1985). In racially mixed schools, low-income students and boys of color are disproportionately represented in the lowest curricular track. Additionally, boys of color are more likely to attend "racially isolated schools where lower-level classes predominate" (Oakes, 1985, p. xi). Therefore, "through tracking, schools continue to replicate existing inequality along lines of race and social class and contribute to the intergenerational transmission of social and economic inequality" (Oakes, 1985, p. xi). In order to fully understand the tracking system, one must pay attention to a "complex set of beliefs and values, while noting carefully the politics of power and privilege" (Oakes, 1985, p. 5). Placement in low-track classes fosters feelings of lowered self-esteem in boys of color, thus hindering their ability to develop positive feelings about their academic performance in school (Oakes, 1985).

Boys of color possess positive experiences during their initial entry (pre-K, kindergarten) into school (Davis, 2003). An overwhelming preponderance (98%) of young boys of color conveyed positive experiences in pre-K and kindergarten, with the vast majority indicating that they liked both their teachers and schools (Davis, 2003). However, Davis (2003) cites Simmons and Grady (1992) in reporting that in the early grades, Black boys were significantly overenrolled in lower-level courses. Simmons and Grady noted that throughout third grade, boys of color perform as well as their peers on mandated assessments in math and reading. However, beginning in the fourth grade, boys of color begin demonstrating evidence of academic decline. Noguera (2003a) references Hillard (1991) and Kunjufu (1985) when suggesting that the academic decline that boys of color begin experiencing in fourth grade "may be explained by the fact that this is the age when Black boys start to look like young men" (p. 455).

Davis (2003), emphasized that "the percentage of boys of color in the top reading group dropped from 23% in Grades 1–3 to 12% in Grade 6" (p. 526). Such declines in academic performance corresponded to the ability grouping of boys of color, which overwhelmingly placed them in lower-level courses. When boys of color have unequal access to high-level curriculum in the early grades, it follows that evidence of "achievement inequalities" will emerge as they progress through institutions of lower education (Davis, 2003, p. 526).

While assignments to lower-class tracks have a deleterious impact on the self-esteem of boys of color, such self-perceptions are exacerbated by the "attitudes of teachers toward those in the lower tracks" (Oakes, 1985, p. 8). In fact, Morrow & Torres (1995) demonstrated that the ethnic and socioeconomic backgrounds of students impact how they are perceived and treated by teachers in the school community. Many boys of color possess tenuous relationships with adults in the school community. The potential to develop meaningful relationships with faculty members is significantly undermined by boys' belief that their teachers are not invested in their success (Metropolitan Life, 2001).

> In MetLife's annual survey on teaching, 39% of students surveyed ($n = 3,961$) indicated that they trust their teachers "only a little or not at all"; when the data from the survey were disaggregated by race and class, minority and poor students indicated significantly higher levels of distrust (47% of minorities and 53% of poor students stated that they trusted their teachers only a little or not at all). (Noguera, 2003a, p. 449)

In his research conducted in California schools, Noguera (2003a) collected evidence indicating that most boys of color "value education and would like to succeed in school" (p. 448). However, Noguera reported a disconnect between minority boys' desire to succeed academically, and the realities of their day-to-day experiences in the school community.

> In a response to a survey about their experiences in school, nearly 90% of the Black male respondents (n = 147) responded "agree" or "strongly agree" to the questions "I think education is important" and "I want to go to college." However, in response to the questions "I work hard to achieve good grades" and "My teachers treat me fairly," less than a quarter of the respondents, 22% and 18%, respectively, responded affirmatively. (Noguera, 2003a, p. 448)

Similarly, Mickelson (1990) found discrepancies between a desire to attain an education and a commitment to hard work among boys of color. Mickelson's findings revealed that while many boys of color value education, they do not believe that education would lead to a better life. We are eager to believe that the process of sorting students into homogenous groups is based on merit and previous accomplishments. We are reticent to consider that ability grouping is based on students' race, ethnicity, or socioeconomic status. However, "factors often influenced by race and class—dress, speech patterns, ways of interacting with adults—often do affect subjective judgments of academic aptitude and academic futures, and that educators allow this to happen quite unconsciously" (Oakes, 1985, p. 13). As a result, poor and minority students are sorted into the lower track, while middle- and upper-class White students are assigned to top-level classes (Oakes, 1985).

As a result, faculty members come to identify students according to the characteristics associated with the respective tracks. Therefore, while White middle- and upper-class students assigned to the upper track are identified as intelligent, determined, and high achieving, boys of color in the low track are labeled slow, unable, and unmotivated.

Boys of color assigned to the lowest track come to experience school very differently than students in other tracks. By tracking boys on their "presumed academic ability and behavior, they develop expectations" regarding their position on the social hierarchy (Noguera, 2003b, p. 344) As boys of color conceptualize their schooling experience, it becomes evident that while the upper curricular tracks lead to success, prosperity, and economic stability, their enrollment in a lower track promises dead-end jobs, low wages, and subordination (Noguera, 2003b). Thus, "the socialization process that accompanies the sorting makes it possible for students to accept the educational trajectory set for them" and boys of color "come to believe that their grades, test scores, and behavior have created a future for them that they deserve" (Noguera, 2003b, p. 344).

With an overwhelming focus on accountability in our schools, the implementation of standards-based learning and high-stakes testing serve as "the vehicle used to sort and stratify students in the name of school reform" (Howard, 2008, p. 978). There exists an inextricable link between student performance on high-stakes tests, socioeconomic status, school performance, and teacher quality. Howard further asserts that, "given the fact that students of color and from low-income backgrounds are more likely to come from poorly funded schools, and have under-qualified and inexperienced teachers," it is hardly surprising that such students score significantly below their White and more affluent peers, who attend schools with greater resources and more qualified teachers (p. 978). Perhaps most appalling is the perpetuation of racist and classist attitudes that assert that students who score poorly on high-stakes tests are "less capable, less intelligent, and inherently less prepared to do well in school and society" (Howard, 2008, p. 979). Doing so "continues to instantiate inequity and validate the privilege of those who have access to cultural capital" (Ladson-Billings, 2004, p. 60). Many boys of color report that their teachers do not hold high expectations for their academic performance and fail to maintain high expectations for the quality of their work. In Noguera's research, he noted,

> It was not uncommon to find students sleeping or playing cards in class, courses where students were made to watch videos that were unrelated to the subject of the class, and students who roamed the hallways freely without concern that they would get into trouble. (2003b, p. 347)

Teachers' attitudes about their students can either encourage or impede students' future academic performance. Teachers who held unfavorable impressions of students' behaviors offered less support in the classroom, thereby creating hostile student-teacher relationships (Meehan, Hughes, & Cavell, 2003). Additionally, negative teacher attitudes have also been linked with punitive classroom management techniques, excessive disciplinary actions, and unnecessary special-education referrals, which can hinder students' academic, social, emotional, and behavioral growth (Roderick, 2003; Thomas & Stevenson, 2009).

Boys of color develop strategies that insulate them from the effects of historic attitudes of racism and classism that perpetuate an antiquated tracking system—one that promotes stereotypes about their academic ability and suppresses their achievement. While all students initially value achievement, constant scrutiny causes boys of color to question their worth in the academic arena, thereby creating disassociation between academic success and self-esteem. McMillian (2004) stated, "While the association between self-esteem and academic achievement in African-American boys decreased between eighth and tenth grade; however, this relationship increased in Caucasian boys during the same time period" (p. 29). Rather than focusing on the presence of an achievement gap, the educational community—researchers and practitioners—must reframe the conversation to focus on the existence of a treatment gap (McMillian, 2004). When achievement is viewed as inferior performance rather than inferior treatment, the achievements of boys of color are being "framed from a deficit-oriented perspective" (McMillian, 2004, p. 30). If members of the school community were willing to consider minority students' "achievement patterns as a treatment gap, it might cause them to focus on African-American schooling experiences and would remove the stigma associated with African-American students"—a stigma that consistently robs boys of color of a high-quality education through their inclusion in the remedial educational tracks (McMillian, 2004, p. 30).

UNKNOWN, MISUNDERSTOOD, AND REJECTED

Youth culture is dynamic, exciting, and characterized by a free flow of ideas, particularly as adolescents begin to think abstractly about identity formation. Noguera (2003a) asserts, "This is particularly true for boys of color, whose speech, dress, music, and tastes often establish trends for young people across America" (p. 452). However, for many adults in the school community, minority culture is impenetrable, bewildering, and intimidating (Noguera, 2003a). Therefore, it is imperative to consider the "ways in which structural and cultural forces shape" Black and Latino boys' experiences in school (Noguera, 2003a, p. 452).

Schools play an important role in socializing students by "teaching the values and norms that are regarded as central to civil society and the social order" (Noguera, 2003b, p. 344). In order to achieve the aforementioned, schools teach "social conventions (e.g., obedience to authority) through implicit and explicit means and by instilling a sense of what it means to be 'normal' in students" (Gottfredson, 2001). However, the norms and social conventions disseminated through schools are deeply rooted in the Anglo-European value system. Historic attitudes of racism and classism have come to permeate our educational institutions, and under the guise of normalizing students according to the prevailing culture, we have developed a method for vilifying and rejecting outsider cultures that threaten the accepted value system. Ladson-Billings (2001) asserted,

> Students of color may become alienated from the schooling process because schooling often asks children to be something or someone other than who they really are . . . It asks them to dismiss their community and cultural knowledge. It erases things that the students hold dear. (p. xiv)

Widespread cultural images and messages portray boys of color as violent, disrespectful, unintelligent, and threatening (Belton, 1995; Blount & Cunningham, 1996; Davis, 2003; Harper, 1996). Such messages continue to exact a deleterious impact on "the ways boys of color are treated, positioned, and distributed opportunities to learn" (Davis, 2003, p. 520). Many of the "Black behaviors" displayed by boys of color in "school hallways, staircases, cafeterias, and parking lots are labeled by school personnel as scary, 'hyper-aggressive,' and gang-like (Solomon & Palmer, 2004, p. 2). White middle-class teachers often perceive Black boys' demeanors as defiant, aggressive, and intimidating (Davis, 2003; Majors, Tyler, Peden, & Hall, 1994; Slaughter-Defoe & Richards, 1994). In fact, White teachers identified Black boys' movement styles (stroll) and cultural expressions (slang) to be high in aggression, and they perceived the boys of color to be lower in academic achievement than their White male counterparts (Neal, McCray, Webb-Johnson, & Bridgest, 2003). Additionally, White teachers often "misinterpret culturally relevant movement and language styles as being aggressive and disrespectful" (Thomas & Stevenson, 2009, p. 168).

Although some researchers have documented that boys of color exhibit behaviors that are viewed as hostile and intimidating by adults in the school community, others assert that boys of color struggle to preserve their dignity and self-respect when confronted with real or perceived iniquities by those in positions of authority (Kunjufu, 1985; Madhubuti, 1990; Majors & Billson, 1992; West, 1993). Such responses on the part of boys of color are rooted in "early, prolonged, or acute rejection experiences with significant others," which inevitably leads to "a heightened sensitivity to rejection" (Noguera, 2003a, p. 454). Thomas and Stevenson (2009) cite the work of Downey, Lebolt, Rincon, and Freitas (1998) when reporting that boys of color develop "expectations of rejection, a lowered threshold for perception of negativity, an increased propensity for personalizing negative cues, and intense affective reactions—all which lead to anxious, hostile, and aggressive interpersonal style emerging during early adolescence" (p. 171).

In order to insulate themselves from harsh treatment from peers, teachers, and administration, many boys of color have learned to "adopt an interpersonal anesthetic in the form of a cold, tough, aloof street-wise demeanor" (Parson, 1994, p. 163). Thomas and Stevenson (2009) cite Swanson, Cunningham, and Spencer (2003) when noting that "hypermasculinity is gender-intensified behavior utilized" by boys of color to "evoke respect and thwart impositions from others, particularly when they feel as though they cannot achieve it effectivly through other orientations or courses of action" (2009, p. 170). Hypermasculinity, which may be disguised as anger, noncompliance, and insubordination, is frequently an ineffective attempt by boys of color to mask feelings of shame, disrespect, and hurt that come along with unfair treatment and practices in the school community (Cassidy & Stevenson, 2005; Noguera, 2003a; Spencer, 1999; Thomas & Stevenson, 2009).

Although discriminatory practices, rejection of culture, and continued marginalization trigger anger responses in boys of color, some contest that acting on such emotions can be detrimental to their academic performance. However, the structure of schooling in the United States "reproduces the current social order where European Americans are the standard and 'others' must live up to this Eurocentric standard," which "reinforces stereotypes about ability" (McMillian, 2004, p. 28). As a result, boys of color have already concluded, through the explicit and implicit messages delivered in the school community, that they are not part of the privileged elite, and therefore education will not lead them to college, entry into the middle class, or economic stability in the future. Therefore, the disengagement, hypermasculinity, and anger displayed by boys of color is an active rejection of the middle-class norms by which they are being judged.

ZERO TOLERANCE IS THE RULE OF LAW

The zero tolerance discipline policy, designed in the mid-1990s to curtail a rising tide of school violence, reflects the dominant social, cultural, and political attitudes in society. According to the Department of Education's Office of Civil Right (OCR) report (2000), boys of color are 2.6 times more likely than White students to be suspended from school, and more likely than any other racial or ethnic group to be expelled from schools. The U.S. Department of Education (2000) reported that boys of color accounted for 34% of all suspensions, and 30% of all expulsions, disproportionally high percentages when considering they compose only 17% of the total student population in the United States. Thomas and Steveson (2009) noted that "the gap in discipline between African American students and other student groups has gained much less attention than that of the achievement gap, which by comparison is widely discussed in the media" (p. 165).

Zero tolerance discipline policies bear remarkable similarities to the Three-Strike law, which seeks to impose harsher penalties on those who commit multiple serious offenses. Chen (2008) reports that although African American men only constitute 3% of the California prison population, they represent 33% of second-strikers, and 44% of third-strikers serving a sentence. Therefore, schools employing zero tolerance discipline policies are complicit in reproducing power and social inequality. Noguera (2003b) cites Singer (1996) when noting that the race, gender, and socioeconomic status of those targeted for punishment in school strongly resemble "smaller versions of the adults who are most likely to be targeted for incarceration in society" (p. 343). Therefore, "the construction of the 'fear' of crime by black youth is used as a justification to police them in schools" (Carby, 1982, p. 207).

School administrators and teachers frequently rationalize the use of zero tolerance policies by citing the need to remove difficult students in order to provide an environment that is conducive for those who want to learn (Noguera, 2003b). Noguera (2003b) refers to such sorting processes as the "triage approach" to schooling, which "requires that we accept the fact that not all students will succeed, and that some students must be deemed expendable so that others can be saved" (p. 346). Ironically, schools boasting high suspension rates of boys of color have been largely unable to create better educational climates for remaining students (Noguera, 2003b).

Zero tolerance policies are generally "least effective for students who are not receiving the benefits of an education" (Noguera, 2003b, p. 344). Once boys of color recognize that the promised rewards of education—access to college, economic stability, entry into the professional class—will elude them, they possess little incentive to adhere to the established rules of the school community (Noguera, 2003b). As a result, Noguera (2003b) cites Brookover and Erickson (1969) in noting that school personnel are likely to label such students "defiant, maladjusted, and difficult to manage, labels that come to encourage boys of color to fulfill the expectations set forth for them by authority figures" (p. 343). As boys of color get older, the frequency and severity of the violations increase, resulting in matriculation to the criminal justice system (Noguera, 2003b).

Urban schools, which serve an exceedingly high number of academically unsuccessful boys of color, often operate more like prisons than schools, particularly as they have moved to fully implement guards, metal detectors, surveillance cameras, and restricted access to bathrooms (Noguera, 2003b). Such processes inoculate boys of color into a prison culture, and although virtually all of the school shootings since Columbine have been carried out by White males, boys of color remain targeted as a criminal group (Algard, 2009).

Zero tolerance is inherently about control and power through domination of a marginalized, oppressed, and subjugated group; in this case, boys of color. Zero tolerance policies prize one set of cultural values and norms over another, where one set of behaviors are correct and all others incorrect. In examining the students—boys of color—who are vilified, it becomes apparent that zero tolerance policies are deeply rooted in the Anglo-Protestant ideals of power, prestige, and privilege. As Jull (2000) argues,

> School discipline policies based on the principles of zero tolerance reinforce Anglo-Eurocentric sensibilities of right and wrong and the authoritative structures within public education. . . . To claim that social justice can be achieved through the implementation of a so-called unbiased zero tolerance school discipline policy is to believe that discriminatory practice can be eradicated by implementing policies that are blind to personal or individual social and/or cultural contexts. . . . Equal treatment in an unequal social and academic environment is discriminatory. (p. 4)

Boys of color who have been suspended or expelled under a zero tolerance policy are more likely to drop out of school and ultimately enter the juvenile justice system (Howard, 2008). Skiba and Noam (2001) examined the outcomes of zero tolerance policies in 37 states in order to assess the impact on academic achievement, behavioral trends, and juvenile incarceration. The data revealed that states with higher rates of suspension from zero tolerance policies were more likely to have a higher rate of juvenile incarceration, and that in virtually every state, boys of color had higher suspension and/or expulsion rates than the general population (Skiba & Noam, 2001). The result of Skiba and Noam's (2001) research is hardly surprising, particularly when considering that "the nature of power and power relations in institutional settings is top-down," and "essential to the maintenance of power and authority is a network of structures: the school, social service agencies, and the criminal justice system that operate in symbiotic relationship with each other" (Solomon & Palmer, 2004, p. 7).

Schools or Prisons? Prisons or Schools?

According to data collected by the U.S. Bureau of Justice, 463,700 African American men were enrolled in institutions of higher education compared to 143,000 who were incarcerated in 1980 (Howard, 2008.) By 2004, data revealed that 758,400 African American men were enrolled in colleges compared to 924,000 who were serving sentences in U.S. prisons (Howard, 2008). Over the aforementioned period, for every Black male who enrolled in college, three entered the prison. Howard (2008) cites Conover (2000) when noting that in California, Black males are five times more likely to be incarcerated than enter college, and in "Illinois, there were 10,000 more African American men in prison than in college" (Howard, 2008, p. 959).

A young boy of color who enters kindergarten at the start of the school year has a better change of being incarcerated than enrolling in college 12 years later (Howard, 2008). Elsner (2004) notes that, "for many young black men, prison is their college" (p. 13). The increasing transference of boys of color from schools to prisons is the result of a "clear relationship between school suspension and juvenile incarceration," and "racial disparities in school discipline and corrections are in fact related" (Skiba et al., 2003, p. 28–29).

Noguera (2003b) describes the argument put forth by sociologist Loic Waquant (2000) in noting the growing correlation between schools and prisons. The physical space of a school mirrors that of a prison: Access is only granted after passing through a metal detector; long, cement, windowless corridors connect a series of isolated classrooms; students, clad in uniforms, are marched single-file through the hallway, often in silence; meals are served in a large, open area that is patrolled and monitored by authority figures. The alarming similarities that exist between schools and prisons can be attributed to what Waquant terms a "deadly symbiosis between ghetto and prison (p. 16)." Noguera (2003b) summarizes Waquant's (2000) argument:

> Since colonial times America has been trapped in a quandary over what to do about the Black people they captured in Africa and enslaved. Slavery was motivated and rationalized by the desire to exploit Black labor, but there was also a competing desire to exclude Black people—except for those in servile role—from all facets of public life. A series of strategies—beginning with slavery, which was followed by legally sanctioned segregation, which in turn was followed by defacto segregation in ghettos—were designed to make it possible for American society to accomplish these contradictory and competing goals. However, over time, each of these strategies proved to be untenable, either because they were morally indefensible, or for practical reasons, difficult to sustain. In the current period the melding of ghetto and prison through various carceral strategies is the latest method devised for achieving these long-standing objectives. The ghettos became more like prisons in the 1970s and 1980s as poverty became more concentrated, Black labor became redundant, and state institutions of social control replaced communal institutions that previously served community needs. (p. 349)

Therefore, schools in poor urban communities no longer function as institutions of learning, but rather one of confinement, where custody, control, and submission are of primary importance.

RECOMMENDATIONS

Despite our best efforts to present a picture of an egalitarian society, where members of all races and ethnicities are valued, race still remains "America's most explosive and difficult dilemma" (West, 2004, p. 1). Howard (2008) notes, "Our failure to honestly and critically examine race and all of its manifestations in many ways has only led to further tension, discrimination, and hostility along racial lines" (p. 960). If we as a nation are to uphold our democratic principles, then we can no longer sit idly by while a group of our citizenry continues to be marginalized, oppressed, and excluded from the promise of life, liberty, and the pursuit of happiness.

School leaders are in a unique position to reverse the exclusionary practices that contribute to the rising tide of underachievement among our boys of color. However, in order to do so, school leaders must realize that assertions about the existence of a color-blind society further "silences the voices of boys of color who continually seek inclusion in schools and society" (Howard, 2008, p. 961). Therefore, in order to reverse the continued exclusion and marginalization of boys of color, school leaders must recognize their "connivance in a social order that has produced institutional structures and ideological paradigms that have directly and indirectly contributed to the disenfranchisement" of our boys of color (Howard, 2008, p. 962).

Some school leaders, knowingly and unknowingly, operate on "dysconscious racism," which is "an uncritical habit of mind (including perceptions, attitudes, assumptions, and beliefs) that justifies inequity and exploitation by accepting the existing order of things as given" (King, 1991, p. 135). Howard (2008) cites King (1991) in asserting that "the pedagogical practices of school personnel are predicated on assumptions about social difference; in this case, black youth and their perceived sub-cultural behaviors that induce fear and require rigidity in discipline" (p. 975).

Educational leaders are called upon to eradicate the historically racist practices that accompany zero tolerance discipline policies and lead to the unjust incarceration of boys of color. School administrators' abdication of their responsibility for students' education and safety has established a clear pipeline from schools to prisons, targeting boys of color for harsh disciplinary practices by security guards, law enforcement agencies, and the juvenile justice system.

To reverse the policy and practice of police intervention in schools, educational leaders need to "distance themselves from prescriptive, authoritative responses to discipline, and engage instead in critical reflective practice" (Solomon & Palmer, 2008, p. 7). Educational leaders need to develop the analytic and moral authority to disassemble racist and classist attitudes about boys of color that have become institutionalized (Solomon & Palmer, 2008). Further, it is incumbent upon educational leaders to support faculty members, many whom have benefited from the social, political, and historical contexts and White privilege attached to educational institutions, in ushering in a paradigm shift that shifts blame from the victim to the structural deficits of our schools (Solomon & Palmer, 2008; Valencia, 1997).

Professional development has always prized the acquisition of technical knowledge over a critical analysis of the sociopolitical factors contributing the underachievement of boys of color. Therefore, educational leaders need to commit to providing faculty members with ongoing professional development that "interrogates the socio-historical context of race, class and gender, and develops strategies to make life equitable for oppressed, marginalized, and dehumanized groups" (Solomon & Palmer, 2008, p. 9).

Educational leaders are called upon to create a safe space in the school community, where boys of color are encouraged to give voice to their experiences as a marginalized group, and challenge mainstream accounts of their experiences. Counterstorytelling emerged from communities of color, where members of the community use "oral means of conveying stories and struggles that are often overlooked by those in positions of power, and it draws explicitly on experiential knowledge" (Howard, 2008, p. 964). The use of counterstories takes place in Black homes, churches, barbershops, and neighborhoods, and enables people of color to share their lived experiences while concurrently analyzing and challenging the privileged discourses (DeCuir & Dixon, 2004; Howard, 2008).

Counterstorytelling gives agency to boys of color to counter the narratives that assassinate their character by identifying them as deficient, deviant, hypersexualized, dangerous, and unintelligent (Howard, 2008). In order for a deconstruction of racism in the school community to occur, boys of color must be empowered to offer a "counterscript to the dominant paradigm" by "uncovering silenced viewpoints" (Howard, 2008, p. 974). At the heart of counterstorytelling is "the question of what counts as truth as who gets to decide" (Sleeter & Delgado Bernal, 2003, p. 249).

CONCLUSIONS

In American history classes, students learn about the immoral practices of slavery, discrimination, and racial segregation, albeit from an Anglo-European perspective. Inevitably, the curriculum introduces Rosa Parks, Martin Luther King, and Thurgood Marshall as Civil Rights superheroes who are credited with eradicating centuries of oppression and marginalization. The curriculum concludes on a high note, wrapped in a pretty bow, proclaiming that we are all equal and will live happily ever after.

In our search for the cause of the underachievement of boys of color, we determined that the problem must lie within the boys. We blamed their socioeconomic status, living conditions, families, genetics, psychological predispositions, and culture. However, never once did we consider that the underachievement of boys is due to the fundamental flaws in our educational institutions. Historic attitudes of racism and classism that have manifested in the form exclusionary practices—of tracking, a rejection of "outsider" cultures, zero tolerance discipline policies, and prison-to-school pipelines—continue to oppress and marginalize our boys of color. Therefore, it is only through an unwavering commitment to dismantling the inherently flawed educational system that we as a nation will be able to reclaim our forgotten sons.

REFERENCES

Algard, A. (2009). Maps of school shootings. *Stoptheshootings.org*. Retrieved from http://www.stoptheshootings.org

Belton, D. (1995). *Speak my name: Black men on masculinity and the American dream.* Boston, MA: Beacon.

Blount, M., & Cunningham, G. P. (Eds.). (1996). *Representing Black men.* New York, NY: Routledge.

Brookover, W., & Erickson, E. (1969). *Society, schools, and learning.* East Lansing, MI: Michigan State University Press.

Carby, V. H. (1982). Schooling in Babylon. In Center for Contemporary Studies. *The empire strikes back* (pp. 187–208). London, UK: Hutchinson.

Cassidy, E. F., & Stevenson, H. C. (2005). They wear the mask: Hypervulnerability and hypermasculine aggression among African American males in an urban remedial disciplinary school. *Journal of Aggression, Maltreatment & Trauma, 11*(4), 53–74.

Centers for Disease Control and Prevention. (2013). National Vital Statistics Reports. *Deaths: Leading Causes for 2010, 62*(6), 1–97.

Chen, E. Y. (2008). Impacts of "three strikes and you're out" on crime trends in California and throughout the United States. *Journal of Contemporary Criminal Justice, 24*(4), 345–370.

Conover, T. (2000). *Newjack: Guarding sing sing.* New York, NY: Random House.

Davis, J. E. (2003). Early schooling and academic achievement of African American males. *Urban Education, 38*(5), 515–537.

DeCuir, J. T., & Dixson, A. D. (2004). So when it comes out, they aren't that surprised that it is there: Using critical race theory as a tool of analysis of race and racism in education. *Educational Researcher, 33*(5), 26–31.

Downey, G., Lebolt, A., Rincon, C., & Freitas, A. L. (1998). Rejection sensitivity and children's interpersonal difficulties. *Child Development, 69,* 1072–1089.

DuRant, R. H., Pendergrast, R. A., & Cadenhead, C. (1994). Exposure to violence and victimization and fighting behavior by urban Black adolescents. *Journal of Adolescent Health, 15,* 311–318.

Elsner, A. (2004). Gates of injustice: The crisis in America's prisons. Upper Saddle River, NJ: Prentice Hall.

Gottfredson, D. (2001). *Schools and delinquency.* Cambridge, MA:Cambridge University Press.

Graham, M., & Robinson, G. (2004). "The silent catastrophe": Institutional racism in the British educational system and the underachievement of Black boys. *Journal of Black Studies, 34*(5), 653–671.

Groves, H. E. (1951). Separate but equal: The doctrine of Plessy v. Ferguson. *Phylon 12*(1), 66–72.

Harper, P. M. (1996). *Are we not men? Masculine anxiety and the problem of African-American identity.* New York, NY: Oxford University Press.

Hawkins, M. (1997). *Social Darwinism in European and American thought, 1860–1945: Nature as model and nature as threat.* Cambridge, MA: Cambridge University Press.

Hilliard, A. (1991). Do we have the will to educate all children? *Educational Leadership, 49*(1), 31–36.

Howard, T. (2008). Who really cares? The disenfranchisement of African-American males in pre-K–12 schools: A critical race theory perspective. *Teachers College Record, 110,* 954–985.

Hutchison, E. O. (1994). *Assassination of the Black male image.* Los Angeles, CA: Middle Passage.

Jackson, J. H. (2008). *Given half a chance: The Schott 50-state report on public education and African American males.* Cambridge, MA: Schott Foundation for Public Education.

Jefferson, T. (1784). *Notes on the State of Virginia, Queries 14 and 19.* Retrieved from http://thefederalistpapers.integratedmarket.netdna-cdn.com/wp-content/uploads/2012/12/Thomas-Jefferson-Notes-On-The-State-Of-Virginia.pdf

Jefferson, T. (1814). Letter from Thomas Jefferson to Peter Carr. *Encyclopedia Virginia.* Retrieved from http://www.encyclopediavirginia.org/Letter_from_Thomas_Jefferson_to_Peter_Carr_September_7_1814

Jull, S. (2000, November 30). Youth violence, schools, and the management question: A discussion of zero tolerance and equity in public schooling. *Canadian Journal of Educational Administration and Policy, 17.* Retrieved from http://www.umanitoba.ca/publications/cjeap/articles/jull.html

King, J. E. (1991). Dysconscious racism: Ideology, identity, and the miseducation of teachers. *Journal of Negro Education, 60*(2), 133–146.

Kunjufu, J. (1985). *Countering the conspiracy to destroy Black boys.* Chicago, IL: African American Images.

Ladson-Billings, G. (2001). *Crossing over to Canaan.* San Francisco, CA: Jossey-Bass.

Ladson-Billings, G. (2004). New directions in multicultural education: Complexities, boundaries, and critical race theory. In J. A. Banks & C. A. M. Banks.

(Eds.), *Handbook of research on multicultural* education (2nd ed., pp. 50–65). San Francisco, CA: Jossey-Bass.

Lewin, T. (2012, March 6). Black students face more discipline, data suggests. *The New York Times.* Retrieved from http://www.nytimes.com/2012/03/06/education/black-students-face-more-harsh-discipline-data-shows.html?_r=1&

Madhubuti, H. R. (1990). *Black men, obsolete, single, dangerous? The Afrikan American family in transition: Essays in discovery, solution, and hope.* Chicago, IL: Third World.

Majors, R., & Billson, M. (1992). *Cool pose: Dilemmas of Black manhood in America.* New York, NY: Simon & Schuster

Majors, R. G., Tyler, R., Peden, B., & Hall, R. E. (1994). Cool pose: A symbolic mechanism for masculine role enactment and copying by Black males. In R. G. Majors & J. U. Gordan (Eds.), *The American Black male: His present status and his future* (pp. 245–259). Chicago, IL: Nelson-Hall.

McMillian, M. (2004). Is no child left behind 'wise schooling' for African American male students? *The High School Journal, 87,* 25–33.

Meehan, B. T., Hughes, J. N., & Cavell, T. A. (2003). Teacher-student relationships as compensatory resources for aggressive children. *Child Development, 74*(4), 1145–1157.

Metropolitan Life. (2012). *The american teacher: Teachers, parents, and the economy.* Washington, DC: MetLife, Inc.

Mickelson, R. (1990). The attitude-achievement paradox among Black adolescents. *Sociology of Education, 63*(1), 44–61.

Morrow, R., & Torres, C. (1995). *Social theory and education a critique of theories of social and cultural reproduction.* Albany: State University of New York Press.

Neal, L. I., McCray, A. D., Webb-Johnson, G., & Bridgest, S. T. (2003). The effects of African American movement styles on teachers' perceptions and reactions. *Journal of Special Education, 37*(1), 49–57.

Noguera, P. (2003a). The trouble with Black boys: The role and influence of environmental and cultural factors on the academic performance of African American males. *Urban Education, 38,* 431–459.

Noguera, P. (2003b). Schools, prisons, and social implications of punishment: Rethinking disciplinary practices. *Theory Into Practice, 42,* 341–350.

Oakes, J. (1985). *Keeping track: How schools structure inequality.* New Haven, CT: Yale University Press.

Parson, E. (1994). Inner city children of trauma: Urban violence traumatic stress response syndrome. In J. Lindy & J. Wilson (Eds.), Countertransference in the treatment of PTSD (pp. 157–178). New York, NY: Guilford.

Race Forward. (2006, April 13). *Historical timeline of public education in the US.* Retrieved June 8, 2014, from https://www.raceforward.org/research/reports/historical-timeline-public-education-us

Roderick, M. (2003). What's happening to the boys? Early high school experiences and school outcomes among African American male adolescents in Chicago. *Urban Education, 38*(5), 538–607.

Simmons, W., & Grady, M. (1992). *Black male achievement: From peril to promise* (Report of the Superintendent's Advisory Committee on Black Male Achievement). Upper Marlboro, MD: Prince George's County Public Schools.

Singer, S. (1996). *Recriminalizing delinquency.* Cambridge, MA: Cambridge University Press.

Skiba, R. J., & Noam, G. (2001). *Zero tolerance: Can suspensions and expulsions keep schools safe?* San Francisco, CA: Jossey-Bass.

Skiba, R., Simmons, A., Staudinger, L., Rausch, M., Dow, F., & Feggins, R. (2003, May 16–17). *Consistent removal: Contributions of school discipline to the school-prison pipeline.* Presentation to the School to Prison Conference, Harvard Civil Rights Project, Indiana Education Policy Center, Indiana University.

Skolnick, J. H., & Currie, E. (Eds.). (1994). *Crisis in American institutions* (9th ed.). New York, NY: HarperCollins.

Slaughter-Defoe, D. T., & Richards, H. (1994). Literacy as empowerment: The case for African American males. In V. L. Gadsden & D. A. Wagner (Eds.), *Literacy among African American youth: Issues in learning, teaching, and schooling* (pp. 125–147). Cresskill, NJ: Hampton.

Sleeter, C. E., & Delgado Bernal, D. (2003). Critical pedagogy, critical race theory, and anti- racist education: Implications for multicultural education. In J.A. Banks & C.A.M. Banks (Eds.), *The handbook of research on multicultural education* (2nd ed.). San Francisco, CA: Jossey-Bass.

Solomon, P., & Palmer, H. (2004). Schooling in Babylon, Babylon in school: When racial profiling and zero tolerance coverage. *Canadian Journal of Educational Administration and Policy, 33.*

Spencer, M. B. (1999). Social and cultural influences on school adjustment: The application of an identity-focused cultural ecological perspective . *Educational Psychologist, 34*(1), 43–57.

Swanson, D. P., Cunningham, M., & Spencer, M. B. (2003). Black males' structural conditions, achievement patterns, normative needs and "opportunities." *Urban Education, 38*(5), 608–633.

Thomas, D., & Stevenson, H. (2009). Gender risks and education: The particular classroom challenges for urban low-income African American boys. *Review of Research in Education, 33,* 160–180.

Terman, L. (1923). *Intelligence tests and school reorganization.* New York, NY: World Book.

U.S. Bureau of Justice Statistics. (2000). *Correctional populations in the United States, 2001.* U.S. Department of Justice. Washington, DC. Retrieved September 1, 2005, from www.ojp.usdoj.gov/bjs/

U.S. Department of Education. (2000). *Fall 1998 elementary and secondary school civil rights compliance report: Projections.* Washington, DC: Office of Civil Rights.

Valencia, R. R. (Ed.). (1997). *The evolution of deficit thinking: Educational thought and practice.* London, UK: Falmer.

Waquant, L. (2000). Deadly symbiosis: When ghetto and prison meet and mesh. *Punishment and Society, 3*(1), 95–134.

West, C. (1993). *Race matters.* Boston, MA: Beacon.

West, C. (2004). *Democracy matters. Winning the fight against imperialism.* London, UK: Penguin.

CHAPTER 10

CHEMICALLY DEPENDENT ADOLESCENT LATINO OFFENDERS

Restorative and Social Justice as Alternatives to Incarceration

Paul M. Marietti
Ventura County Office of Education

Janice Tucker
California Lutheran University

Anthony H. Normore
California State University Dominguez Hills

ABSTRACT

Latino adolescent substance abuse and the need for treatment are of growing concern. Research indicates that Latinos are more likely than non-Latinos to need treatment for substance abuse and are less likely than non-Latinos to receive treatment (e.g., Falck, Nahhas, Li, & Carlson, 2012). Further research

Inclusive Practices and Social Justice Leadership for Special Populations in Urban Settings, pages 189–212
Copyright © 2015 by Information Age Publishing
All rights of reproduction in any form reserved.

shows Latino youth having disproportionately high contact with the juvenile justice system, and that they would benefit from greater access to community-based preventive services and alternatives to detention (Moeller, 2011). Intervention and treatment options as alternatives to incarceration have shown great promise (Holleran Steiker, 2009). Across the country, treatment-oriented juvenile drug courts and recovery programs have shown the capacity to provide therapeutic experiences as a response to substance abuse and as an alternative to incarceration. The increased use of restorative justice principles within the juvenile justice system have been demonstrated through the implementation of drug court and recovery programs (Schetly, 2009). The restorative justice models emphasized by treatment-oriented drug courts and recovery programs promote social justice through an attempt to reintegrate offenders back into the community and go against traditional educational policies at the federal, state, and local levels, which tend toward retributive justice. This chapter examines Latino adolescents, substance abuse, treatment options, the degree to which those options are restorative, and implications for social justice leadership.

Conceptual in nature, this chapter provides a review of literature surrounding adolescent substance abuse in relation to Latino juvenile offenders and their treatment options to reduce both drug use and rates of incarceration. Keeping in line with the scope of this book, we consider this group a special population. First, we present an overview of adolescent substance abuse and the need for treatment with a focus on Latino youth. Then, a synopsis of the incarceration of Latino youth will be discussed with an emphasis on the needs of these adolescent offenders. Next, intervention and treatment literature pertaining to alternatives to incarceration will be analyzed, with a focus on drug courts and recovery programs. Finally, social justice literature will be reviewed, with an emphasis on connections to retributive justice, restorative justice, educational leadership, and collaboration efforts in supporting recovery for Latino dependent adolescent offenders.

ADOLESCENT SUBSTANCE ABUSE, LATINOS, AND THE NEED FOR TREATMENT

Adolescent Substance Abuse

There is a substantial amount of research concerning substance abuse among adolescents. Adolescents account for the highest use of alcohol, tobacco, and illicit drugs in the United States (Sussman & Ames, 2008). Johnston, O'Malley, and Bachman (1999) found in their national drug use survey that the onset of substance abuse typically occurs between 13 and 15 years of age and peaks between 18 and 24 years of age. In a more recent study, Johnston, O'Malley, Bachman, and Schlenberg (2004) found further evidence that substance abuse is high among teens and emerging adults. By the age of 18, a majority of adolescents in the United States will have tried a mind-altering substance. Of those, 50% use it at least once a month (Sussman, Lisha, & Griffiths, 2011). Research has clearly established the connection between adolescent drug use and detrimental conditions, including morbidity and mortality. Newcomb and Bentler's foundational work (1988a, 1988b) identified teen substance use and related conditions, including poor academic performance, job instability, delinquency, and violence. Some 20 years later, Sussman and Ames (2008) validated the previous research associating teen substance abuse with teen pregnancy, sexually transmitted diseases, and delinquency.

According to the 2010 U.S. Census, Latinos are the fastest growing minority population in the United States. Of the 308.7 million people residing in the United States, 16% (or 50.5 million) are of Latino origin (U.S. Department of Commerce, 2011). The Latino population increased by 15.2 million between 2000 and 2010, accounting for over half of the 27.3 million increase in the total population of the United States (U.S. Department of Commerce, 2011). The increasing population overall also means an increase in the number of Latino adolescents, a population that raises particular concerns with regard to substance abuse. There is evidence that drug use among Latino adolescents has surpassed that of White adolescents. Differences exist for Latinos with regard to susceptibility to drug use, attitudes toward drugs, and treatment strategies (Prado et al., 2007). New data indicate Latino youth having a greater use of all substances except amphetamines when compared to other racial and ethnic groups (Johnston, O'Malley, Bachman, & Schulenberg, 2011).

Substance Abuse Among Latinos and the Need for Treatment

The extent to which ethnic differences contribute to the susceptibility of substance use and abuse is an ongoing question. Longitudinal survey data by the Substance Abuse and Mental Health Service Administration (SAMHSA) point to a substance abuse problem in the Latino community and a need for treatment options. According to the National Survey on Drug Use and Health (NSDUH, 2009), 25% of Latino youth have used some type of illegal substance in a given month. The survey goes on to identify 9.4% of adolescent Latinos in need of treatment for substance abuse and found that Latinos born in the United States are 6.4% more likely to need treatment when compared to Latinos not born in the United States (NSDUH, 2009). The National Survey on Drug Use and Health (2012), combining 2003–2011 data, asserts that Latinos were more likely than non-Latinos to have needed treatment for substance abuse in the past year. For Adolescents 12 or older who are in need of treatment, Latinos are less likely than non-Latinos to have received treatment (NSDUH, 2012). Overall, in 2011 an estimated three million Latinos needed but did not receive specialty treatment for substance abuse (NSDUH, 2012). Regardless of ethnicity, treatments for chemically dependent adolescents have traditionally focused on substance-related issues and are closely aligned with adult treatment methods. A focus on education is one area where adult and adolescent treatments can differ (Balsa, Homer, French, & Weisner, 2009). Adolescent treatment programs centered on school engagement, as opposed to employment, show increased outcome benefits, including lifetime earnings, cognitive functioning, and health, while adult programs show a connection between employment and reduced substance abuse (Balsa et al., 2009).

Adolescents, as opposed to adults, need treatment programs connected to an academic component. For adolescents, treatment programs centered on school engagement, as well as academics, drug counseling, and behavioral therapy, can be the most effective. Examining how these programs operate can lead to the development of more effective drug treatment programs for chemically dependent adolescents. For chemically dependent adolescents of all ethnicities, there is a connection between positive outcomes and treatment programs which include an academic component.

INCARCERATED LATINO YOUTH

Contact With the Juvenile Justice System

According to the U.S. Department of Justice's Office of Juvenile Justice and Deliquency Prevention, the juvenile arrest rate for all offenses in the United States reached its highest level in the 1990s, and then declined 43% by 2010. In 2010, there were 4,857 arrests for every 100,000 youths ages 10 through 17 in the United States (U.S. Department of Justice, 2012). However, when collecting juvenile arrest rates for all crimes in the nation by race, the U.S. Department of Justice fails to disaggregate the data for Latinos. The Office of Juvenile Justice and Delinquency Prevention justifies this failure to identify juvenile arrest rates for Latinos by concluding that persons of "Hispanic" ethnicity may be of any race, that is, White, Black, Native American, or Asian (U.S. Department of Justice, 2012). The data collected on the federal level does not provide an accurate understanding of Latino youth in the juvenile justice system; however it is estimated that 18,000 Latino youth are incarcerated each day in the United States (Saavedra, 2010). Although an estimate of 18,000 demonstrates a large number of youths being placed into custody, due to difficulties obtaining data related to Latinos, most experts in the field see this number as significantly underestimated. In a 2009 interview with Dr. David Springer, Holleran Steiker reported,

> If we want our neighborhoods and communities to be safer, we must be more than tough on crime, we must be smart on crime. This is a tough population to treat, and it requires expertise. Whenever possible, families should be involved in treatment. This means that we must keep juvenile offenders as close to their home communities, and their families, as possible. Of course, the research shows that the most effective way to treat a substance abusing juvenile offender is in his or her community, not in prison-like institutional settings. The evidence about what works is very clear. Study after study indicates that prevention and treatment programs are more effective than incarceration, and that it is cheaper and more effective to keep less serious juvenile offenders in the community, where they can access needed services and avoid or limit disruption in their home lives. The evidence also shows that it is ineffective to lump delinquent kids together in large institutions far from home. The challenge remains in reforming the juvenile justice system, which takes a shifting of resources, and political will. (pp. 136–138)

While the number of Latino youth grows rapidly in the United States, research into juvenile arrests rates and contact with the juvenile justice system for Latino youth is limited. As the number of Latino youth continues to grow, more are coming into contact with the juvenile justice system. In California, where data on Latinos are tracked, the Latino youth population grew from 4.4 million in 2002 to 4.9 million in 2008. Arrests of Latino youth rose during the same period, from 85,284 in 2002 to 121,120 in 2008, and Latinos represent 52.9% of all youth arrested in California in 2008 (California Department of Justice, 2009). The data collected by the U.S. Department of Justice prevents us from tracking the problem at the national level and therefore fails to make clear Latino youth and their contact with the juvenile justice system. Although California does a better job tracking arrest for Latino youth, there is still a limited amount of research into Latino youth residing in the juvenile justice system.

Latino Juvenile Incarceration

Without national data, it is difficult to get a clear understanding of the scope of the problem faced by Latino youth in the juvenile justice system. Moeller (2011) attributes this to data-collection methods which hide Latino youth presence in the system. Moeller argues that the available data show Latino youth having disproportionately high contact with the juvenile justice system. Evidence also suggests that Latino youth are harmed by policies and practices at the state and local levels, such as treating youth as adults in criminal court, and would benefit from greater access to community-based preventive services and alternatives to detention (Moeller, 2011).

Research into youth residing in the juvenile justice system reveals some of the realities they face. In a study of characteristics of juvenile offenders in a large juvenile justice system, building upon basic characteristics of juvenile offenders from previous studies, Martin Martin, Dell, Davis, and Guerrieri (2008) found that the most serious youth offenders enter the juvenile justice system with histories that include physical and sexual abuse, witnessing violent acts, parental substance abuse and neglect, and numerous mental health, developmental, and emotional issues (Martin et al., 2008, p. 608) Martin et al. (2008) make it clear that there is a strong relationship between trauma, delinquency, and mental health, and that to focus primarily on the delinquency without a deeper understanding of the whole child is ineffective.

Previous studies address the need to understand incarcerated youth in order to limit and reduce delinquency (Jenson, Potter, & Howard, 2001; Snyder & Sickmund, 2006). Research by Jenson et al. (2001), Baer and Maschi (2003), as well as Dixon, Howie, and Starling (2005) indicates adolescents adjudicated for serious offenses, including Latinos, enter the juvenile justice system with high rates of physical abuse, sexual abuse, emotional issues, neglect, and parental substance abuse.

Research also reveals a connection between depression and substance abuse with juvenile delinquency and adolescent incarceration. Caufmann, Feldman, Waterman, and Steiner (1998), Leve and Chamberlain (2004), and Ritakallio, Kaltiala-Heino, Kivivuori, Luukkaala, and Rimpela (2006) all connect delinquency to depression, finding that between 10% to 30% of incarcerated juveniles exhibit symptoms of depression. Previous research by Brook, Whiteman, Finch, and Cohen (1996) and Jenson et al. (2001) identified high rates of substance abuse in samples of incarcerated youth. More recent research into substance abuse by incarcerated adolescents reveals substance abuse as a predictor of incarceration (Tripoli, Springer, & Corcoran, 2007). For adolescents entering incarceration, including Latinos, trauma has consistently been found to be present.

The examination of incarcerated youth and the causes of delinquency provide us an opportunity to change the focus of juvenile justice from retributive incarceration and punishment to restorative identification and treatment (Moeller, 2011). The extensive amount of trauma found in incarcerated youth, including Latino youth, must be identified, taken into consideration, and provided treatment. If the expectation for the youth exiting the juvenile justice system is not to reoffend, the juvenile justice system must provide the services and attention necessary while they are incarcerated (Moeller, 2011).

INTERVENTION AND TREATMENTS FOR LATINO JUVENILE OFFENDERS

Latinos and a Need for Treatment

Getting youth, including incarcerated youth, into treatment programs for substance abuse is an important first step for their recovery. For Latino youth residing in our juvenile justice system, getting access to treatment and staying in treatment is a real challenge (Holleran Steiker, 2009). One of the ways to provide treatment, and treatment retention, is for our juvenile system and courts to make treatment a priority over incarceration.

There are a limited number of drug-based prevention and treatment programs that target minority youth (Goldbach, Thompson, & Holleran Steiker, 2011). Research on substance abuse treatments for Latino adolescents is also limited; however there has been some examination of drug abuse treatment for Latino youth in relation to family therapy. Santisteban, Dillon, Mena, Estrada, and Vaughan (2005) examined ethnicity-related factors that impact treatment for Hispanic substance abusing adolescents and found that there was a need for specialized engagement interventions that could offset psychiatric and parenting factors that serve as obstacles for engagement in treatment. Santisteban, Mena, and McCabe (2011) examined family-based interventions for Latino adolescents and concluded that it was possible to enhance the effects of family therapy on both drug use and parenting practices by adding components that strategically target drug, cultural, and parenting processes.

There is little research related to treatment, retention, and engagement for substance abusing minority offenders. Springer, Rivaux, Bohman, and Yeung, (2006) examined adolescent substance abuse treatments for Latino, Anglo, and African American juvenile offenders, focusing on the impact of retention and therapeutic engagement. Conclusions by Springer et al. support previous studies that substance abuse interventions with at-risk Latino youth are more effective when they center on culture. The study suggests that family therapy is an essential part of effective treatment components for Latino juveniles (Springer et al., 2006). Rivaux, Springer, Bohman, Wagner, and Gil (2006) explored successful treatment outcomes for high-risk, substance abusing Latino, Anglo, and African American juvenile offenders. The study found evidence of positive results for treatments focused on the identification of individuals in certain ethnic groups and their responsiveness. The study also found that greater family problems were related to recidivism among Latino juvenile offenders and that treatment focused on family history and dynamics offered the greatest benefit (Rivaux et al., 2006).

Szapocznik et al., (2006) examined evidence-based drug abuse treatments for Latino adolescents and found family based approaches have the greatest potential to treat drug abuse in Latino adolescents. Szapocznik, Lopez, Prado, Schwartz, and Pantin (2008) explored drug abuse in African American and Latino adolescents, finding that results support the implementation of family-based interventions. Therapy should involve multiple family members and address family relationships in addition to the influence of peers and bonding with school (Szapocznik et al., 2008).

For Latino adolescents incarcerated in the juvenile justice system, family-based approaches to treatment are seen as the most promising approach, however providing family-based substance abuse treatment poses a challenge. Research into treatment for substance abuse for Latino adolescents does not reveal any single approach to be effective, but some of the most promising interventions for incarcerated adolescents of any ethnicity include outpatient family-based interventions, problem solving, and social skills training (Holleran Steiker, 2009).

Drug Court

Drug courts for both adults and juveniles operate in very similar ways. They attempt to combine judicial monitoring with substance abuse treatment for drug offenders. The process includes a drug offender coming before a judge in a courtroom setting and in most cases involves a collaborative approach between prosecution and defense. The offender is required to receive access to comprehensive treatment, participate in frequent drug testing, and receive sanctions for infractions and rewards for achievements. Drug courts across the nation vary greatly in design and specific treatment options and supervision components (Lindquist, Krebs, Warner, & Lattimore, 2009). There is research suggesting that drug courts are effective at reducing recidivism and substance abuse of drug-involved offenders, but there is no single effective drug court model, and fully implemented programs are not well documented (Lindquist et al., 2009). Current research into drug courts focuses on the validity of programming and the effects of drug courts on substance abuse and recidivism. The current goal is to determine specifically which components contribute to an effective program, including treatment, testing, supervision, and collaboration between organizations (Taxman & Bouffard, 2005).

Although drug courts vary throughout the United States, they do have several commonalities relating to duration, type, and intensity of substance abuse treatment that is required (Lindquist et al., 2009). Most programs require participation for a 12-month period before participants can graduate; programs either provide a recovery program for participants or send them to a community-based program. Participants are supervised by the court and are routinely drug tested (Lindquist et al., 2009).

A key component found in the drug courts' structure includes the use of recovery phases consisting of 2 to 6 months each. Success in individual programs was then measured based upon participants moving through phases of recovery (Taxman & Bouffard, 2005). Taxman and Bouffard (2005) suggest that regardless of the conditions of the drug court program, or the requirements for success, government-run drug court treatment programs succeed in holding offenders more accountable in terms of commitment to the treatment and recovery process. Although it is clear that drug court programs hold offenders accountable, the study fails to determine if, or how, the quality of the various drug treatment programs affect the progress offenders make in the program (Taxman & Bouffard, 2005). In their comparison between drug court and non–drug court adult participants, Lindquist et al. (2009) concluded that drug court participants receive more intense treatment and increased supervision than those not involved in drug court, and cite several studies that report significantly lower recidivism rates among drug court participates when compared to nonparticipates. Like Taxman and Bouffard (2005), the research also called for future exploration into drug court treatment on the outcomes of substance use and recidivism. Research by Deschenes, Ireland, and Kleinpeter (2009) reinforces the previous literature supporting the effectiveness of drug courts and counseling, in addition to education and vocational resources, as components to increasing retention and graduation from drug court.

Although the literature supports favorable outcomes of adult drug courts, the literature to support juvenile drug courts is not as strong. Aos, Miller, and Drake (2006) and D.K. Shaffer (2006) both found only a modest impact of juvenile drug courts in their meta-analyses. In the most up-to-date research, Henggeler, McCart, Cunningham, and Chapman (2012) studied strategies for enhancing the capacity of juvenile drug courts to reduce substance use and criminal behavior by incorporating components of evidence-based treatments into their existing services. The study of family engagement (CM-FAM) produced results demonstrating that evidence-based substance abuse treatment can be integrated effectively into the juvenile justice system (Henggler et al., 2012).

Through the review of literature, it is clear that juvenile drug courts have the capacity to provide therapeutic experiences as a response to substance abuse and provide alternatives to incarceration. Treatment-oriented juvenile drug courts provide adolescent substance abusers with an alternative to incarceration, while providing them with much-needed treatment for their addictions. The types of structure and treatment programs offered by adult and juvenile drug courts thought the United States vary, but the literature surrounding effective methods and programs remains limited, as are known examples of evidence-based treatments.

School-Based Recovery Programs

Currently in the United States, there are 30–35 known programs within high schools providing academics and services for students in recovery from drug and alcohol addiction (de Miranda & Williams, 2011). These programs began in the late 1970s, when it was recognized that a need existed for "sober schooling" to serve high school-aged children. Recovery schools catered to adolescents exiting formal residential treatment for substance abuse. Research into the effectiveness of recovery schools is limited. In a cursory study of 17 recovery high schools, Travis (2010) found a significant reduction in substance and mental health symptoms among participating students. The effectiveness of these recovery programs was seen as derived from adolescents not having to return to the same environment where the abuse took place.

For chemically dependent adolescents, regardless of ethnicity, high school is one of the largest threats to relapsing (Moberg & Finch, 2007). This is due in part to high schools as places where adolescents have established their social network, and if their network is composed of substance abusers, it is hard to break the cycle of abuse. Recovery schools are designed to reduce the risk of relapse by removing the adolescents from their destructive social networks and creating an environment of support, treatment, and social bonding. Although recovery programs differ from school to school, they all have some basic similarities. These include targeting multiple areas of health, including education, emotional, physical health, psychiatric, vocational, and legal, all during the school day (Moberg & Finch, 2007).

Until this decade, recovery programs on school campuses and standalone recovery schools existed mostly in isolation. Like the juvenile courts, these recovery programs and schools operate with unique requirements and treatment options. In 2002, the Association of Recovery Schools was formed with the purpose of advocating, promoting, and strengthening recovery programs and schools across the United States (de Miranda & Williams, 2011). The Association of Recovery Schools convenes annually to discuss the current state of programs across the nation and to examine the latest research to inform practice. Participates in the annual conference consist of public and private recovery schools, and recovery programs that exist on college campuses.

Attempts to address the effectiveness of recovery schools are limited and have produced mixed results. Recovery High School (RHS) in Albuquerque, New Mexico, was an alternative school for chemically dependent adolescents funded by the Robert Wood Johnson Foundation and emphasizes therapy over education (Moberg & Finch, 2007). An evaluation of the program by Moberg and Thaler (1995) focused on the feasibility of replicating the program model and concluded that the ARHS model was feasible programmatically, with impressive evidence of therapeutic effectiveness. It was also concluded that although highly therapeutic, the model's educational outcomes were limited (Moberg & Thaler, 1995).

Chicago Preparatory Charter High School is also an example of an alternative recovery school but unique in that it emphasized a rigorous educational program over therapy. An evaluation of the program by Moberg (1999) focused on the evaluation of the model based on implementation, feasibility, and preliminary effectiveness. Unfortunately, the school was closed prematurely resulting in Moberg not implementing the evaluation (Moberg, 1999).

Recovery High School, a private high school for students who volunteer to attend and agree to work "programs of recovery" for substance abuse. In a study utilizing ethnographic data, Finch (2003) examined the dynamics of recovery within the RHS model. A key finding of the study centered on the effectiveness of boundaries on the sense of place within the school. RHS established boundaries to support the recovery of students and to define a sense of place in the community. It was found that for some students, threats did not align with boundaries, while other students found rigid structures helpful. This resulted in staff and students determining the appropriate level of structure and flexibility needed to create a healthy learning environment (Finch, 2003).

Past research on individual recovery schools focused on initial implementation and feasibility of the programs. All three schools for adolescents recovering from substance abuse disorders presented here provided for both substance abuse treatment and education; however they differed greatly in what they emphasized, and their results were unclear.

RETRIBUTIVE AND RESTORATIVE JUSTICE

Retributive Justice

Herman Bianchi (1994) suggests that scholars are so connected to our current retributive model of criminal justice, that they are unable to accept the effectiveness of other models in other times and places. While Jon Braithwaite (1997) argues that through the history of the world, restorative justice has been the dominant model of criminal justice, and as such, a move toward a restorative justice model is a return to our roots and not the latest attempt to solve our ailing justice system. Restorative justice is not a new idea but a prominent concept of justice visible throughout most of human history (Llewellyn & Howse, 1999).

Prior to our modern system of state-centered public justice, the administration of justice was not simply about applying rules. Instead, it was a mediating and negotiating process known as community justice (Zehr, 1990). Community justice grew out of the need for communities to resolve disputes, reconcile harm, and to maintain relationships, the use of retributive justice or forced resolution were used as a last resort. As governments grew, they began the process of replacing community with courts for the administration of justice. Courts established rule of law and applied the rules, established guilt, and set penalties. Victims, offenders, and the community lost control of disputes; instead, punishment served the interest of the state while doing nothing to address the harm caused by the wrongdoing (Llewellyn & Howse, 1999).

The retributive approach to justice is the philosophy that has underlined our Western systems of criminal justice and one that relies on third-party sanctions and punishment to address societal wrongs (Duff, 2003). A retributive model of justice measures wrongdoing through a system of rules associated with particular consequences, establishes the wrongs committed, and assigns guilt. The traditional retributive model has the offender as the focus and does not consider the needs of the victim or the community. In addition, it does not take into consideration the view of offender as a victim or the stigma that comes with labeling a person as a criminal (Calhoun & Pelech, 2010). The traditional use of retributive justice pratices has led to issues beyond the punishment of the offender and the returing of status and power to the victim. Today, the U.S. criminal justice system is burdened by the cost of high rates of incarceration and the maitainence of the world's largest prison system. In addtion, there is the stigmatization and marginalization of prisioners, which limits their opportunities upon release. As a response to these issues, and a growing emphasis on human rights, movements have begun to replace this retributive system of justice with restorative justice.

Restorative Justice

Restorative justice models of criminal justice are increasingly advocated as the preferred alternative to retributive justice (Johnstone, 2003; Sullivan & Tifft, 2001). The term "restoratve justice" can be used when referring to both criminal and civil matters, and is a process in which parties involved in a specific offense work collectively to find resloution. A wider more comprehensive defintion provided by Gilbert and Settles (2007) "views crime as a harm to individuals, their neighborhoods, the surrounding community and even the offender. Crimes produce injuries that must be repaired by those who caused the injury" and that "crimes are more than violations of law, and justice is more than punishment of the guilty," They further posit that restorative justice "strives to promote healing through structured communication processes among victims, offenders, community representatives and government officals . . . to accomplish these goals in a manner that promotes peace and order for the community, vindication for the victim, and recompense for the offender" (p. 7).

There is no definitive restorative justice model in place. But if restorative justice is a process of bringing all parties involved in an offense together for resolution and reintegration into the community, then restorative justice should be measured by its ability to restore relationships. Although models of restorative justice differ, there are several common components to how parties work toward restoration. The process of restorative justice must be voluntary and must include telling the truth. The only way to repair the wrong is to know and understand what has happened. At the heart of the restorative justice process is encounter. The process must include an encounter, which involves sharing the truth in the presence of the offender, victim, and community. Sharing the truth allows the community to see the truth, allows the offender to see the harm inflicted, and allows the victim to see the offender as a person. For the encounter to be successful, it must include a facilitator, who serves as the symbolic representation of the community and who allows the participants to decide what is important and what the right resolution is. Through a series of encounters, healing can begin and agreements can be reached. Through listening and understanding, participants can commit to restoring their relationship to one of dignity, concern, and respect (Llewellyn & Howse, 1999). Finally, the restorative justice process empowers the offender and the victim to take an active role in the justice process. In order for a program to be completely restorative, it must include 11 components:

- Involves all parties with a stake in the resolution of the conflict. The victim, perpetrator, and the community must each be involved and enabled to participate fully in the process.
- Recognizes and seeks to address the harms to one another, remembering that harm is not restricted to the victim but can be expressed by the offender and the community.
- Is voluntary. Participation cannot be the result of coercion, fear, threats, or manipulation brought to bear on either the victim or the offender.
- Is premised on and includes truth telling. Truth telling in the form of an admission of responsibility for what happened on the part of the perpetrator is a precondition for a restorative process; truth telling in the form of honest relating of one's story and experience by all parties is a fundamental part of the process.

- Involves encounter, a face-to-face sharing of stories and experiences between victim/offender and community.
- Protects the rights of victims and offenders.
- Involves a facilitator who can ensure a broader social perspective.
- Aims for reintegration of the victim and offender into the community.
- Develops a plan for the future or agreement for resolution out of negotiation.
- Does not involve punishment.
- Is evaluated by its results, whether it restores or not. (Llewellyn & Howse, 1999, p. 73)

Drug Court Recovery Programs as Restorative

Arguments for drug courts as restorative come from Bazemore (1999), who concluded that the restorative justice model can be used to rehabilitate offenders, and Braithwaite (2001), who suggested that restorative justice can be an appropriate model for dealing with drug abuse. The recovery programs associated with drug courts have a strong connection to Braithwaite's concept of reintegrative shaming (Miethe, Lu, & Reese, 2000). Reintegrative shaming consists of initial social disapproval of the offender's deviant behavior followed by the acceptance of the offender back into the community (Braithwaite, 1989). Drug courts assign chemically dependent adolescent drug offenders to treatment programs after they have admitted to their violations. After completing treatment, participants are recognized with a graduation ceremony symbolizing acceptance back into the community.

Fulkerson (2009) emphasizes that an intervention which provides treatment to those addicted to drugs is by nature a restorative sanction. Roche (2001) previously concluded that the community orientation and the reintegrative shaming in drug court programs demonstrate restorative values. It could be argued that the restorative justice definition is malleable, and programs such as drug court and their recovery programs share enough restorative properties for us to consider further adaptation of the restorative justice theory (Fulkerson, 2009, p. 258).

SOCIAL JUSTICE AND RESTORATIVE JUSTICE

The term "social justice" is evoked daily in literature and the news media; however it can be difficult to define. Murrell (2006) argues that "social justice involves a disposition toward recognizing and eradicating all forms of oppression and differential treatment extant in the practices and policies of institutions, as well as a fealty to participatory democracy as a means of this action" (p. 81).

Narrowing the definition of social justice from the world stage to the classroom does not make the task any easier. How social justice relates to and influences educational areas such as program development, curricula, practicum opportunities, educational philosophies, and social vision is a large conversation (Hytten & Bettez, 2011). What can be said is that education plays a part in promoting justice and the development democratic citizenship. Michelli and Keiser (2005) see this educational commitment to social justice diminished through our current political environment of emphasizing curriculum tied to basic literacy and numeracy and not much else.

In addition to a modern emphasis on academic success in the face of globalization, countries throughout the world continue to adopt the social justice principal of universal education for all children. This increasing inclusiveness has led to challenges of diversity, individuality, and discipline. Schools must now weigh the needs of the many with the needs of the few. An individual student's right to an education must weighed against the majority of students' right to a safe and affirming educational environment (Wearmouth, Mckinney, & Glynn, 2007a). To combat these challenges, schools in Europe, Australia, New Zealand, and North America are implementing restorative practices in the form of victim-offender conferences as a process for conflict resolution and student discipline (Wearmouth et al., 2007a). Teachers and staff are trained as mediators and lead restorative circles, bringing together the offender, victim, and community members in an effort to turn injury into personal healing and community development (Wearmouth, McKinney, & Glynn, 2007b).

Within the Unites States, it is understandable that a restorative approach to discipline could be perceived as a realistic alternative to zero tolerance retributive polices, which mandate suspension and expulsion, and disproportionately target minority students. Specifically, Latino youth are disproportionately represented in the number of school suspensions, expulsions, and referrals to the juvenile justice system. Restorative justice is increasingly being implemented as an alternative to retributive school discipline polices and a social justice response to the school-to-prison pipeline. Sumner, Silverman, and Frampton (2010) state that there is little research on school-based restorative justice and even less on its implementation and efficacy in schools serving youth of color (p. 4). However, one example of restorative justice policies reducing violence, suspensions, and referrals to the juvenile justice system can be found in the Oakland Unified School District. In a 2007 case study conducted by the Thelton E. Henderson Center for Social Justice at the University of California, Berkeley, Cole Middle School in west Oakland's restorative justice program, created as an alternative to zero tolerance disciplinary polices, was found to resolve conflict and build school community. The process for implementing a restorative justice approach to student discipline began with the training of all teachers and staff at Cole Middle School on the practice of disciplinary circles and community building activities (Sumner, Silverman, & Frampton, 2010). This new restorative discipline program then became the primary way of resolving disciplinary issues at Cole. Students were also offered an elective restorative justice class and a full-time disciplinary case manager was funded through the City of Oakland (Sumner et al., 2010). Students participated in restorative circles, which included students, teachers, and staff. The circles were led by a circle keeper to ensure everyone had an opportunity to speak. The morning advisory period was utilized as time to hold restorative circles and address disciplinary infractions. The study concluded that the restorative justice program strengthened school relationships, helped students and adults deal with violence in their community, reduced suspensions by 87% and expulsions to zero, and saw increased student responsibility and autonomy (Sumner et al., 2010).

Restorative justice programs implemented in schools provide students with the opportunity to confront the harm they have caused, and in the process, students learn empathy and accountability (Sumner et al., 2010). Restorative justice practices are well suited for school campuses because they have the ability to support student learning by providing an alternative to retributive discipline and creating a supportive atmosphere. The restorative justice models emphasized by drug courts and recovery programs promote social justice through an attempt to reintegrate offenders back into the community and goes against the current educational policies at the federal, state, and local levels, which tend toward retributive justice.

CONCLUDING THOUGHTS

As restorative justice programs are taking hold in classrooms in the United States and abroad, they are also being implemented within juvenile justice systems. These reforms target the process of justice for incarcerated youth, their families, and their communities. In the United States, evidence-based practices are being implemented and replicated. These practices focus on a set of guiding principles articulated by the Catherine T. MacArthur Foundation and their *Models for Change* program. The principles include fundamental fairness to youth, families, victims, and communities; understanding; developmental differences between youth and adults; acknowledgement of individual strengths and needs; belief in youth potential; expectation that individuals, communities, and the justice system have responsibilities; and commitment to safety for communities and individuals (Models for Change, 2014).

States across the country are participating in the Models for Change Initiative, which applies the concepts of social justice to juvenile justice settings. The Initiative supports a network of organizations and indiviuals working together to hold juveniles accountable for their offenses while being treated fairly throughout the juvenile justice process (Models for Change, 2014) One aspect of the Models for Change Initiative is the Disproportionate Minority Contact (DMC) Action Network and the Juvenile Detention Alternatives Initiative (JDAI). Started in 2007, the networks attempt to reduce the number of youth in the juvenile justice system and specifically the disproportionate number of racial and ethinic minorities in the juvenile justice system. This incudes the tracking and reporting of data, incresed culural competencies, responsiveness, and community-based and culturally relevant alternatives to incarceration (Models for Change, 2014).

Collaboration and Leadership

The literature from the 1990s shows a movement to provide comprehensive services that would be coordinated among providers and be delivered effectively to youths and their families (Holden, Friedman, & Santiago, 2001; Kagan & Neville, 1993; Pumariega & Winters, 2003). Pires (2002) described this movement found in the literature as a "system of care." This system of care refers to a variety of services which are coordinated to meet the multiple and changing needs of children and their families (Stroul & Friedman, 1994).

In order to provide consistently effective restorative justice programs founded on social justice for chemically dependent Latino adolescents, there must be a collaborative effort between several organizations. Unfortunately, very few of the nation's juvenile drug courts implement evidence-based programs for youth caught in the cycle of drug dependency (Nissen, Merrigan, & Kraft, 2005). In order to create more effective comprehensive systems of care, leaders must create a more coordinated effort at the local, state, and federal levels, bringing together public and private community organizations (Nissen et al., 2005). Educational leaders working both inside and outside detention facilities must take into consideration education and corrections.

Mackey (2011) established that it is unclear how these two organizations can and should work together. This partnership is hindered due to the influence of governmental policies, the media, and specific organizations and advocates (Mackey, 2011). This means that educational leaders in these settings must maneuver between two very different organizations, with two very different agendas. Strong educational leaders committed to social justice and restorative solutions are needed. Stefkovich and Begley (2007) see a genuine regard for a student's best interests as a major part of principal leadership. Ethical educational leaders working within the context of juvenile justice must engage in active inquiry and self-reflection in order to make decisions that represent the best interests of the student and be willing to stand up against those that do not (Stefkovich & Begley, 2007). Stronger educational leaders and increased collaboration with and between judges, attorneys, law enforcement, behavioral health organizations, and researchers can reduce the fragmentation found in drug courts and recovery classrooms, and implement effective evidence-based programs that reduce recidivism and lead adolescents to recovery.

The published literature presented in this chapter clearly demonstrates a need for further research into substance abuse, Latino youth, and treatment options. Although the research suggests that treatment for Latinos include a family component, there are also other areas that are in need of exploration. These include treatment models, outcomes, and success rates for Latino students. Research is also needed for current treatment options and the degree to which they are restorative, impactful, and culturally appropriate for substance abusing Latino students.

Finally, limited research appears to have been done on school-based recovery programs. The research does not go much further than that recovery schools and programs exist and vary greatly. There was minimal literature found on school-based recovery programs that are provided through drug courts as an alternative to incarceration. It is clear that much research is needed in the area of recovery schools, including the various models and their requirements for student entry and treatment, recovery schools as tools to support abstinence, relapse, avoidance, education, the effectiveness of recovery schools on reducing substance abuse and educating students, comparing recovery programs to each other and to students in community-based treatment, examining racial and ethnic diversity in specialty treatment programs and recovery school communities, and what treatment options would be most effective.

The literature reviewed clearly calls for a need to unite juvenile detention centers, drug courts, treatment programs, and schools both individually and collaboratively. Through greater research and understanding, leadership within organizations, and between organizations, can grow and improve. A closer examination of recovery programs through the restorative justice lens and in relation to the organizations they collaborate with will inform leadership and lead to more effective and dynamic programs.

The Recovery Classroom unites adolescent substance abusers, juvenile drug courts, schools, and adolescent substance abuse treatment providers in an effort to educate, provide treatment, and connect teens to positive activities and caring adults. This chapter examined the relevant literature regarding adolescent drug addiction, drug courts, treatment programs, and restorative justice. The literature explored adolescent drug use among

Latino adolescents and the response, both punitive and restorative. The research provides the conceptual framework for the study of chemically dependent adolescent offenders in an alternative community school to illustrate and inform their impact and the implications for leadership.

There is currently no research examining Latino adolescents in recovery programs or their outcomes, either therapeutic or educational. Research is needed to have a clearer picture and greater understanding of recovery schools and programs, and their effectiveness with Latino youth. Further research should include how schools and programs operate academically; provide greater detail about the students they serve, the effects of the programs on academic achievement and the reductions of substance abuse; and how these program differences affect outcomes (Moberg & Finch, 2007). By examining how recovery schools and drug courts fit into a restorative justice model, we can move closer to discovering an evidenced-based treatment program that can be applied impactfully.

REFERENCES

Aos, S., Miller, M., & Drake, E. (2006). *Evidence-based public policy options to reduce future prison construction, criminal justice costs, and crime rates.* Olympia: Washington State Institute for Public Policy.

Baer, J., & Maschi, T. (2003). Random acts of delinquency: Trauma and self-destructiveness in juvenile offenders. *Child and Adolesent Social Work Journal, 20*(2), 85–98.

Balsa, A. I., Homer, J. F., French, M. T., & Weisner, C. M. (2009, January). Substance use, education, employment, and criminal activity outcomes of adolescents in outpatient chemical dependency programs. *Journal of Behavioral Health Services & Research, 36*(1), 75–99.

Bazemore, G. (1999). After shaming, whither reintegration: Restorative justice and relational rehabilitation. In G. Bazemore & L. Walgrave, *Restorative juvenile justice : Repairing the harm of youth crime* (pp. 155–194). Monsey, NY: Criminal Justice Press.

Bianchi, H. (1994). *Justice as sanctuary: Toward a system of crime control.* Bloomington: Indiana University Press.

Braithwaite, J. (1989). *Crime, shame and reintegration.* Cambridge, UK: Cambridge University Press.

Braithwaite, J. (1997). *Restorative justice: Assessing an immodest theory and a pessimistic theory.* Review essay prepared for University of Toronto Law Course, Restorative Justice: Theory and Practice in Criminal Law and Business Regulation.

Braithwaite, J. (2001). Restorative justice and a new criminal law of substance abuse. *Youth and Society, 33*(2), 227–248.

Brook, J., Whiteman, M., Finch, S., & Cohen, P. (1996). Young adult drug use and delinquency: Childhood antecedents and adolescent mediators. *Journal of American Academy of Child and Adolescent Psychiatry, 35*(12), 1584–1592.

Calhoun, A., & Pelech, W. (2010). Responding to young people responsible for harm: A comparative study of restorative and conventional approaches. *Contemporary Justice Review, 13*(3), 287–306.

California Department of Justice. (2009, July). *Juvenile justice in California 2008, Table 1*. Retrieved from http://ag.ca.gov/cjsc/publications/misc/jj08/preface.pdf

Cauffman, E., Feldman, S., Waterman, J., & Steiner, H. (1998). Posttramatic stress disorder among female juvenile offenders. *Journal of the American Academy of Child and Adolescent Psychiatry, 37*(11), 1209–1216.

de Miranda, J., & Williams, G. (2011, April). Youth in recovery. *The Prevention Researcher,* 16–19.

Deschenes, E. P., Ireland , C., & Kleinpeter, C. B. (2009). Enhancing drug court success. *Journal of Offender Rehabilitation, 48*(1), 19–36.

Dixon, A., Howie, P., & Starling, J. (2005). Trauma exposure, posttraumatic stress, and psychiatric comorbidity in female offenders. *Journal of the American Academy of Child and Adolescent Psychiatry, 44*(8), 789–806.

Duff, R. A. (2003). Probation, punishment and restorative justice: Should altruism be engaged in punishment? *Howard Journal of Criminal Justice, 42*(2), 181–197.

Falck, R. S., Nahhas, R. W., Li, L., & Carlson, R. G. (2012, May). Surveying teens in school to assess the prevalence of problematic drug use. *Journal of School Health, 82*(5), 217–224.

Finch, A. J. (2003). *A sense of place at Recovery High School: Boundary permeability and student recovery support.* Unpublished PhD dissertation, Vanderbilt University, Nashville, TN.

Fulkerson, A. (2009). The drug treatment court as a form of restorative justice. *Contemporary Justice Review, 12*(3), 253–267.

Gilbert, M. J., & Settles, T. L. (2007). The next step: Indigenous development of neighborhood-restorative community justice. *Criminal Justice Review, 32*(1), 5–25. doi:10.1177/0734016806297645

Goldbach, J. T., Thompson, S. J., & Holleran Steiker, L. K. (2011). Special consideration for substance abuse intervention with Latino youth. *The Prevention Researcher, 18*(2), 8–11.

Henggler, S. W., McCart, M. R., Cunningham, P. B., & Chapman, J. E. (2012). Enhancing the effectiveness of juvenile drug courts by integrating evidence-based practices. *Journal of Consulting and Clincal Psychology, 80*(2), 264–275.

Holden, E. W., Friedman, R. M., & Santiago, R. L. (2001). Overview of the national evaluation of the Comprehensive Community Mental Health Services for Children and Their Families program. *Journal of Emotional and Behavioral Disorders, 9*(1), 4–12.

Holleran Steiker, L. K. (2009). Substance-abusing incarcerated youth: An interview with Dr. David Springer. *Journal of Social Work Practice in the Addictions,* (9), 135–139.

Hytten, K., & Bettez, S. C. (2011, Winter-Spring). Understanding education for social justice. *Educational Foundations,* 7–24.

Jenson, J., Potter, C., & Howard, M. (2001). American juvenile justice: Recent trends and issues in youth offending. *Social Policy and Adminsitration, 35*, 48–68.

Johnstone, G. (2003). *Restorative justice reader: Texts, sources, context*. Portland, OR: Willan.

Johnston, L., O'Malley, P., & Bachman, J. (1999). *National survey results on drug use from the Monitoring the Future study, 1975–1998, Volume I*. Washington DC: National Institute on Drug Use, Publication no.99-4660.

Johnston, L. D., O'Malley, P. M., Bachman, J. G., & Schlenberg, J. E. (2004). *Monitoring the Future national survey results on drug use, 1975–2003, Volume I: Secondary school student*. Bethesda, MD: National Institute on Drug Abuse.

Johnston, L., O'Malley, P., Bachman, J., & Schulenberg, J. (2011). *Monitoring the Future: National survey results on drug use, 1975–2010*. Ann Arbor: University of Michigan Institute for Social Research.

Kagan, S. L., & Neville, P. (1993). *Integration services for children and families*. New Haven, CT: Yale University Press.

Leve, L., & Chamberlain, P. (2001). Female juvenile offenders: Defining an early-onset pathway for delinquency. *Journal of Child and Family Studies, 13*(4), 439–452.

Lindquist, C. H., Krebs, C. P., Warner, T. D., & Lattimore, P. K. (2009). An exploration of treatment and supervision intensity among drug court and non-drug court participants. *Journal of Offenders Rehabilitation, 48*(3), 167–193.

Llewellyn, J., & Howse, R. (1999). *Restorative justice: A conceptual framework*. Ottawa: Law Commission of Canada.

Mackey, H. J. (2011). Youth detention facilities and restorative justice: Lesson for public education. In A. H. Normore & B. D. Fitch (Eds.), *Leadership in education, corrections and law enforcement: A commitment to ethics, equality and excellence* (pp. 229–245). Bingley, UK: Emerald.

Martin, D., Martin, M., Dell, R., Davis, C., & Guerrieri, K. (2008). Profile of incarcerated juvenile: Comparison of male and female offenders. *Adolescence, 43*(171), 607–622.

Michelli, N. M., & Keiser, D. L. (2005). *Teacher education for democracy and social justice*. New York, NY: Routledge.

Miethe, T., Lu, H., & Reese, E. (2000). Reintegrative shaming and recidivism risks in drug court: Explanations for some unexpected findings. *Crime and Delinquency, 46*(4), 522–541.

Moberg, D. P. (1999). *Evaluation of Chicago Preparatory Charter High School. Final grant report to the Robert Wood Johnson Foundation*. Madison: Wisconsin Center for Health Policy and Program Evaluation.

Moberg, D. P., & Finch, A. J. (2007). Recovery High Schools: A descriptive study of school programs and students. *Journal of Groups in Addiction & Recovery, 2*(2/4), 128–161.

Moberg, D. P., & Thaler, S. L. (1995). *An evaluation of Recovery High School: An alternative high school for adolescents in recovery from chemical dependence*. Madison: University of Wisconsin Center for Health Policy and Program Evaluation.

Models for Change. (2014). *About: Models for Change: Systems reform in juvenile justice*. Retrieved from http://www.modelsforchange.net/about/index.html?utm_source=%2fabout&utm_medium=web&utm_campaign=redirect

Moeller, M. (2011, February). Reauthorizing the Juvenile Justice and Delinquency Prevention Act: The impact on Latino Youth. *National Council of La Raza*.

Retrieved from http://www.nclr.org/images/uploads/publications/Reauthorizing_the_JJDPA_The_Impact_on_Latino_Youth_1.pdf

Murrell, P. J. (2006). Toward social justice in urban education: A model of collaborative cultural inquiry in urban schools. *Equity and Excellence in Education, 39*(1), 81–90.

National Survey on Drug Use and Health (NSDUH). (2009, July 16). Substance use treatment need and receipt among Hispanics. *Substance Abuse and Mental Health Services Administration.* Retrieved from http://www.taadas.org/publications/prodimages/The%20NSDUH%20Report%20July%2016,%20 2009%20Substance%20Use%20Treatment%20Need%20and%20Receipt%20 among%20Hispanics.pdf

National Survey on Drug Use and Health (NSDUH). (2012, October 25). Need for and receipt of substance use treatment among Hispanics. *Substance Abuse and Mental Science Administration.* Retrieved from http://www.samhsa.gov/data/sites/default/files/NSDUH117/NSDUH117/NSDUHSR117HispanicTreatmentNeeds2012.pdf

Newcomb, M. D., & Bentler, P. M. (1988a). *Consequences of adolescent drug use: Impact on the lives of young adults.* Newbury Park, CA: Sage.

Newcomb, M. D., & Bentler, P. M. (1988b). Impact of adolescent drug use and social support on problems of young adults: A longitudinal study. *Journal of Abnormal Psychology, 97,* 64–75.

Nissen, L. B., Merrigan, D. M., & Kraft, K. M. (2005, March/April). Moving mountains together: Strategic community leadership and change. *Child Welfare,* 125–140.

Pires, S. A. (2002). *Building systems of care: A prime .* Washington DC: Georgetown University Child Development Center.

Prado, G., Pantin, H., Briones, E., Schwartz, S. J., Feaster, D., & Huang, S. (2007). A random controlled trial of a parent-centered intervention in preventing substance use and HIV risk behaviors in Hispanic adolescents. *Journal of Consulting Clinical Psychology, 75*(6), 914–926.

Pumariega, A. J., & Winters, N. (2003). *Handbook of children and adolescent systems of care: The new community psychiatry.* San Francisco, CA: Jossey-Bass.

Ritakallio, M., Kaltiala-Heino, R., Kivivuori, J., Luukkaala, T., & Rimpela, M. (2006). Delinquency and the profile of offences among depressed and non-depressed adolescents. *Criminal Behavior and Mental Health, 16,* 100–110.

Rivaux, S. L., Springer, D. W., Bohman, T., Wagner, E. F., & Gil, A. G. (2006). Differences among substance abusing Latino, Anglo, and African American juvenile offenders in predictors of recidivism and treatment outcome. *Journal of Social Work Practice in the Addictions, 6*(4), 5–29.

Roche, D. (2001). The evolving definition of restorative justice. *Contemporary Justice Review, 4*(3/4), 341–353.

Saavedra, J. (2010, March). *Just the facts: A snapshot of incarcerated Hispanic youth.* Washington, DC: Council of La Raza.

Santisteban, D. A., Dillon, F., Mena, M. P., Estrada, Y., & Vaughan, E. L. (2005). Psychiatric, family, and ethnicity-related factors that can impact treatment utilization among Hispanic substance abusing adolescents. *Journal of Social Work Practice, 5*(1/2), 133–155.

Santisteban, D. A., Mena, M. P., & McCabe, B. E. (2011). Preliminary results for an adaptive family treatment for drug abuse in Hispanic youth. *Journal of Family Psychology, 25*(4), 610–614.

Schetly, D. H. (2009, September). Restorative justice: An alternative model whose time has come. *The Brown University Child and Adolescent Behavior Letter, 25*(9), 5–7.

Shaffer, D. K. (2006). *Reconsidering drug court effectiveness: A meta-analytic review.* Unpublished doctoral dissertation, College of Education, Criminal Justice and Human Services, University of Cincinnati, OH.

Snyder, H., & Sickmund, M. (2006). *Juvenile offenders and victims national report, Chapter 3: Juvenile offenders.* Washington DC: Department of Justice, Office of Justice Programs, Office of Juvenile Justice and Delinquency Prevention.

Springer, D. W., Rivaux, S. L., Bohman, T., & Yeung, A. (2006). Predicting retention in three substance abuse treatment modalities among Anglo, African American, and Mexican American juvenile offenders. *Journal of Social Service Research, 32*(4), 135–155.

Stefkovich, J., & Begley, P. T. (2007). Ethical leadership: Defining the best interests of students. *Educational Management Administration & Leadership, 35*(2), 205–224.

Stroul, B. A., & Friedman, R. M. (1994). *A system of care for severely emotionally disturbed children and youth.* Washington DC: Georgetown University Development Center.

Sullivan, D., & Tifft, L. (2001). *Restorative justice: Healing the foundations of our everyday lives.* New York, NY: Willow Tree.

Sumner, M. D., Silverman, C. J., & Frampton, M. L. (2010). *School-based restorative justice as an alternative to zero-tolerance policies: Lessons from west Oakland.* Berkeley, CA: University of California, Berkeley, School of Law, Thelton E. Henderson Center for Social Justice.

Sussman, S., & Ames, S. L. (2008). *Drug abuse: Concepts, prevention, and cessation.* New York, NY: Cambridge University Press.

Sussman, S., Lisha, N., & Griffiths, M. (2011). Prevalence of the addictions: A problem of the majority or the minority. *Evaluation and the Health Professionals, 34*(1), 3–56.

Szapocznik, J., Lopez, B., Prado, G., Schwartz, S. J., & Pantin, H. (2006). Outpatient drug abuse treatment for Hispaic adolescents. *Drug and Alcohol Dependence, 84*, S54–S63.

Szapocznik, J., Robbins, M. S., Turner, C. W., Dillon, F. R., Mitrani, V. B., & Feaster, D. J. (2008). The efficacy of structural ecosystems therapy with drug-abusing/dependent African American and Hispanic American adolescents. *Journal of Family Psychology, 22*(1), 51–61.

Taxman, F. S., & Bouffard, J. A. (2005). Treatment as part of drug court: The impact on graduation rates. *Journal of Offender Rehabilitation, 42*(1), 23–50.

Travis, T. (2010). In my own words: Celebrating students' stories of recovery: A compilation of essays by high school and college students . *Addiction Technology Transfer Center Network, 14*.

Tripoli, S. J., Springer, D. W., & Corcoran, K. (2007). Determinates of substance abuse among incarcerated adolescents: Implications for brief treatment and crisis Intervention. *Brief Treatment and Crisis Intervention, 7*(1), 34–39.

U.S. Department of Commerce. (2011, May). The Hispanic population: 2010. *U.S. Census Bureau.* Retrieved from http://www.census.gov/prod/cen2010/briefs/c2010br-04.pdf

U.S. Department of Justice. (2012, December 17). Statistical briefing book. *Office of Juvenile Justice and Delinquency Prevention.* Retrieved from http://ojjdp.gov/ojjstatbb/crime/JAR_Display.asp?ID=qa05200

Wearmouth, J., Mckinney, R., & Glynn, T. (2007a). Restorative justice: Two examples from New Zealand. *British Journal of Special Education, 34,* 196–203.

Wearmouth, J., Mckinney, R., & Glynn, T. (2007b). Restorative justice in schools: A New Zealand example. *Educational Research, 49,* 37–49.

Zehr, H. (1990). *Changing lenses: A new focus for crime and justice.* Scottsdale, PA: Herald.

CHAPTER 11

IMPLEMENTING A HOLISTIC APPROACH TO ENHANCE CAREER OPPORTUNITIES FOR TRANSITION STUDENTS WITH DISABILITIES

Susan Stuntzner and Bryan Austin
University of Idaho

ABSTRACT

Transition services are vitally important and an essential component of successful employment, career planning, self-determination, and independent living for students with disabilities. Public schools strive to meet the federal mandates placed upon them to help this group of students reach graduation and beyond. However, students with disabilities oftentimes fall short and do not succeed following high school. In an effort to change this trend, information pertaining to transition services and ways it can be enhanced are provided. This chapter addresses the necessity of transition services and its relationship to federal legislation, barriers that inhibit students' successful transition to adult life, and the current climate of the public educational system. A framework of recommendations is provided for educators assisting students with disabilities.

Inclusive Practices and Social Justice Leadership for Special Populations in Urban Settings, pages 213–233
Copyright © 2015 by Information Age Publishing

Transitioning from high school to the adult world that awaits developing and young adults is a major developmental milestone or marker for all students. For many students, this is that point in time when they leave home, go off to college, enter the military or another training program, travel, and have new life experiences. Due to the plethora of choices and possibilities available, it is an exciting time for many, but what about the experiences and needs of students with disabilities or those who need additional assistance and preparation so they can achieve the opportunities and goals they seek following high school? Do students with disabilities have the same opportunities available to them post–high school compared to their same-aged peers without disabilities? Does their educational training and experience adequately prepare them to be employed or independent, choose occupational and career directions that are interesting and meaningful, become well-informed decision makers and self-advocates, and to pursue life goals successfully?

Many helping professionals and educators probably hope that is the case, but the reality is that many students with disabilities are not adequately prepared for life after high school; nor are they provided adequate opportunities or exposure to the multiple life- and career-planning experiences afforded to their same-aged peers without disabilities. Although it is understood that educators work hard to teach and address the needs of their students, the educational, developmental, and vocational planning processes of students with disabilities oftentimes are not where they need to be in order to ensure adequate and successful transition from high school. While there is legislation and educational mandates to promote equitable access to education for students with disabilities, it is important for us to recognize and admit that legislation and mandates are not enough to effectively meet the transitional needs of students with disabilities; more still needs to be done. Part of this is related to the fact that many social injustices are still experienced by persons with disabilities. Some of these injustices can be understood as inequities in educational practices; training opportunities; employment versus unemployment rates (Wagner, Newman, Cameto, Levine, & Garza, 2006); career exploration experiences; access to and knowledge of resources and supports available following high school (Riesen, Schultz, Morgan, & Kupferman, 2014); personal, professional, or societal biases about the abilities of persons with disabilities (Smart, 2009); and varying degrees of expectations held toward persons with disabilities.

In an effort to decrease the margin of inequities sometimes experienced by students with disabilities, this chapter provides an in-depth discussion of legislation and appropriate services as it relates to this population. We focus on several areas, including the (a) role of vocational rehabilitation (VR) and interagency collaboration, (b) necessity of transition services as a means to improve employment outcomes following high school, (c) barriers that may inhibit successful transition, and (d) importance of the educational climate, followed by several recommendations.

SOCIAL JUSTICE: A SOCIETAL CONCERN FOR STUDENTS WITH DISABILITIES

Social justice is an issue of concern and of relevance for students with disabilities and society. Oftentimes, social justice is described as a value and a paradigm used by professionals and agencies to pursue and achieve equitable opportunities for people or groups of people who do not typically have them (Rawls, 2011). Bankston (2010) expands this concept by stating that "social justice involves a redistribution of goods and services to improve the state of people who are disadvantaged" (p. 165). When considering the needs and issues of students with disabilities within the educational system, the redistribution of goods and services should not be equated with negative connotations such as a "free handout" or entitlement. Rather, the provision of quality services is related to the idea that all persons, including students with disabilities, have the ability to help themselves achieve independence, employment, self-actualization, and a better quality of life when they receive the proper education, guidance, and opportunities afforded to their same-aged peers.

Social justice and its relationship to personal empowerment can be an instrumental perspective for educational professionals to understand. From this view, we are not denying the reality that many students with disabilities do not receive equitable attention, services, or training throughout their lifespan; nor are we stating that everyone will reach the same level of equity and quality of living if they receive additional support and guidance. What we are trying to stress is the fact that options are available and should be promoted among students with disabilities to bridge the gap and to narrow the void so they are given more opportunities to learn the skills deemed adequate and necessary to live as independently as possible and to achieve the best quality of life they can. Furthermore, it is through this process of experiencing success throughout their life that students with disabilities become empowered and oftentimes "come to believe" that a better way of life is possible.

Being more conscious and equitable in the approaches used and the services offered to students with disabilities does more than enhance their lives; it also has the potential to positively impact society. For example, students who successfully graduate and transition to the adult world of work and achieve employment become better integrated into society. Through societal integration, persons with disabilities become employees, economic consumers, role models, and potential agents of societal change—all of which benefit society. More specifically, students with disabilities who become successfully employed start to give back to society rather than take away from it as is sometimes the case when they are relegated to living off of social security. Those who earn an income typically spend money on products and services, which also gives back to society. Furthermore, students with disabilities who receive adequate training become employed, living independently, and may serve as role models to other students with disabilities. Opportunities to role model success and societal integration when living with a disability helps students with and without disabilities understand the positive impact persons with disabilities can have on society when they are given an equitable opportunity to succeed.

FEDERAL LEGISLATION
AND STUDENT TRANSITION SERVICES

Making the transition from adolescence to adulthood is one of the biggest adjustments for all young people in America today. For students with disabilities (ages 16 to 24), this transition becomes an even greater challenge. For example, there have been long-standing negative societal attitudes toward the abilities and potential of people with disabilities that remain prevalent (Smart, 2009). Students with disabilities also have a wide array of physical, cognitive, and emotional/behavioral disabilities that oftentimes require a multitude of service needs. To address these primary challenges, two landmark pieces of disability legislation originally were passed and necessarily amended overtime; the Rehabilitation Act of 1973 and the Education for All Handicapped Children Act of 1975.

In 1973, the Rehabilitation Act was passed, mandating the state and federally funded VR programs to provide services to consumers with the most severe disabilities and involve VR consumers to a greater degree in the rehabilitation planning process (Peterson & Aguiar, 2004).

In 1975, with the passage of the Education for All Handicapped Children Act, youth with disabilities were afforded the right to a free and appropriate public education, the same as young people without disabilities, in an integrated and least restrictive environment (Peterson & Aguiar, 2004). In 1990, this act was amended and renamed the Individuals with Disabilities Education Act (IDEA) and for the first time required public schools to develop Individual Education Plans (IEPs) with students by age 16 to include documentation of transition services that target postschool outcomes, such as vocational training, postsecondary education, employment, independent living, and other community-based services (Morningstar, Kleinhammer-Tramill, & Lattin, 1999). Further, these act amendments mandated schools to invite the student, family, school personnel, adult service providers, and other community participants to be part of the transition team (Morningstar et al., 1999). Following suit, the Rehabilitation Act, reauthorized and amended under the Workforce Investment Act (WIA) of 1998, made interagency collaboration an explicit priority by mandating VR to work more closely with schools to better ensure an uninterrupted delivery system of services that more effectively promote students' transition from school or work. The National Council on Disability (NCD) (2008) provides a list of such VR mandates and are bulleted below:

- VR agencies must coordinate with educational personnel and enter into a formal interagency agreement with state education agencies;
- use student information from education programs for eligibility and vocational planning purposes;
- develop and write an Individual Plan for Employment (IPE) before the student leaves high school;
- collaborate with state education programs in providing transition services; and
- provide outreach and identify students with disabilities who may need transition services. (pp. 19–20)

Along with this mandate for interagency collaboration, WIA mandated One-Stop Centers throughout the United States, including programs designed to meet the needs of youth (including transition students) with and without disabilities that provide access to and participation in both youth and adult services such as training, job placement, and other career-related resources (Luecking, Crane, & Mooney, 2002).

Following this 1998 amendment of the Rehabilitation Act, the IDEA, again amended and renamed in 2004 as the Individuals with Disabilities Education Improvement Act (IDEIA), also mandated public schools to provide transition services to include interagency collaboration (Oertle & Trach, 2007). Currently, the IDEIA defines transition services as

a coordinated set of activities for a child with a disability that:
- Is designed to be within a results-oriented process, that is focused on improving the academic and functional achievement of the child [student] with a disability to facilitate the child's movement from school to post-school activities, including postsecondary education, vocational education, integrated employment (including supported employment); continuing and adult education, adult services, independent living, or community participation;
- Is based on the individual child's needs, taking into account the child's strengths, preferences, and interests; and
- Includes instruction, related services, community experiences, the development of employment and other post-school adult living objectives, and, if appropriate, acquisition of daily living skills and functional vocational evaluation.

[34 CFR 300.43 (a)] [20 U.S.C. 1401(34)] (U.S. Department of Education, Office of Special Education Programs, 2007, Regulation 3)

As can be seen with this definition and legislative amendments presented, transition services require a considerable amount of attention and interdisciplinary expertise to help students with disabilities be successful and prepared as they embark upon their future careers, education, and daily living. Thus, the importance of helping young people prepare for and succeed in adult life must be a focal point in both public schools and VR.

How Vocational Rehabilitation Can Help

VR can be a critical resource and service provider to students with disabilities and their efforts to make the successful transition from school to work and adult life. VR assists people with disabilities who require services to overcome their disability-related barriers to obtain or maintain employment. VR focuses on consumers' vocational interests, abilities, and skills, and works with other adult agencies to help consumers achieve their career potential. Services may include, but are not limited to assessment, vocational counseling and guidance, job search assistance, job placement, rehabilitation technology (assistive technology), transportation, on-the-job support, job-readiness training, occupational/vocational training, and college or university training. There is also a substantial research base to validate the efficacy of VR services that are positively associated with employment outcomes for various disability populations (Austin & Lee, 2014; Saunders, Leahy, McGlynn, & Estrada-Hernandez, 2006).

VR agencies hire VR counselors who have specialized expertise in providing direct services to people with disabilities in the primary areas of vocational assessment, career counseling, case management, and job placement. Consequently, VR counselors who work with high schools, transition specialists, and who have transition students in their caseloads can be an integral part of the IEP team (Oertle, Trach, & Plotner, 2013). Further, VR counselors may also be nationally certified rehabilitation counselors (CRCs), which means they have met knowledge and competency standards for VR practice established by the profession. Certified counselors are required to adhere to a professional code of ethics (Commission on Rehabilitation Counselor Certification, 2009) and must also complete a minimum of 100 hours of continuing education credits every five years to maintain their certification credential. Both of these requirements raise the bar for VR counselors and ensure they keep up with current trends and update their skills to provide quality and ethical rehabilitative services.

Interagency Collaboration

Interagency collaboration by school transition programs is a particularly crucial component in providing individualized services for students with disabilities and may have the most positive upside for helping students achieve their transition goals (Morningstar et al., 1999). Oertle and Trach (2007) suggest that formalized transition planning can produce positive results for both transition students and communities because of the connections made to work and educational training. *Interagency collaboration* can be defined as

> interactions and activities between special educators and rehabilitation professionals such as working as a team, sharing information, attending transition planning meetings, combining resources, and establishing and utilizing effective lines of communication to benefit students with disabilities as they transition from high school to the adult world (p. 37)

There are many potential benefits of interagency collaboration between state VR and school transition programs. Both VR and school transition programs are able to meet their federal mandates as stated by law (Edmondson & Cain, 2002). Students and educators can benefit from the vocational expertise provided by VR counselor to assist with transition planning. Collaboration can also be increased through student and family involvement with VR agencies who can provide linkages to other adult agencies during the transition process, which can lead to greater student success in achieving not only employment goals, but also goals in independent living and postsecondary education (Oertle et al., 2013).

Despite the importance of interagency collaboration, barriers remain that impede effective collaboration between school transition programs and VR agencies. Ashby and Bensberg (as cited in Edmondson & Cain, 2002) suggested that one of the barriers of collaboration between school transition and VR agencies has been the interpretation by both systems of the IDEA and Rehabilitation Act and deciphering who should do what and when. Benz and Lindstrom (1999) concluded in their review of the research that interagency collaboration does not happen regularly because of misperceptions by schools, students, and parents about the nature and scope of VR services and lack of formalized procedures to facilitate student referrals to VR agencies. A survey of VR counselors and special educators showed that most educators did not (or rarely) invited VR counselors to be part of the transition team (Agran, Cain, & Cavin, 2002). It was inferred from this same study that VR counselors may not be invited because "(a) teachers did not believe they could be of much assistance, (b) they were not aware of the valuable information they could potentially provide, or (c) because they did not know who to contact" (Agran et al., 2002, p. 152). An absence of well-established relationships between VR counselors and educators may also explain this disconnect (Oertle et al., 2013). In a similar study, lack of knowledge of community-based supports (i.e., VR, social security benefits, on-the-job training, and other disability resources) were perceived as "high impact" barriers to transition (Riesen et al., 2014).

NECESSITY OF TRANSITION SERVICES FOR STUDENTS WITH DISABILITIES

Current practices that support the transition of students with disabilities have been shown to be effective and lead to positive postschool outcomes. Evidence-based transition practices are an example of services that have led to positive outcomes for students with disabilities in the areas of employment, independent living, and postsecondary education. For example, inclusion in general education, paid employment/work experience, parental/family involvement, student support, interagency collaboration, career awareness, self-advocacy/self-determination, social skills, vocational education, community experiences, exit exam requirements/high school diploma status, self-care/independent living skills, transition programming, and program of study and work study (Test & Cease-Cook, 2012; Test et al., 2009) have been linked to positive postsecondary outcomes for transition students with disabilities. Moreover, inclusion in general education, paid employment/work experience, self-care/independent living skills, and student support during the school years may have an even greater impact for improving student outcomes across all three transition domains: employment, independent living, and postsecondary education (Test et al., 2009).

The National Alliance for Secondary Education and Transition (NASET, 2005) provided a comprehensive research document that incorporates many of these evidence-based transition practices and serves as the basis for the National Standards for Secondary Education and Transition. They include *Schooling, Career Preparatory Experiences, Youth Development and Youth Leadership, Family Involvement,* and *Connecting Activities.* Schooling ensures students are provided access to the general curriculum and held accountable to a standards-based education with the use of assessments, including alternative formats when needed, that uphold high expectations and performance standards (academic and nonacademic) for all students (NASET, 2005).

Career preparatory experiences are summarized as being both school and community-based opportunities that provide access to many of the careers and occupations available to students (NASET, 2005). Youth development and youth leadership are based on the idea that youth with disabilities should take an active role in directing services and decisions that affect their lives (NCWDY, 2010). Critical to this process, students need to be supported in developing self-advocacy and self-determination skills and be given the opportunity for person-centered planning (NASET, 2005). Family involvement is important throughout the transition process. Morningstar,

Turnbull, and Turnbull (as cited by NASET, 2005) found that youth with disabilities want guidance and input from family members about their futures. Connecting activities are "collaborative approaches [that] bring together community agencies to focus their collective expertise and combined resources to improve the quality of transition planning and services for youth" (NASET, 2005, p. 44).

Employment Outcomes for Students With Disabilities

Despite the evidence to support current practices, it is unclear how often and to what extent these practices are being delivered as part of transition services in schools. In relation to employment outcomes, lower employment rates and outcomes for transition students with disabilities remains a significant concern nationally (NCD, 2008; Wagner et al., 2006). Employment outcomes for transition students with disabilities, although improving, remain well below that of their same-aged peers without disabilities (Blackorby & Wagner, 1996; Wagner et al., 2006). In the National Longitudinal Transition Study-2 (NLTS2), Wagner et al.'s (2006) findings suggest that it continues to be significantly more difficult for transition students with disabilities to achieve or sustain a successful employment outcome; for example, youth with disabilities had an employment rate of approximately 40% versus 63% for same-aged peers in their study of a sample of more than 11,000 youth receiving special-education services. Further, state VR agencies may be serving only a small percentage of youth that could benefit from VR transition services (NCD, 2008). Combined, transition students with disabilities are significantly more likely to be unemployed, underemployed, or underrepresented in the current U.S. labor force.

ADDITIONAL BARRIERS TO SUCCESSFUL TRANSITION

Barriers to successful transition can present themselves from multiple directions. Beyond those already discussed, barriers may come from (a) the student with a disability; (b) others in the external environment (i.e., family members, professionals, agencies); (c) societal attitudes and beliefs about the abilities of persons with disabilities (i.e., employer bias and attitude); (d) lack of educational opportunities, training, or knowledge; and (e) school-to-work transitional services and coordinated practices (Riesen et al., 2014; Smart, 2009; Stuntzner, 2012). For example, are the prominent barriers emanating from the beliefs held by the student with a disability about his or her abilities? Are there attitudinal obstacles originating from within the family, other helping professionals, or employers? Do any of these individuals hold lower expectations of the student with a disability because of the particular situation or the disability? If lower or different expectations are held and promoted, how might these affect the success of students' transition from high school to the adult world of work?

Educators who teach and assist students with disabilities can assist the students they work with by identifying the areas or domains mentioned above which are most disconcerting and problematic. Educators may first consider whether the barriers experienced are self-induced, other induced, or both. Stuntzner (2014, in press) explains that *self-induced* barriers are those created by persons with disabilities that promote further obstacles to overcome, such as the belief and practice of self-fulfilling prophecies. *Other-induced* barriers are the obstacles within the external environment and those promoted from others outside of persons with disabilities such as inaccurate beliefs about the abilities of persons with disabilities or employer bias (Stuntzner, in press). In many instances, both of these barrier types coexist and promote one another, so the task is to determine which ones to address first.

Identifying and understanding the source of barriers is essential for successful transition to occur. Educators can assist students by helping them recognize areas within themselves or their life which need to be addressed sooner rather than later throughout the educational process. Beyond the internal barriers sometimes experienced and perpetuated by persons with disabilities are those observed and personally encountered externally (Stuntzner, in press). External barriers typically receive more recognition because they are concrete and observable. Some of the barriers typically encountered by persons and students with disabilities are discussed throughout the literature and may include (Riesen et al., 2014; Stuntzner, 2012, in press; Stuntzner & Hartley, 2014) attitudes and bias; lack of physical access; inadequate educational-, training-, and employment-related opportunities; poor understanding of one's disability or diagnosis and its effects; low parental expectations of students with disabilities; inadequate understanding of self-advocacy skills; lack of understanding about how to access needed services (i.e., VR, assistance with learning in colleges and universities); and educators not feeling fully prepared to provide adequate transition services, just to name a few.

Compounding these issues is the reality that transition services may not be addressed or fully considered until students are approaching their junior year in high school. While many students may be on an IEP throughout their schooling, students with disabilities oftentimes proceed through the educational system without fully understanding their disability (Schreiner, 2007), what it means, and how it may affect their future; nor are they given adequate exposure to training, employment, or career-related opportunities or skills pertaining to self-advocacy (Gil, 2007; McCarthy,

2007; Stuntzner & Hartley, 2014). Students who do receive such services may not begin to have exposure until they are close to graduating, and by this time, many are not prepared for the realities that await them post–high school. For these reasons, it is essential that educators and school systems consider the transition needs and skills of students with disabilities earlier in their educational process.

VALUE OF THE EDUCATIONAL CLIMATE

Educators, similar to other helping professionals, choose their career path to make a difference in the lives of the people they serve. For educators, this means many choose this occupation because they want to help shape the hearts and minds of students with the hope it will lead to personal well-being, independence, and positive societal change. While meeting the needs of all students is often a challenge, it is an expectation and responsibility held by professionals who teach. Educators are asked to consider how to teach and to promote a learning environment that is inclusive of all students—one that is of high quality and value to both students with and without disabilities (Gillies, 2013).

Educators—not only special educators—have a responsibility to address the educational and learning needs of students with disabilities. Promotion of social justice, equitable services, empowerment, and successful transition services is a value which must be embraced throughout the school setting (Brooks, 2012); it is an attitude of expectation and hope that can be embraced and extended throughout the school district and the various school environments (Theoharis, 2009). School districts that value, integrate, and encourage the promotion of social justice and equity of high-quality services (i.e., education, career exploration, self-knowledge) become a model or environmental framework to help guide the decisions and actions of administrators, educators, and staff (Capper & Young, 2014) which, in turn, can affect learning and training expectations and opportunities.

Due to the reality that professional attitudes and expectations are communicated, directly or indirectly, from administrators to teachers and staff, it is essential for everyone concerned to consider whether their district, school setting, classroom, or they themselves approach their work with students with disabilities from a positive or negative stance. Similarly, it is important for educator professionals to understand their own values and expectations and how those may be communicated throughout the educational process.

For example, what are the expectations of students with disabilities to learn, graduate, and/or to become productive members of society? Are students with disabilities given equitable opportunities compared to their peers without disabilities to learn, to explore vocational interests and career options, and to build life skills relevant to their independence following high school? Are the needs and abilities of students with disabilities tended to throughout the educational system so they will be as prepared as possible to transition to adulthood following high school? Does the school system approach education and learning opportunities from an empowerment perspective—one that focuses on the abilities and strengths of students with disabilities? Do the schools hold different educational, employment, or independent-living expectations of females with disabilities than their male counterparts with disabilities or females without disabilities (Stuntzner, Ricks, & Dalton, 2014). If so, what are these differences and how do they present themselves throughout the educational or career exploration experiences? Or does the school system address the needs of students with disabilities from a less desirable standpoint, such as promoting the notion that providing them services as outlined in the IEP or helping them graduate is sufficient.

Asking these questions may be uncomfortable for some professionals, but it is a necessary endeavor because a person's attitude and expectations, spoken or not, are conveyed to students. Such attitudes and expectations have the ability to positively or negatively shape those held by students with disabilities and their families. For this reason, understanding our own expectations and those of the school system is essential for the promotion of social justice and for successful transition to occur.

HOLISTIC FRAMEWORK FOR EDUCATORS

Educators interested in meeting the needs of students with disabilities throughout the transition process can review the main tenets provided in the following sections. Although the needs of many students are vast and situations are individualized, several of these recommendations are relevant to administrators, educators, allied helping professionals (i.e., transition specialists, rehabilitation counselors), family members, and to students with disabilities. Some of the recommendations provide for a potential framework that may be more salient to some people than to others, but the intent is to provide an array of options so that those involved in the transition process can understand how change can occur from both a social justice and a transitioning from high school perspective. In both instances, the primary goal is to learn and incorporate strategies to assist students with disabilities in pursuing and achieving equitable opportunities (Rawls, 2011) that are available to their peers without disabilities and to provide services that can assist students with disabilities in improving their overall quality of life.

Communication and Early Planning: An Essential Skill

As indicated earlier and as is evident throughout the literature, personal and familial involvement is essential for successful transition to occur (Test et al., 2009). For optimal education, training, and employment opportunities to occur following high school, students with disabilities and their family members need to be encouraged and invited to participate and take ownership of their future at an earlier time in the educational process; most likely while still in elementary school.

Due to the multiple layers of barriers and needs often associated with disability, transition planning and post–high school training options should not be postponed until the junior year of high school (Fabian, 2007). A more proactive and engaging choice is for educators to communicate to students and their family members plans and options pertaining to their future. This means discussions should take place earlier rather than later regarding a student's future training, employment and career directions, mentorship needs and options (Noonan et al., 2004), independent-living desires, and essential life skills needed for successful living. Educators may need to tailor the content and information communicated so that it is developmentally appropriate based on the student's chronological age and abilities; however, it is a way of approaching one's future and life choices that is more inclusive and empowering.

Beginning the communication and planning process earlier rather than later gives students time to learn about their desires, interests, and needs, and to fully understand their disability and what it means so they can then learn how to effectively self-advocate (Fabian, 2007; NCWDY, 2010). Understanding one's own disability is essential because many graduate high school without fully knowing what their disability means and how it may affect them as adults; therefore, they mature and become adults who have little or negative information about their disability (Schreiner, 2007; Stuntzner & Hartley, 2014). This lack of information may translate into having an inadequate foundation for knowing how to successfully self-advocate (McCarthy, 2007). Further, early planning can assist students and their families in gaining exposure to employment and work-related opportunities and to successful persons with disabilities who may serve as mentors or role models (Noonan et al., 2004). Such experiences may drastically change the way students with disabilities view themselves and their future.

Person-Centered Planning

A person-centered approach in transition planning has been gaining in popularity and is designed to empower individuals with disabilities who have multifaceted service needs in the transition to adult life (Hagner, Kurtz, May, & Cloutier, 2014). According to Claes, Hove, Vandevelde, Loon, and Schalock (2010), the main goals of person-centered planning are to "develop collaborative, goal-oriented, and individualized programs that are focused on community presence, community participation, positive relationships, respect, and competence" (p. 432). The idea behind person-centered planning is that the consumer of services (e.g., transition student) and his or her parents or family members are empowered to choose and direct the planning and service delivery process and goals of their IEP (Kosciulek, 1999). Although this approach has been more widely used for individuals with developmental and intellectual disabilities (Claes et al., 2010) and transition students with autism spectrum disorders (Hagner et al., 2014), it should considered for use with all transition students. For example, the research suggests that the use of person-centered planning may improve social networks, community involvement, choice making, knowledge about leisure activities, work-related activities and social support, teamwork and family involvement, and reduce challenging behavior (Claes et al., 2010).

When incorporating person-centered planning into the transition process, the student, family, and teacher select important significant others, advocates, and other related support staff who intimately know the student who is the focus of services. Gathering data about the student from others who know the student best better ensures that information collected is more accurate and practical to best meet the needs of the student. Sensitivity to the student's language and his or her family culture (Callicott, 2003) is a key aspect in the development of IEP goals and services that match a student's unique interests, assets, and capabilities across areas of employment, independent living, and postsecondary education.

When working on vocational-related goals, the use of person-centered planning may be particularly useful when students are connected to a VR agency. A person-centered plan or written document that results from this planning process can be used to help with determining a suitable employment goal with the VR counselor. Further, incorporating person-centered planning as part of students' VR participation may lead to more successful job placements (Migliore, Butterworth, Nord, & Gelb, 2012).

Internal Social Justice Change Opportunities

Transition services and opportunities for social justice change can also be discussed from an internal environmental approach. From this perspective, the emphasis is on what is or can take place within the school district or system to promote social justice opportunities for students with disabilities (Brooks, 2012) as well as more successful and meaningful transition outcomes. For starters, it is essential for school districts and administrators to take an active role and interest in the services provided to students with disabilities (Capper & Young, 2014). When a discrepancy in the amount or quality of educational and training services is found, school administrators are in a position to create change. More specifically, administrators have the authority to review, restructure, and possibly reprioritize resources so that more emphasis and importance is given to students with disabilities and their future. Such restructuring and reprioritizing efforts have the potential to effect teachers and staff attitudes and expectations of students with disabilities, which then translates into more focus on quality educational and training opportunities and higher expectations held for students with disabilities.

Internal change may also be addressed through the curriculum and taught to students in the classroom. While having a quality education should be of high importance for all students, it is also recommended that school districts, administrators, and teachers consider the importance and value of teaching students about disabilities and the importance self-advocacy.

The precise methods used to approach this topic and skillset may vary based on the school setting, but it is an area which needs to be better addressed among students with disabilities. Some school districts may discover ways to infuse the topic and discussion of disability into the educational curriculum so that it benefits all students and learners. In these instances, both students with and without disabilities are afforded the opportunity to learn about the capabilities and abilities of persons with disabilities and skills to effectively advocate for one's own needs. Students learn to view disability as a more normalized experience rather than a pathological one as well as the value of how to advocate for one's own needs. In other settings, administrators and educators may develop and infuse additional learning opportunities for students with disabilities so they can more fully understand their own unique condition or diagnoses, how it affects them, and what they can learn to effectively manage their life in a positive way. Educators may work collaboratively with other team members to construct reading or writing assignments that help promote students' understanding of disability as well as skills pertaining to self-advocacy.

External Solutions for Collaboration and Societal Change

The research shows positive benefits from incorporating career development activities as part of the transition process that can give students career information and work-based experiences they need to make informed choices about their futures (NCWDY, 2014). Activities should be designed to build self-awareness, vocational skills, and the competencies necessary for employment and tailored to each student's interests, strengths, and individualized needs (NCWDY, 2010). Self-awareness activities facilitate students' knowledge of their interests, strengths, and values and give students opportunities to better understand what it takes to work in a profession as well as make connections from the coursework to their life goals outside the classroom (NCWDY, 2014).

Vocational skill activities support student experiences within their schools and community that further help clarify their career-based interests, strengths, values, and skillsets needed for identified careers, and educational/training requirements to enter a chosen career (NCWDY, 2014). Competency-based activities encourage students to develop work-related and career decision-making skills that can serve as foundational skills throughout their lives (NCWDY, 2014). Further, students develop job-search and work-readiness skills as well as work habits and behaviors necessary to do well in their job and also become knowledgeable of the job market and future career opportunities to maximize their employability (NCWDY, 2014).

Collaboration with VR

Interagency collaboration resulting from a strong partnership between the public school system and VR can lead to positive transition outcomes for students (Benz, Lindstrom, & Yovanoff, 2000; Fabian, 2007). Johnson, Zorn, Tam, Lamontagne, and Johnson's (2003) study revealed seven factors that can guide efforts for successful interagency collaboration: (a) commitment, (b) communication, (c) strong leadership from key decision makers, (d) understanding the culture of collaborating agencies, (e) engaging in serious preplanning, (f) providing adequate resources for collaboration, and (g) minimizing turf issues. Another suggestion is to seek out opportunities that enhance transition knowledge and competencies that clarify information about VR and the role and involvement of the VR counselor as part of the IEP team (Oertle et al, 2013). Educators and VR counselors share mutual responsibility during the transition process and therefore should both take a leadership role by initiating contact with each other. If the outcome of successful transition from school to adult life is to be achieved, interagency collaboration between schools and VR must be of high quality (Oertle & Trach, 2007).

Student Work Experience and Job-Readiness Skills

There is considerable evidence that supports the relationship between paid employment during the school years and positive employment outcomes for transition students following exit from the public school system (Carter et al., 2010; Fabian, 2007; Test et al., 2009). To aid in this effort, educators should initiate career development activities with potential transition students and initiate communication with VR agencies before students reach the age of 16 (Fabian, 2007). Further, developing knowledge of the local One Stop Center and its WIA-funded youth programs will also aid students by helping them get involved in community-based programs intended to enhance their career development (Luecking et al., 2002). Given the limited resources by both schools and VR agencies, WIA can share its resources and possibly some the costs of job-related programming (e.g., career assessments, paid internships with employers, job coaching, job placement) that can further facilitate students' development of job-readiness skills. In addition, the importance of family involvement and support may be central to some students' ability to access and follow through on their community-based and employment commitments (Carter et al., 2010). Therefore, engaging parents or family members in the transition process from the beginning and eliciting their support in their child's transition program can be crucial.

Principles of Person-Centered Planning

The research highlights the importance of student involvement, empowerment, and self-determination as core values (Test et al., 2009) necessary to effectively prepare students for independence and success in their transition to adult life. To practically apply this underlying philosophy, which adheres to the "spirit of the law" (Edmondson & Cain, 2002), educators should consider training in person-centered planning. Such training can enhance educators' empathy for their students and families and provide a platform for internalizing person-centered values, essential to this approach (Amano & McBride, 2001). Educators may also have an opportunity to build upon their group leadership skills and acquire important knowledge of the person-centered planning process.

Websites and Links for Resources

A final area of interest pertains to the ways educators can enhance their understanding of the needs and practices promoted in relation to transition services. Five websites and resource options are provided below. These links can assist educators in obtaining information about promising transition practices, one-stop centers, evidence-based practices to support transition strategies, and transition training offered on person-centered planning.

- RSA (Rehabilitation Services Administration): Promising Practices for Basic VR Agencies Helping Transition Age Youth: http://www2.ed.gov/rschstat/eval/rehab/promising-practices/transition-age/index.html

- U.S. Department of Labor, Division of Youth Services:
  http://www.doleta.gov/youth_services
- One-Stop Centers:
  http://www.onestops.info/
- Evidence-Based Practices in Secondary Transition:
  http://www.nsttac.org/content/evidence-based-practices-secondary-transition
- University of Idaho's Center on Disabilities and Human Development free online transition training in person-centered planning:
  http://moodle.idahocdhd.org

FINAL REFLECTIONS

For students with disabilities, the act of experiencing and achieving adequate and equitable transition assistance from high school to the adult world of formalized education or work is not an automatic process. While legislation exists and is mandated to promote the educational and transition rights afforded to students with disabilities, these legislative acts are not sufficient; further collective action must be taken and promoted by schools, administrators, teachers, allied helping professionals, students with disabilities, and family members of students. Everyone involved has an important role and contribution to make to ensure the transition needs of students with disabilities are equitable, meaningful, and directly related to the post–high school needs, desires, and goals of this group of students. More candidly, this means that the traditional way of approaching transition services beginning at the age of 16 (Fabian, 2007) should not be encouraged. Rather, the holistic process of considering the interests and desires of students with disabilities should be discussed and encouraged at a much younger age in the educational process.

Educators and professionals working with students with disabilities may find this change in thinking and approach to be more work initially, but it is likely the best course of action for students with disabilities, their families, and for society. Given the specific needs of students with disabilities, they need more than an equitable education. They need to understand (a) their disability and how it affects them and their future life choices, (b) the potential obstacles they may encounter in the future so they can learn how to effectively self-advocate (Test et al., 2009), (c) that they have choices in relation to employment, training, career-related opportunities, and independent living, (d) the ways they can access community-based support and vocational assistance following high school (Carter et al., 2010), (e) how to access role models or positive supports as they work toward their life goals (Riesen et al., 2014), and (f) their role in making decisions, taking actions, and creating the life they want to have (NCWDY, 2010). In essence, their transition process needs to be approached from a holistic and inclusive manner—one that begins sooner rather than later.

REFERENCES

Amado, A. N., & Mc Bride, M. (2001). *Increasing person-centered thinking: Improving the quality of person-centered planning: A manual for person-centered planning facilitators.* Minneapolis: University of Minnesota, Institute on Community Integration.

Austin, B. S., & Lee, C. (2014). A structural equation model of vocational rehabilitation services: Predictors of employment outcomes for clients with intellectual and co-occurring psychiatric disabilities. *Journal of Rehabilitation, 80*(3), 10–19.

Agran, M., Cain, H. M., & Cavin, M. D. (2002). Enhancing the involvement of rehabilitation counselors in the transition process. *Career Development for Exceptional Individuals, 25,* 141–155.

Bankston, C. L., III (2010). Social justice: Cultural origins of a perspective and theory. *The Independent Review, 15*(2), 165–178.

Benz, M. R., & Lindstrom, L. (1999). Improving collaboration between schools and vocational rehabilitation: The youth transition program model. *Journal of Vocational Rehabilitation, 13,* 55–63.

Benz, M. R., Lindstrom, L., & Yovanoff, P. (2000). Improving graduation and employment outcomes of students with disabilities: Predictive factors and student perspective. *Exceptional Children, 66*(4), 509–229.

Blackorby, J., & Wagner, M. (1996). Longitudinal post-school outcomes of youth with disabilities: Findings from the national longitudinal transition study. *Exceptional Children, 62*(5), 399–413.

Brooks, J. S. (2012). *Black school White school: Racism and educational (mis)leadership.* New York, NY: Teachers College Press.

Callicott, K. J. (2003). Culturally sensitive collaboration within person-centered planning. *Focus on Autism and Other Developmental Disabilities, 18*(1), 60–68.

Capper, C. A., & Young, M. D. (2014). Ironies and limitations of educational leadership for social justice: A call to social justice educators. *Theory Into Practice, 53*(2), 158–164.

Carter, E. W., Ditchman, N., Sun, Y., Trainor, A. A., Sweeden, B., & Owens, L. (2010). Summer employment and community experiences of transition-age youth with severe disabilities. *Exceptional Children, 76*(2), 194–212.

Claes, C., Hove, G. V., Vandevelde, S., Loon, J. V., & Schalock, R. L. (2010). Person-centered planning: Analysis of research and effectiveness. *Intellectual and Developmental Disabilities, 48*(6), 432–453.

Commission on Rehabilitation Counselor Certification. (2009). *Code of professional ethics for rehabilitation counselors.* Schaumburg, IL: Author.

Edmondson, C. A., & Cain, H. M. (2002). The spirit of the individuals with disabilities education act: Collaboration between special education and vocational rehabilitation for the transition of students with disabilities. *Journal of Applied Rehabilitation Counseling, 33*(4), 10–14.

Fabian, E. S. (2007). Urban youth with disabilities: Factors affecting transition employment. *Rehabilitation Counseling Bulletin, 50*(3), 130–138.

Gil, L. A. (2007, November/December). Bridging the gap from high school to college: Preparing students with disabilities for a successful postsecondary experience. *Teaching Exceptional Children,* 12–15.

Gillies, R. M. (2013). Making reasonable adjustments: What can we do for students with disabilities? *International Journal of Disability, Development, and Education, 60*(4), 291–294.

Hagner, D., Kurtz, A., May, J., & Cloutier, H. (2014). Person-centered planning for transition-aged youth with autism spectrum disorders. *Journal of Rehabilitation, 80*(1), 4–10.

Johnson, L. J., Zorn, D., Tam, F. D. Y., Lamontagne, M., & Johnson, S. A. (2003). Stakeholders' views of factors that impact successful interagency collaboration. *Exceptional Children, 69,* 195–209.

Kosciulek, J. F. (1999). The consumer-directed theory of empowerment. *Rehabilitation Counseling Bulletin, 42*(3), 196–214.

Luecking, R. G., Crane, K., & Mooney, M. (2002, December). Addressing the transition needs of youth with disabilities through the WIA system. *National Center on Secondary Education and Transition, 1*(6), 1–4. Retrieved from http://www.ncset.org/publications/info/NCSETInfoBrief_1.6.pdf

McCarthy, D. (2007, November/December) Teaching self-advocacy to students with disabilities. *About Campus,* 10–16.

Migliore, A., Butterworth, J., Nord, D., & Gelb, A. (2012). Improving the employment outcomes of job seekers with intellectual and developmental disabilities: A training and mentoring intervention for employment consultants. *Journal of Rehabilitation, 78*(2), 20–29.

Morningstar, M. E., Kleinhammer-Tramill, P. J., & Lattin, D. L. (1999). Using successful models of student-centered transition planning and services for adolescents with disabilities. *Focus on Exceptional Children, 31,* 1–19.

National Alliance for Secondary Education and Transition (NASET). (2005). *National standards and quality indicators: Transition toolkit for systems improvement.* Minneapolis, MN: University of Minnesota, National Center on Secondary Education and Transition.

National Collaborative on Workforce and Disability for Youth (NCWDY). (2010). *Guideposts for success: Second edition.* Retrieved from http://www.ncwd-youth.info/sites/default/files/page/2009/02/guideposts_0.pdf

National Collaborative on Workforce and Disability for Youth (NCWDY). (2014, March). *Understanding the new vision for career development: The role of family.* Retrieved from http://www.ncwd-youth.info/sites/default/files/Infobrief%20Career%20Development%20-%20Family%20Role.pdf

National Council on Disability (NCD). (2008). *The Rehabilitation Act: Outcomes for transition-age youth.* Retrieved from http://www.ncd.gov/publications/2008/10282008

Noonan, B. M., Gallor, S. M., Hensler-McGinnis, N. F., Fassinger, R. E., Wang, S., & Goodman, J. (2004). Challenge and success: A qualitative study of the career development of highly achieving women with physical and sensory disabilities. *Journal of Counseling Psychology, 51*(1), 68–80.

Oertle, K. M., & Trach, J. S. (2007). Interagency collaboration: The importance of rehabilitation professionals' involvement in transition. *Journal of Rehabilitation, 73*(3), 36–44.

Oertle, K. M., Trach, J. S., & Plotner, A. (2013). Rehabilitation professionals' expectations for transition and interagency collaboration. *Journal of Rehabilitation, 79*(3), 25–35.

Peterson, D. B, & Aguiar, L. J. (2004). History and systems: United States. In T. F. Riggar & D. R. Maki (Eds.), *Handbook of rehabilitation counseling* (pp. 50–75). New York, NY: Springer.

Rawls, J. (2011). *The theory of justice* (5th ed.). New Delhi, India: Universal Law.

Riesen, T., Schultz, J., Morgan, R., & Kupferman, S. (2014). School-to-work barriers as identified by special educators, vocational rehabilitation counselors, and community rehabilitation professionals. *Journal of Rehabilitation, 80*(1), 33–44.

Saunders, J. L., Leahy, M. J., McGlynn, C., & Estrada-Hernandez, N. (2006). Predictors of employment outcomes for persons with disabilities: An integrative review of potential evidenced-based factors. *Journal of Applied Rehabilitation Counseling, 37*(2), 3–20.

Schreiner, M. B. (2007). Effective self-advocacy: What students and special educators need to know. *Intervention in School and Clinic, 42*(5), 300–304.

Smart, J. (2009). *Disability, society, and the individual* (2nd ed.). Austin, TX: Pro-Ed.

Stuntzner, S. (2012). *Living with a disability: Finding peace amidst the storm.* Ahmedabad, Gujrat, India: Counseling Association of India.

Stuntzner, S. (2014). *Reflections from the past: Life lessons for better living.* Ahmedabad, Gujrat, India: Counseling Association of India.

Stuntzner, S. (in press). *Resiliency and coping with disability: The family after.* Ahmedabad, Gujrat, India: Counseling Association of India.

Stuntzner, S., & Hartley, M. (2014, September). Balancing self-compassion with self-advocacy: A new approach for persons with disabilities to enhance their process of learning to self-advocate. *American Association of Integrative Medicine.*

Stuntzner, S., Ricks, S., & Dalton, J. (2014). *Shades of grey in the ivory tower: Mentorship and women with disabilities.* Manuscript submitted for publication.

Test, D.W., & Cease-Cook, J. (2012). Evidence-based secondary transition practices for rehabilitation counselors. *Journal of Rehabilitation, 78*(2), 30–38.

Test, D. W., Mazzotti, V. L., Mustian, A. L., Fowler, H. C., Kortering, L., & Kohler, P. (2009). Evidence-based secondary transition predictors for improving post-school outcomes for students with disabilities. *Career Development for Exceptional Individuals, 32*(3), 160–181.

Theoharis, G. (2009). *The school leaders our children deserve: Seven keys to equity, social justice, and school reform.* New York, NY: Teachers College Press.

U.S. Department of Education, Office of Special Education Programs (2007, February 1). *IDEA regulations: Secondary transition.* Retrieved from http://idea. ed.gov/explore/view/p/%2Croot%2Cdynamic%2CTopicalBrief%2C17%2C

Wagner, M., Newman, L., Cameto, R., Levine, P., & Garza, N. (2006). An overview of findings from wave 2 of the national longitudinal transition study-2 (NLTS2). (NCSER 2006-3004). Menlo Park, CA: SRI International.

ABOUT THE CONTRIBUTORS

Bryan S. Austin earned his PhD in Rehabilitation Counselor Education from Michigan State University and is assistant professor of Rehabilitation Counseling and Human Services at the University of Idaho, Boise. Dr. Austin is a Licensed Professional Counselor (LPC) in the State of Idaho and nationally Certified Rehabilitation Counselor (CRC). Bryan has worked in rehabilitation for over 18 years and has extensive clinical experience providing direct services to individuals with disabilities in a variety of practice settings in the fields of mental health, developmental disabilities, and vocational rehabilitation. Bryan has worked as an educator, researcher, clinical supervisor, vocational rehabilitation counselor, behavior specialist, and consultant. Bryan's research interests include clinical judgment skill competencies/counselor debiasing techniques, clinical supervision, rehabilitation counselor professional identity, and employment for individuals with intellectual and co-occurring psychiatric disabilities. He has published recent articles including "A Structural Equation Model of Vocational Rehabilitation Services: Predictors of Employment Outcomes for Clients with Intellectual and Co-occurring Psychiatric Disabilities" (2014, *Journal of Rehabilitation, 80*(3), 11–20) and "A Qualitative Analysis of Vocational Rehabilitation Counselor Perceptions of Clinical Supervision" (2012, *Journal of Applied Rehabilitation Counseling, 43*(3), 25–33). Bryan has served as a vocational rehabilitation policy advocate for the National Rehabilitation Association (NRA), Government Affairs Summit, in Washington, DC. He was also recently appointed as a member of the Public Policy and Legislation Standing Committee for the American Rehabilitation Counseling Association,

Inclusive Practices and Social Justice Leadership for Special Populations in Urban Settings, pages 235–243
Copyright © 2015 by Information Age Publishing
235

responsible for monitoring and informing the Executive Council of any issues or developments in the area of human rights that relate to disabilities or rehabilitation.

Mere Berryman completed her PhD in education at the University of Waikato, New Zealand, where she currently serves as associate professor and is the director of the Building on Success program. Dr. Berryman has extensive experience as a teacher and researcher in English and bilingual settings and in special education. Her work has been published in peer-reviewed journals such as *Teaching and Teacher Education, Teacher Development, Journal of Māori and Pacific Development, Canadian Journal of Native Education,* and *International Journal of Bilingual Education and Bilingualism,* and she has co-authored a number of books. She co-edited (with SooHoo and Nevin), *Culturally Responsive Methodologies* (2013, Emerald Group Publishing).

Jeffrey S. Brooks is Professor of Educational Leadership in the Faculty of Education at Monash University. He is a J. William Fulbright Senior Scholar alumnus who has conducted studies in the United States and the Philippines. His research focuses broadly on educational leadership, and he examines the way leaders influence (and are influenced by) dynamics such as racism, globalization, distributed leadership, social justice, and school reform. Dr. Brooks is author of two full-length books based on his research: *The Dark Side of School Reform: Teaching in the Space Between Reality and Utopia* (Rowman & Littlefield Education) and *Black School, White School: Racism and Educational (Mis)leadership* (Teachers College Press). He is also co-editor of the volumes *What Every Principal Needs to Know to Create Equitable and Excellent Schools* (with George Theoharis), *Confronting Racism in Higher Education: Problems and Possibilities for Fighting Ignorance, Bigotry and Isolation,* and *Anti-Racist School Leadership: Toward Equity in Education for America's Students* (both with Noelle Witherspoon Arnold). Dr. Brooks has written articles in leading educational research journals, including *Teachers College Record, Educational Administration Quarterly, Educational Policy, Journal of Educational Administration, Science Education, Journal of Research on Leadership in Education,* and the *Journal of Values and Ethics in Educational Administration.* He has also contributed many chapters to scholarly edited volumes and written several entries for reference works. Dr. Brooks is Series Editor for the *Educational Leadership for Social Justice* book series. He has served in several leadership positions in universities and educational research organizations, including AERA Division A (Administration, Organizations and Leadership) and the AERA Leadership for Social Justice Special Interest Group.

Brantley R. Choate has 23 years of experience working in the field of educational administration. Since 2003, Dr. Choate has worked in the field of adult education managing both California adult schools as well as university programs. He was the Director of Inmate Education for the Los Angeles County Sheriff's Department from 2011 to 2014. Recently, California's Governor appointed Dr. Choate as the State Superintendent of Correctional Education to lead academic and career technical programs for all 35 state prisons for over 50,000 students. Dr. Choate holds a Bachelor of Science degree from Brigham Young University in Educational Psychology and a Masters and Doctorate from Saint Mary's College of California in Educational Leadership.

Theresa Garfield Dorel holds an EdD from University of Texas at San Antonio. She is Assistant Professor of Special Education in the College of Education at Texas A&M University-San Antonio. Prior to her appointment at Texas A&M-San Antonio, Dr. Garfield Dorel spent 8 years teaching in an urban setting working with diverse populations at the elementary school level and 9 years teaching and serving as department chair at a community college. Her research interests include learning disabilities, social justice, multicultural special education, urban education, and teacher preparation. She has published articles on examining subjectivities and community-based experiential learning and has presented on a variety of topics. She currently holds leadership positions in several national and state organizations.

M. C. Kate Esposito is professor at California State University, Dominguez Hills in the special education program. Dr. Esposito conducts and publishes research in the areas of inclusion, efficacy beliefs, teacher preparation, and educational practices within correctional settings. She has worked with exceptional students for over 20 years. Dr. Esposito has conducted workshops in the areas of bullying, best inclusionary practices, response to intervention, and complying with special education law. She received her BA and MA from Loyola Marymount University and her PhD from the University of Southern California. She holds Multiple Subject and Mild/Moderate Teaching Credentials. She currently serves on editorial boards for scholarly journals and the California Education Research Association Executive Board.

Therese Ford has a background in classroom teaching and senior school leadership in both primary and secondary schools in New Zealand. She has a master's degree in educational leadership and currently works as a professional development facilitator within the Building on Success project team at the University of Waikato. Building on Success is a professional development project that seeks to support teachers and school leaders to develop and implement culturally responsive learning contexts that facilitate the achievement of Māori students. In her role as a professional development facilitator, Therese works to support leaders in schools to develop their capacity to collaborate with Māori whānau (families) and communities. This work is informing her PhD research, which investigates how schools in New

Zealand develop partnerships with their Māori whānau and communities that enable Māori students to achieve education success as Māori. She published a chapter in *Culturally Responsive Methodologies* (2013, Emerald Group Publishing).

Susanne Foulk is currently an adjunct assistant professor at the USC Rossier School of Education where she has been teaching since 2008. She has served on dissertation committees at Rossier, which addressed literacy and motivation for youth in at-risk circumstances. Dr. Foulk's research interests include foster youth mentoring, motivation, literacy, self-regulation, and self-efficacy development for children and adolescents with special needs. Dr. Foulk's 25-year professional experience in education includes founding a school, which included students of various cultural backgrounds, physical disabilities, and learning, behavioral, and emotional challenges. Dr. Foulk went on to found a nonprofit educational organization in 1999, Foundation for Greater Opportunities in Learning (FFGOIL). Her work ranges from serving as director of educationally structured, inclusive early education programs to launching a literacy project for children and adolescents in foster care for Edelman Children's Court in the County of Los Angeles, Department of Children and Family Services. Dr. Foulk received both her Doctorate of Education and Master of Science degree in the division of Educational Psychology and Technology from the Rossier School of Education at the University of Southern California and her Bachelor of Science degree in psychology from the University of LaVerne.

Nicole Limperopulos is the associate director of the Summer Principals Academy at Teachers College, Columbia University, which is the largest university-based principal preparation program in the nation. In her role as associate director, she is responsible for operations oversight, fiscal management, and student recruitment. Dr. Limperopulos took an early leadership role in conducting a feasibility study and establishing partnerships that led to the successful launch of the Summer Principals Academy New Orleans. She also manages program accreditation and led the Summer Principals Academy to secure full national accreditation through NCATE. Dr. Limperopulos completed her doctorate at Teachers College, and her research focuses on the effects that chronic exposure to community violence has on the lives of urban male adolescents. After completing an initial study on violence exposure in the South Bronx, Dr. Limperopulos is currently replicating the study in New Orleans, Chicago, Detroit, Washington, DC, Miami, and Los Angeles. Prior to her work at Teachers College, Dr. Limperopulos spent 8 years as a teacher in the New York City Department of Education. She holds an MA in history education from the City University of New York (CUNY), an MEd in education leadership, and an EdD in interdisciplinary studies from Columbia University.

Paul M. Marietti is the Director of Student Achievement and School Support for the Ventura County Office of Education in Camarillo, California. Prior to his present position he served as a high school social science teacher in Los Angeles and as a comprehensive high school Principal. Paul is currently a doctoral candidate in the educational leadership program at California Lutheran University, Thousand Oaks, California.

Peter McLaren is distinguished fellow in critical studies, College of Education, at Chapman University. Dr. McLaren holds a PhD from the University of Toronto. He is the author and editor of nearly 50 books, and his writings have been translated into over 20 languages. Five of his books have won the Critic's Choice Award of the American Educational Studies Association. His book, *Life in Schools: An Introduction to Critical Pedagogy in the Foundations of Education* (1998, Allyn & Bacon), has been named one of the 12 most significant writings by foreign authors in the field of educational theory, policy, and practice by the Moscow School of Social and Economic Sciences. He taught at the University of California, Los Angeles from 1985 to 2013 as a professor in the Division of Urban Schooling at the Graduate School of Education and Information Studies. Professor McLaren taught elementary and middle school from 1974 to 1979, and most of that time was spent teaching in Canada's largest public housing complex located in Toronto's Jane-Finch Corridor. *Cries from the Corridor*, McLaren's book about his teaching experiences, made the Canadian bestseller list and was one of the top ten bestselling books in Canada in 1980 (*MacLean's Magazine*), initiating a countrywide debate on the status of inner-city schools. Renowned internationally for his fellowships, affiliations, and awards, Dr. McLauren was named 2013 Outstanding Educator of America Award by the Association of Educators of Latin America and the Caribbean; 2013 Lifetime Achievement Award by Pedagogy and Theater of the Oppressed, Inc., and Miami University of Ohio; and the 2014 Critics Choice Book Award by the American Educational Studies Association.

Ann Nevin, PhD, is professor emeritus at Arizona State University and faculty affiliate of Chapman University in Orange, California. Dr. Nevin is a hearing-impaired monolingual female from second-generation family of American Irish and German descent; a daughter, a sister, a wife, a mother, a grandmother and great-grandmother, and a colleague. Ann's work experiences include substitute teaching in rural and suburban schools, teaching remedial math classes at a rural high school, teaching special and general educators in Hawaii, Arizona, and Florida. Instead of working as a special education teacher, she helped establish a new consultative role and worked as a consulting teacher in Vermont schools to integrate students with special needs. Ann's research interests began with identifying variables that favorably affect the academic and social progress of students with disabilities in general-education environments using single-subject designs and simple statistical models. Since 1999, working with colleagues, she moved to ethnographic case study approaches, then, in 2009, she explored how to apply principles from critical pedagogy for inclusive special education when she joined the Chapman University faculty and doctoral students in applying a disabilities studies approach. Over a lengthy career span (1969–present), Ann has authored books, research articles, chapters, and federal and state grants and co-developed various innovative teacher education programs in Vermont, Arizona, California, and Florida to ensure that students with disabilities succeed in normalized school environments. Ann co-edited (with Berryman and SooHoo), *Culturally Responsive Methodologies* (2013, Emerald Group Publishing) and co-authored the third edition of *A Guide to Co-teaching: Practical Tips for Facilitating Student Learning* (with J. Thousand and R. Villa, published by Corwin Press). Recent articles have appeared in *Issues in Teacher Education*, the *Journal of Teaching and Teacher Education*, and the *International Journal for Researcher Development.*

Anthony H. Normore (Tony) holds a PhD from the University of Toronto. He is a Professor of Educational Leadership, and Department Chair of Special Needs Services at California State University Dominguez Hills (CSUDH) in Los Angeles. Dr. Normore has been a visiting professor of ethics and leadership at Seoul National University, a visiting professor in the Department of Criminal Justice Studies at University of Guelph/Humber. He is also a graduate professor of law, ethics, and leadership for the Summer Leadership Academy at Teachers College-Columbia University. His 30+ years of professional education experiences has taken him throughout North America, south-central Asia, eastern Asia, UK, continental Europe, and the South Pacific. Tony's research focusses on urban leadership preparation, growth, and development in the context of ethics and social justice. He is the author 15+ books, including *What the Social Sciences Tell us About Leadership for Social Justice and Ethics* (2014, Information Age Publishing), *Moral Compass for Law Enforcement Professional* (2014, International Academy of Public Safety), and *Collective Efficacy: An Interdisciplinary Approach to International Leadership Development* (2013, Emerald Group Publishing). He was recently appointed as Chief Leadership and Ethics Officer, and the Chairman of the Criminal Justice Commission on Credible Leadership Development at the International Academy for Public Safety

Catherine O'Brien is assistant professor of educational leadership in the Department of Education at Gallaudet University. She holds a PhD from the University of Missouri-Columbia. She is the winner of the 2012 AERA Division A Dissertation of the Year Award for her study, *The Influence of Deaf Culture on School Culture and Leadership: A Case Study.* Her research interests include school culture, culturally relevant leadership, distributed leadership, principal preparation, Deaf culture and schooling, social justice, school improvement, school reform, and the improvement of educational outcomes for Deaf children. Dr. O'Brien's work has been published in the *Journal of Excellence and Equity,* and she has several other manuscripts in various stages of preparation. Dr. O'Brien has contributed a book chapter to the edited volume *Continuing to Disrupt the Status Quo* and contributed a book review of *Culturally Relevant Leadership* to the *American Annals of the Deaf.* She also has submitted entries to the *Deaf Encyclopedia,* "Language Attitudes: Oralism v. Manualism and the Current Status of Schools for the Deaf." She has numerous peer-reviewed presentations at AERA, UCEA, AESA, and the World Congress of Sociology.

Irina S. Okhremtchouk is assistant professor in the Mary Lou Fulton Teachers College at Arizona State University, Tempe. She earned her PhD in education with a focus on School Organization and Policy from the University of California, Davis. Her research interests include classification/stratification practices for language minority students, school organization, school finance, and assessment practices for preservice teachers. In addition to her academic work and research activities, Dr. Okhremtchouk has over 12 years of experience working in 6–12 education settings as a schoolteacher, program coordinator, and school board member.

Edlyn Vallejo Peña is assistant professor of Higher Educational Leadership in the Graduate School of Education at California Lutheran University. She holds a PhD from the University of California. Her research and work in the autism community centers on supporting the educational success of students with autism in P–20 contexts, with a particular emphasis in postsecondary education. Dr. Peña has published her research on autism and disability issues in journals like the *Journal of College Student Development* and *Journal of Applied Research in Community Colleges.* Her dedication to providing resources to the autism community has earned her recognition at the state level in California and at the national level.

Melissa Spence is currently an Autism Support Teacher for the Los Angeles Unified School District. She previously spent 7 years teaching in a moderate/severe classroom for students with ASD and 2 years working as a behavioral therapist within both schools and homes. Her research and professional interests are focused on the nonverbal population of students with ASD. Dr. Spence earned her doctorate in education at California Lutheran University and her dissertation focused on reading comprehension strategies for nonverbal students with ASD.

Suzanne SooHoo is the Hassinger Chair of Culture, Community, and Collaboration in the College of Educational Studies and the co-director of the

Paulo Freire Democratic Project at Chapman University in Orange, California. In this capacity, she conducts research and teaches classes in critical pedagogy, culturally responsive and socially responsible research methodologies, and multicultural education. As a former school principal, Dr. SooHoo is committed to the multivocality of democratic engagement as it plays out in K–12 communities. She is a published author with theoretical, methodological, and theory/practice-based works and is the co-editor of the peer-reviewed journal *Issues in Teacher Education*. Her most cherished work is the cultural work she does with doctoral students and families from the community. From this base and faculty collaborations across the world, she co-edited *Culturally Responsive Methodologies* (2013, Emerald Group Publishing) with Mere Berryman and Ann Nevin. Her current research interests include student voice in school reform, socially responsible research methodologies, and the intersections of race and identity formation in schools, the community, and the academy.

Susan Stuntzner is assistant professor in Rehabilitation Counseling and Human Services at the University of Idaho-Coeur d'Alene. Dr. Stuntzner holds a PhD in rehabilitation psychology from University of Wisconsin-Madison. She is also a Licensed Professional Counselor (LCC) for the State of Idaho, a Certified Rehabilitation Counselor (CRC), and a Nationally Certified Counselor (NCC). She has been in the field of rehabilitation counseling for over 30 years. During this time she has worked as a counselor, vocational evaluator, psychology staff member, and educator and has vast experience in working with numerous individuals with disabilities. Dr. Stuntzner has researched and written on topics related to adaptation and coping with disability, resilience, self-compassion and compassion, forgiveness, and has developed a resilience intervention for individuals with disabilities. The resilience intervention she developed is a 10-week intervention designed to teach and enhance individuals' skills pertaining to resilience and coping well with life following disability. It is currently being pilot-tested among a diverse group of individuals. Additionally, she has written three books pertaining to coping and adaptation as well as resilience-based skills. Her works are entitled *Living with a Disability: Finding Peace Amidst the Storm*, *Reflections from the Past: Life Lessons for Better Living*, and *Resiliency and Coping: The Family After*.

Armando Tejeda (MA, Special Education, University of Texas at San Antonio) is a lecturer in the College of Education and Human Development at Texas A&M University-San Antonio, teaching special education and education courses. He taught special education in K–12 in two San Antonio school districts and specialized in teaching students with learning and emotional/behavioral disabilities. Mr. Tejeda has extensive experience in working with underprivileged and underserved populations in urban and suburban areas in San Antonio in education and social service. He is currently working on an interdisciplinary PhD with a concentration in higher education. His research interests include pedagogical practices using various modalities for children with special needs, ethics in special education practice, special education advocacy, and leadership.

James Thing is a postdoctoral research fellow in the Norton School of Family and Consumer Science at the University of Arizona. He earned his PhD in sociology with a Certificate in Gender Studies from the University of Southern California. Dr. Thing's research broadly examines social inequality, focusing more specifically on lesbian, gay, bisexual, and transgender populations and health disparities. He is currently working on two qualitative projects. The first, in collaboration with Bienestar Human Services, explores coming out to family processes among young Latino men. The second is a multisite mixed-methods study of three cohorts of LGB persons. His research has been published in *Social Identities, Drug and Alcohol Addiction, Substance Use and Misuse,* and *Perspectives on Sexual and Reproductive Health.*

Janice L. Tucker is an Associate Professor in Educational Leadership at California Lutheran University in Thousand Oaks, California. She earned her doctoral degree in educational leadership (EdD) from Indiana University, Bloomington, Indiana. Dr. Tucker teaches courses in organizational change, policy, and international comparative educational practices in the Graduate School of Education. Her research interests include educational change and reform, international policy studies and women in leadership. She brings experience as a classroom teacher and administrator in K–12 schools, as a curriculum consultant in elementary education and eight years in senior administration at the district level as assistant superintendent of Elementary Education and the Assistant Director of Programs (K–12).

CPSIA information can be obtained at www.ICGtesting.com
Printed in the USA
BVOW08s0748120515

399918BV00004B/34/P